A
Healer's Pathway

Don Greenbank.

A
Healer's Pathway

An examination, explanation and irrefutable
proof of the healing of illness by spiritual means.

by

DON GREENBANK

Regency Press (London & New York) Ltd.
125 High Holborn, London WC1V 6QA

ISBN 0 7212 0813 4

Printed and bound in Great Britain by
Buckland Press Ltd., Dover, Kent.

This book is dedicated in gratitude to my two dear friends

Karen and Maggie

who proved so loyal in the rough times.

You know your friends better in the first few moments of meeting, than you will an acquaintance in a lifetime, also a friend is someone you need never say 'sorry' to!

CONTENTS

LIST OF ILLUSTRATIONS

INTRODUCTION
by the healer

"Health is a crown on a person's head
– but only a sick person can see it".

AVAILABLE to the do-it-yourself enthusiast are a host of manuals that cover every subject under the sun. These can range from how to fly an aircraft, right down to repairing a burnt out vacuum cleaner or clearing a blocked drain.

Up until now there has been little positive information, on the important subject, especially if you are a sensitive person, of how best to live life without experiencing too many painful traumas, and how to avoid having yourself slowly eaten alive by a system that is as heartless as any you could find in your local wild jungle or nature reserve.

In this country alone, there are millions upon millions of good, kind and honest people. Described rather patronisingly by the news media as 'The common masses' the majority of them harm no one as they drift quietly through life, living low key lives. They will never be household names or hit the headlines of the newspapers; they toil, sweat, worry and donate their lives in large numbers in the wars which politicians enter into at regular intervals. The true meaning of life and why they are here in a physical body is very much a mystery to them, as they gently and quietly work their way through their lifespan.

Classified as ordinary and looked down upon by the intellectual elite, they are confronted constantly by a set of blatantly false values that are based on outright materialism, which extols the virtues of selfish behaviour, pride of possessions, and the encouragement of selfishness. The various media's news outlets enthusiastically stress that these ideals are the only sensible ones and that they should be accepted by everyone in their entirety. No heed is paid to Mr Average's finer inner instincts, for his higher spiritual nature is completely ignored by this system, which says with confidence that the death of his body is also the death of himself.

To fill in this discrepancy in the do-it-yourself field, I have written this manuscript, which is essentially a manual for living. Its chief concern is to spell out in simple language to the common man, for whom I have great sympathy, the real facts concerning his present life and his future life after he has discarded his body. My answers, the product of a life's experiences, could prove to be far more important to the inner person, than any other book read previously.

The first part of this manuscript concerns myself and the strange pathway that the fates have made me walk along. It contains a full description of healing by the spiritual energy that is transmitted through me, as I am able to convey into words.

If you have ambitions to be a healer, remember that what one person can do, others can emulate *if* you can follow to the exact letter the golden rules regarding the transmission of healing. Be warned though: it is not an easy task that you are contemplating. The experience of practising healing is bound to change you by making you more sensitive and thereby even more vulnerable to worldly pressures.

The second part is a detailed manual for living life; it directly concerns the inner person. I can assure you that within these pages is contained all the necessary information to take you safely from the cradle to the grave. This book answers in full many of the questions that seemingly have no logical answers that must arise from time to time in every thinking person's mind.

It is no exaggeration to say that the healing of sickness in the very special form I practise has the potential of being the most powerful health recovery agency ever offered to the human race. Contained within these pages is the sum total of a lifetime's application of healing by myself. None of my words are available for anyone to either debate, ridicule or cast any doubtful slur upon for they are extraordinary, factual events that have happened to me. By placing the mantle of a 'Healer of sickness' on my shoulders, I have gained access to certain timeless spiritual truths that will be just as valid in ten thousand years time as they are this day. I am duty bound to tell you of some in these pages.

There are good, concrete reasons why you are living in a body undergoing a mixture of experiences that range from the blissful to the downright painful.

The art of healing I practise is not a 'magic bullet' with the ability or even the outright intention of wiping out all the ailments that afflict humanity. It is a force of goodness that operates within the bounds of certain inflexible natural laws. However, within their bounds, much is possible. Its practical, main purpose is to help *you* get through life without too many problems, making you a happier person in the process. The key to perfect health is inner happiness. The only time happy people fall terribly ill is to terminate their lifespan, they having completed and fulfilled their life's experience.

Healing is not a fit subject to be placed under the caustic eye of science for the gaining of a greater common understanding. The general attitude of science, based as it is on the confines of a physical universe, is not at the moment sympathetic towards spiritual healing, though the future may be a completely different story.

I have always remained untroubled by the musings of the academic mind in its conceited and (what I consider) rather impertinent and patronising efforts to understand healing and from where it emanates.

There is a lovely divine reason behind healing's formation for it is one of God's gifts to mankind to give the recipient of healing an inner reassurance regarding the act of living in a body. As such, it goes far beyond the removal of pain and distress for these things are the important issues of the moment. A successful healing invariably gives the patient a quiet inner awareness that the Almighty is concerned about his or her welfare.

I hotly refute the argument that a healer uses any form of suggestion in his work. In fact, some of the more spectacular cures that have happened through my gift have been from people who prior to receiving healing were entirely cynical and thought my work was a load of 'cod's wallop'.

Healing as I practice it, is a spiritual science, not something that is completely

10

devoid of both common sense and logic. My dedication to the work has given me much knowledge regarding illness and its cure that is completely unknown to medical science. In many cases it is the complete opposite to what is wrongly taught at every medical school in the world.

Everyone would accept that we are gifted at birth with five senses . . . sight, hearing, taste, touch and smell. In these writings I shall explain about other invisible senses that each of us has but which only a very few knowingly use. In a purely worldly manner, these hidden senses are used by every successful business man. He plays his hunches; he trusts certain people because his instincts tell him that a particular person is a good man for the job. He senses rises and falls in the world markets, in some cases months before they happen, yet he would laugh his head off if it was suggested he were using spiritual gifts.

A healer's attitude and approach is the complete opposite. He 'knowingly' tunes in to these hidden powers of the mind and as a consequence he is able to help sick people in the form of a health-giving energy that he channels through his mind and body. Incidentally this energy is of such a nebulous character that it will only flow freely where there is neither controversy, debate or suspicion.

The truth of my words is reflected through 100,000 patients who have been cured with my gift. It is something I prove daily as the cures continue to flow from under my hands.

The reality of the world of spirit, into which every living thing is linked, due to our dual natural composition of being both physical body and spiritual entity, is as real to me as the world of matter is to you. The proof of any theory is in the results. If your views and beliefs are different to mine, you are in the unfortunate position of being unable to provide any proof that they are correct, not even to yourself. I regularly prove my beliefs, by the continuous stream of happy, cured patients that leave my sanctuary.

Chapter One

THE AWAKENING

AWAKENING slowly from the soundest and deepest sleep I could ever remember, I lazily stretched myself and opened my eyes. Streaming through the open window was a beam of bright sunlight and from outside I could hear a sweet chorus of birds singing their hearts out.

Looking around the room I saw that none of my surroundings looked at all familiar. My brain was not ticking over yet for it looked exactly like one of my former wartime billets when I was in the Royal Air Force. Glancing round the room, I noted that the furniture was sparse and simple. The bed looked as though it was service issue, although it felt a lot more comfortable.

At that moment there came a soft tap on the door which then opened to expose the smiling face of a batman, carrying in one hand a pot of steaming tea, with a newly pressed uniform draped neatly over his other arm. His face looked vaguely familiar.

"I hope you slept well, Sir", he said. "It's a lovely day outside. I have been told to tell you there is no rush, just get ready in your own good time then the interrogation officer would like a word with you. His office is the first room down the next corridor." With another beaming smile he went whistling on his way; it was a tune I remembered well.

Memory flooded back. I recalled him now. It had been at Upwood bomber station in the RAF. That must be over sixty years ago now. Strangely he didn't look a single day older.

I sat on the side of the bed and drank the pot of tea. It tasted like nectar and was strong enough in which to stand up a spoon. I tried to muster my thoughts but my brain seemed to be in neutral, like a bad hangover without the upset, for I felt wonderful in myself. I decided I must have been involved in some sort of car accident that had caused me to have slight amnesia.

"Ah well," I thought. "Let's see what it's all about." I staggered over to a wash-basin that stood in the corner of the room in my usual first-thing-in-the-morning manner and splashed the crystal sparkling water that came gushing out of the tap over my face. "That's strange," I thought as I rubbed my hand over my face. "There's no stubble." Glancing in the mirror I had another shock, for this was a face I had not seen for a long, long time, youthful and without a single line on it and my hair had lost all trace of greyness. Explanations were demanded.

I quickly dressed myself in the uniform that had been laid out for me. It fitted

13

like a glove and felt good, like the old days, but with no medal ribbons or rank ensignas, just a single air gunner's brevet and the small golden wings of the Pathfinder Force.

I stepped out of the room into a milling crowd of young, fresh faced fliers. Obviously by their uniforms they had come from many different countries. There were English, American, Russian, French, Polish, and even some in German and Japanese uniforms.

"Must be prisoners," I thought to myself though they were all mixing together as if they were long lost friends, for everyone was cheerful and full of comradeship. I felt so completely happy in myself, with an inner feeling of coming home.

I was directed to the interrogating officer's room and entered to be confronted with this kindly faced chap wearing a huge handlebar moustache on his weathered face. He was dressed in a well worn old fashioned first world war Royal Flying Corp uniform.

"Sit down", he said indicating an easy chair. "I won't be a moment" he added, as he shuffled through a huge pile of semi-transparent folders. "Rushed off our feet. Must be the silly season caused by all the bad weather out there," he added as he eventually found my particular documents and became lost in thought as he scanned through them.

"Can I ask you a question?" I said. "What year is this?" He looked up at me, puzzled.

"It's 1944 out there; here you are in a timeless zone," he answered. "Surely you know that." As he read deeper into my notes he said, "No, of course you don't. To you, it's sometime in the 21st century. You are one of those funny ones who went right over our heads to receive special dispensation." He pointed his index finger upwards. "It's all right for you, but it plays havoc with our records."

"I must tell you, if you have not already guessed. Your physical body has worn out and died. In special cases, such as yours, it is the edict of natural law that when you have finished your tour of duty on earth you are automatically returned to the actual year when you should have gone back to the world of spirit. Time can work both ways.

The Red Indian warriors of North America had a saying for the debriefing you are going through at this moment. They called it their 'Song of life'. I want to hear yours in full, now, to enable us to keep the Akashic records straight before you leave this staging post and swan out to meet all your old friends and start enjoying yourself. It will not take you long to forget all those little bits of earthly life's experience that have no value here, but they can often prove to be very useful to souls who are waiting to go into a fresh body to live another life experience."

I started to tell him and if my memory serves me correct, this is how it was.

I lay in the dark, comfortable warm womb, quietly sucking my thumb, waiting patiently to be born. Might as well review the equipment provided to live the life that lay ahead of me. I shuffled through the self-destruct notes printed of ectoplasm, notes you cannot take with you, regarding this new life that awaited me!

"Keen sense of humour." Very necessary to face hardships with. Good. I have been given a strong one.

"Nature. Rebellious against conformity." Oh yes, I like that. At least they don't toast you alive in this era.

"Skin colouration – white." Well at least that will be different.

"Financial prospects of parents – poor." Said with a sigh. Well they do maintain it's good for the soul, but it's only rich people who say it.

"Optimistic in character." Good. A bubbly nature is an essential weapon to overcome negativity.

"Intelligence – reasonable." At least I would not be a moron.

"Guts, not just the physical type." Essential, for I could tell it was going to be one of those funny lives.

"Stubbornness – like a mule." An essential quality for I understand this society likes to impose its own brand of rules.

The genetic strain of my allocated parents showed that I would have a strong, well constructed body; that too would be helpful, for this was a working life ahead of me.

"Will I be happy?" Silly question to ask, as always in snatches. Well at the very least it should be an interesting experience.

Here we go. Already past memories that belong to the higher mind are filtering out of my awareness. Faintly I hear comments from my friends I am leaving behind. They were saying, "Tell them the truth and tell it loud, for some of them haven't the brains they were born with." Their voices fade away to nothing as the limitations imposed by matter and earthly life fix me in its mould. Once again, I have to conform to the laws of the physical. That was written down exactly as it was given to me in a dream vision. The following was what I actually experienced in life.

The act of birth takes place normally. This you do understand, for you must have been through exactly the same thing. It isn't at all painful for the baby, but what a noisy brash world I find I have entered!

I took an instant dislike to it. Much later I was told by my mother that at the actual moment of birth, the bells from a local church were ringing out their Sunday morning peals. I have detested that sound ever since.

Childhood was uneventful, bar the daily beatings at one of my schools by a particularly sadistic headmaster who taught with fear and ruled with a cane. It annoyed him constantly because I would not kowtow to his bullying. Years later he met my father in the street and enquired how I was getting on in life. When hearing that I was doing well he said that, "One had to admire a rebel."

Growing up was normal, with never a hint given regarding my future work as a healer of sickness. Well, perhaps just one. This happened when my mother was impressively pregnant with me. She visited a local healer by the name of Jack Rachford for treatment of a minor condition. After he had cured the condition, he told her: "You are going to have a boy child who will be blessed with many gifts of the spirit. One day he will have world-wide fame as a healer of sickness." Mother forgot this for a long time and did not mention it to me until long after I had started my healing ministry.

It is said that "life begins at forty." Well in my case I can only say that to me, life really began to swing when I was eighteen years of age. The war by this time was at its height. What mainly caught my imagination were the newsreels of war in the air that were shown weekly in our local cinema. At this early period of the war the films mostly consisted of obviously posed scenes, showing members of a

15

bomber aircrew busily occupied in hurling out bundles of leaflets over Germany, telling residents in no uncertain terms not to be so silly as to take on the might of Britain. If they had only known how poorly equipped we were as a nation, the outcome may have been vastly different.

The booming voice of the commentator especially captivated myself and my friends as we stared fixedly at the screen with our eyes stuck out like chapel hat pegs. To us that voice carried with it both the conviction and impact of God speaking to Moses on that mountain top. His carefully chosen words of propaganda usually ended with, "So we say farewell to those intrepid aviators, who night after night, in all weathers, fight their way across the war torn skies of Europe to take back Britain's answer to the Third Reich, and return you to the studio."

Those passionate, emotive words were so effective that at exactly seventeen years and three months of age to the day, I was beating on the doors of the recruiting office, begging to go that instant to where the action was. The kindly-faced recruiting sergeant gave me a knowing wink and in a confidential voice said to me: "Put in for training as a navigator, lad. Two or three years in South Africa in the sunshine – smashing! What more could you ask?"

With the innocence of the young, I asked what would be the quickest way to join the action. "Air gunner," he replied. "Six months to sergeant; seven months and they could be washing your remains out of a turret with a pressure hose. But don't worry. You will not feel a thing."

I accepted that grim prospect and in turn was taken on by the RAF in that very role. Eventually, after a few month's impatient wait, I received a jolly little note requesting my presence to serve both my King and country.

Scrubbing – and thereby ruining – beautiful wooden parquet floors in a ex-luxury flat in London's select St. John's Wood seemed not only sacrilege, but a most curious way to fight a war. Happily that part only lasted about three weeks. In that time, I did somehow learn to march in step and swing my arms, have inoculation needles stuck in my arm, be issued with a uniform and became the proud wearer of a white aircrew flash in my cap.

Then it was on to flying school where I soon learnt how to shoot holes in a drogue with paint coated bullets that was towed behind our weaving aircraft. I somehow earned the title of being an ace gunner, when they found a hundred and ten bullet holes in my drogue . . . when I had only fired a hundred rounds! I had not the heart to tell them that to while away the time when waiting to have the drogue checked, I added another fifty holes by pushing a bullet through the fabric! I offered the lame excuse that they must have been the new boomerang bullets. I loved both the flying and the comradeship. My idealistic nature was joyful and felt it had at last come home. Everything we had was shared. Property was communal and a bond of complete brotherhood was forged, held together by the daily facing of danger.

This was a strange new world I had entered, with its own special vocabulary. Inside a few days such slang words as 'Wizzo', 'Browned off', 'Rodger' for 'Yes', and 'As dim as a Tock H lamp', dropped off my tongue with the ease of a lifetime's usage.

The exaggeration of the young was voiced when talking of someone who had been in the service for many years, such as "Oh he's been in the RAF so long he knew Pontius when he was a Pilot," or "When he joined up, they didn't have service numbers because everybody knew each other."

The select few who were put on instructor's duties after completing a tour of operations could do even better with – line shooting. We newcomers would listen open mouthed and wide eyed to such examples as "There we were at twenty thousand feet, nothing on the clock but the maker's name, shot so full of holes that we did not cast a shadow", or "The flak was so thick you could actually get out and walk on it."

In those early days shortly after I joined up, I was introduced to the service motto that kept hands from being idle and minds from thinking. It was and still is, "If it doesn't move, then paint it white." Have you ever seen white-washed coal? Well I have!

I received some good advice from an old sweat on how best to get on in the service. He told me: "No matter what you do in the forces, always have an excuse, no matter how feeble it may sound. If you do not like going on parades, walk around with a clipboard and look as though you have an important task well in hand. Nobody will ever question what you are doing." Both these pieces of advice worked wonders for I never attended another parade, except the one in which I was presented with my half wing as an air gunner and three stripes.

Regarding the 'feeble excuse' part of his advice, this came in very handy in the following happening.

Guard duty in the sentry box at the main gate was a rare privilege, or so the guard sergeant told me. He also said that sleeping while on duty was an act punishable by being tied to a cannon and shot, and that it happened quite regularly. This remark puzzled me somewhat as the only cannon I had seen had taken the church parade the previous Sunday.

Having a healthy respect for my skin, I stood alert and poised, covering the local scenery which consisted of a typical Welsh mountainside, mainly scree, with just the odd bush leaning permanently away from the prevailing wind. The sun dropped like a hot red penny over the horizon. Night had come. The drone of voices from the camp slowly died away and my tensions eased.

Being a creature of habit, at night I usually sleep. I was torn between habit and duty and compromised by standing with eyes closed, but with ears very alert.

It is a well-known fact that a Sten gun is a very fickle weapon, both for friend and foe alike, and will often, if dropped, start firing temperamentally on its own. Perhaps I did slip into an unconscious sleep state for a moment because as the sten gun slipped out of my unfeeling fingers, the trigger may well have caught on one of my greatcoat buttons. The next moment the still night was shattered by the rat-a-tat of the gun as it stitched a row of very precise neat holes through the roof and down one wall of the sentry box, with yours truly dancing around in a manner that would have drawn a round of applause from any Cossack dance troupe.

Red faced, I was quickly surrounded by a group of half asleep warriors convinced that the Germans, in sheer frustration at being unable to bring London to its knees, had launched a full scale attack against our little camp. For once in my life I was quick thinking. My explanation that I thought I had seen something moving in the darkness was received with some relief, though one cultured and very English voice remarked that, "A Sten gun is not really the thing with which to shoot rabbits." Luckily there had been a party the previous evening in the sergeant's mess. A brief hunt amid the debris of empty bottles at the rear of the

17

mess provided me with a handful of corks. A few moments work with the corks, a razor blade and some boot blacking quickly camouflaged the damning evidence. I found it rather curious that I was never offered guard duty ever again.

I still have in my possession a photograph of those who graduated with me from the air gunnery course. Of the whole course there were only two of us to survive, the other person, being of a fearful temperament, elected to go on to ground duties rather than fly on operations against the enemy. You see, all aircrew members were volunteers. As such we had the option of being grounded any time we felt we could not endure the dangers and rigours of operational flying any longer.

The service had, as is usual, an answer for those whose nerve went. It was nothing as subtle as sending you a white feather through the post, but in its own way just as heartless. They simply stamped the letters LMF on all your documents, meaning 'Lack of Moral Fibre.' They stripped you of your rank, precious wings and any gallantry medals awarded. You were than given the dirtiest jobs available, the implication being that, in their eyes, you were a coward. They knew full well that most young people would rather face death than be branded with such a title. I have seen an entire crew elect to go LMF. They all trooped out of a fully bombed up Lancaster as it was waiting at the end of the runway all ready to take off on their first mission, which happened to be Berlin.

Operational fatigue, which is the limit of an individual's capacity to cope under extreme conditions of danger and stress, is now recognised as a clinical fact. Full allowances are made today for a person in such a state.

My ever strong instincts regarding self-preservation were reflected in my 'attempted to shoot down' record. I do admit I had a habit of shooting first and verifying later. I was certainly not the best air gunner in the RAF but think that I was probably the keenest.

If it had been known at the time it would certainly have raised a cheer in the echelons of the German High Command, for they included one British Mosquito, mistaken for an ME110 on the darkest of nights over the target area, and one American Flying Fortress, mistaken for a FW Condor in the dim light of very early dawn as we were returning from a raid. In our opinion it had no right to be there. Also there were two British barrage balloons which I shot down in the Thames Estuary, shush – don't tell. This was a complete error of navigation, according to our navigator we were over Northern Germany, and I shot at the North Star several times. If you stare at stars long enough, they do move, but they have never been known to shoot back!

Rear gunners had a favourite saying, "We could not see where we were going but could sure see where we had been!"

Our bomb aimer had us nearly in hysterics several times in his keenness to gain a direct hit on the target. This night in particular time after time he had us flying round and round the target. Finally, we gave him the 'hard word' to drop the bombs and let us go home. We started on the final bombing run, with bomb doors open – "Left, left steady." "Right, right steady." You must have heard a similar patter in the old films. Then out it came, "Go back a bit."

The dangers of wartime operations over Germany grow dim in people's memories. Mention the word 'dangerous' and most would say something like, 'Crossing the M1 or M25 during peak rush hour traffic.' The dangers of flying in

'Near Miss'. Lancaster struck by bomb dropped by friendly aircraft. Just one of wartime flying dangers.

wartime were a completely different kettle of fish. My personal war was tame in comparison with many who gave the ultimate sacrifice – their lives.

Simple things sometimes made all the difference between living and dying, like the tossing of a coin with a friend to see who would fly on a combat operation with a brand new crew on their first operation whose rear gunner had gone sick. I won, he lost and was killed a few hours later as his aircraft crashed into a mountain in Scotland on their way home after the raid, two hundred miles off course.

Under such conditions, death could come in a thousand different ways and with frightening suddenness. Once on the finals of our bombing run on a daylight raid, I was flying in the mid-upper turret. I glanced upwards and saw that about two hundred feet directly above us, seemingly oblivious to our presence, was another Lancaster bomber with its bomb doors gaping open like a great maw. Out of it's vast bomb bays a four thousand lbs 'Cookie' began to emerge which came lumbering down towards us like a huge bath tub, closely followed by a stick of smaller bombs. I shouted over the intercom to our pilot to swerve starboard. He reacted instantly. A stream of bombs headed by the 'Cookie' fell between our wing and tail only a few feet away, or so it seemed.

Another time our aircraft was hit repeatedly by flak whilst over a target. As a result of the damage, the bomb doors would not open. Most of the plane's hydraulics were shot to pieces whilst one of our engines caught fire. The other gunner and myself waited trembling at the rear of the plane ready to bail out into the pitch darkness if the fire continued. The pilot managed to feather the engine and fortunately the fire then went out. Losing height all the way, we crawled back to England with a full bomb load . . . and only three engines.

We barely scraped over the cliffs on the East coast at a point near Bridlington, with not enough height for anyone to be able to bail out and headed for the nearby emergency crash drome at Carnaby, which had a special five-mile long runway for war damaged aircraft to land. Some of our crew managed to lower the undercarriage, be it reluctantly. We landed safely after a heart-stopping few moments in which we used all the runway length, with no brakes, no flaps, a full bomb load and seven very terrified men!

Eventually I graduated on to the famous elite Pathfinder force. Our task in Lancasters was to illuminate all of the target area at the onset of the raid, while Mosquito aircraft would fly in at rooftop height and pin-point various strategic works and buildings with different coloured flares. The whole operation was under the control of a master bomber who stage managed the raid by directing the incoming waves of bombers to bomb a particular coloured flare he thought was receiving less than its fair share of attention.

On one such raid I overheard what I shall always remember as the coolest and bravest act amongst my memories. The master bomber directing the raid came on the radio. In a matter of fact voice he told the deputy master bomber to prepare to take over command. "We have been hit badly," he said. "I am going down in flames. The escape hatch has jammed." Then speaking to the main bomber force on a different radio channel, he added; "Come on in chaps! Bomb the red flares.There is only slight opposition." Switching radio channels back to the one used by the Pathfinder crews, he said: "I am just about to hit the ground. Over to you deputy. Rodger and out. Be seeing you." Then came silence. Far below we could see a ball of fire erupt as his aircraft hit the ground. So died two very brave young Englishmen.

On another occasion on our bombing run, we were hit by flak in the body of our aircraft. As a result the bomb bay doors would only open partially. The bomb aimer nevertheless released his bombs, which tore off one of the bomb bay doors. Afterwards, trying to assess the damage, I shone a torch through an inspection window of the bomb bay . . . and found that one of our load of 500 lbs bombs was rolling around in the hollow of the other bomb door – loose and probably live!

There was no access to the bomb bay from the inside of the plane so our pilot had to resort to performing violent aerobatics over the target in a desperate effort to dislodge it, banking over steeply at a one hundred and eighty degree angle, first one way and then the other. With a crash that shook the whole plane, the remaining bomb bay door tore itself loose . . . and the live bomb sped away into the darkness. Phew, that was a close call!

Most members of aircrew adopted a devil-may-care attitude to the rest of the world. This was a merely a mask to cover our fears. The fear in me at times of operational stress was so great that I would often tremble all over in uncontrollable spasms. This persisted at odd times long after the war was over. I was not alone in experiencing this nervous effect, as several other ex-aircrew members have told me since. In fact, one person who flew many scores of highly dangerous missions said that he thought he was the only coward in the RAF.

Over Northern Germany nearly at the end of the war on a daylight raid, we lost half of our force of twenty-two bombers in a matter of a few moments. We were attacked by a pack of the then new German ME262 jet fighters. I had to smile later at what our wireless operator said as he kept a look-out from the astrodome. Seeing this mass of enemy aircraft diving down on us he remarked, "Oh look, there are a lot of Avro Ansons (training aircraft) coming towards us," which merely endorsed our view that wireless operators in general, are lousy at aircraft recognition.

We had little defence against such speed in our, by comparison, lumbering aircraft. Our pilot, on seeing the losses and in complete disregard of the accepted form of defence flying which was a cork screw movement, literally stood the Lancaster on its nose and dived for the cover of the ground twenty thousand feet below.

The wings fluttered: the whole aircraft shook from end to end as the crew in the front of the plane fought to regain some control. We were nearly down to ground level before this was achieved, our hearts in our mouths and the inside of the plane at the front end covered in spent cartridge cases from the front turret guns. The bomb aimer vowed never to use the canvas bags – designed to collect the spent cartridge cases, to hold his sandwiches and thermos flask ever again.

We flew out across the town at chimney top height, with bombs exploding all around us, then out over the sea, gradually regaining our operational height of twenty thousand feet just in time to drop our bomb load with the last of the main force, accompanied by our late arriving escort of Mustang fighters, for by this time the raid was nearly over.

Danger often followed us back to this country. Even when we were over our home base we still couldn't breath freely. Once when we were on our landing finals, just about to touch down on the runway after returning from a bombing raid, every landing light on it and the airfield suddenly went out. At the same instant, a stream of cannon shells splashed and exploded on the runway directly in front of us, fired by an enemy intruder aircraft.

We overshot the field and fled into the pitch black night, flying to the safety of a far away airfield. Such encounters played havoc' with your nerves. It was quite common for aircrew to develop severe nervous facial ticks and mannerisms.

The loss of aircraft on raids was horrific, to say the least. To allay our fears we were told by High Command that the Germans had a new secret device that they called a 'Scarecrow'. This was shot up into the bomber stream where it exploded and came down slowly on a parachute, simulating in every way an aircraft going down in flames. Its purpose, we were told, was to frighten our aircrew into dropping their bombs on the open countryside and send us scuttling back to the safety of England.

Often on a raid we would say to each other, "Jerry is wasting a lot of Scarecrows tonight." It wasn't until after the war had finished that we learned that the Germans had no such device. They were *real* planes we had seen going down in flames.

Truth is often far stranger than any fiction. There is an old First World War saying that, 'If a bullet has your number on it, you will get it.' I once knew a person who was actually struck by a spent cannon shell. Luckily, it was a dud and it didn't explode, but lodged itself in his parachute harness, the impact knocking him unconscious. He nearly fainted on examination of the spent shell when he returned to base as he discovered it was stamped with the last three letters of his service number.

As part of such an elite force, every member of aircrew who was on flying operations was cossetted with lots of perks. For instance we were issued with a pint of milk a day and fruit, also a meal of eggs (rationed to civilians) every time we flew. We were also given sweets and bars of chocolate to help while away the monotony of long hours of flying. Lord Nuffield personally inspired a special fund that gave each member of aircrew extra money when on leave or a holiday in one of his palatial homes.

After each operation over enemy territory, on our return we were given a large tot of navy rum. Often the last crew to land would polish off the jug and finish up plastered – together with the padre and any intelligence officers who were in attendance for the aircrew debriefing.

To retract, my first day on a heavy bombing squadron was one of the red letter days of my life. I gazed in awe at dozens of huge aircraft that looked so awkward on the ground but which when airborne immediately were transformed into creatures of immense grace and beauty. Another air gunner took me on a guided tour of the Lancaster aircraft that I would later fly on operations against the enemy.

It was pointed out that the RAF Roundel was painted directly under the mid-upper turret and was often used by attacking enemy fighters coming in off the beam as an aiming point. I was told jokingly by my guide, "If you are attacked and flying in the mid-upper turret, bring your knees up by your ears."

I viewed with bemused interest the huge, thick armour plated doors that protected the rest of the crew from an attack from the rear, then finally, the flimsy plywood doors and the wooden slide down which the gunner slid down into his turret. "Go on and have a look at your future home," said my guide.

So with great difficulty I eased myself down into this strange contraption. "What protection is there for the gunner?" I asked in my innocence, seeing only perspex and aluminium. "You are looking right at it," was the reply. I looked dubiously at a tiny six inch square of armour plating which, with a bit of luck, would save the gunner's face from irreparable damage – and that was all. It was at that point a stray thought hit me to the effect that the 'powers that be' obviously thought air gunners were expendable – which does not do a lot for your self esteem!

"There is one other thing I should tell you, and most of the other gunners do it," my friend continued. "Take your steel helmet with you on operations. Don't put it on your head, but for the sake of bettering your prospects of raising a family if you are lucky enough to survive, hang the helmet under your seat. Light flak usually comes up, not down."

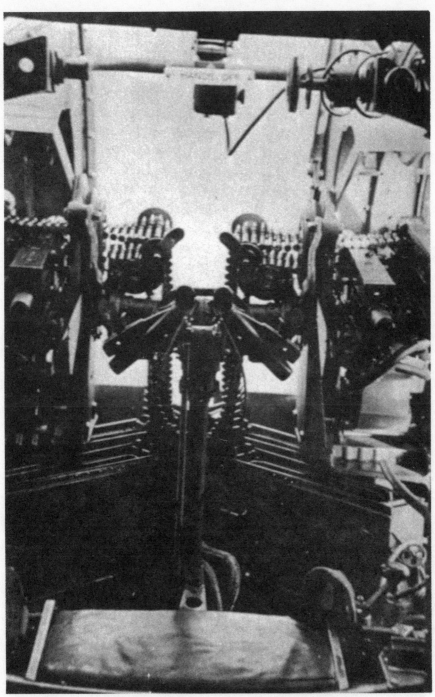

My home in the sky. Rear turret of Lancaster aircraft.

Glancing around as I crawled out of the turret, I noticed for the first time a strange looking device with a red handle. "What is that for?" I asked. My new found friend coughed nervously and said: "I didn't really want to mention it, but since you ask, it's what we call 'The dead man's handle.' If a gunner is killed or wounded and the turret is on the beam, by operating that handle we can centralise the turret and remove his body." I gulped; just what had I let myself in for? War certainly could be hell.

To recapture the moment of truth that opened my mind to the many caring energies that keep a loving eye on man's welfare, you will have to return to the airfield on which I was based in 1944. The traumatic experience that was to follow culminated in myself developing a unique gift of being able to heal sickness, a special faculty that would later prove to be my life's vocation.

I had been ordered to attend the briefing for this raid, as a spare gunner, just in case an air gunner reported sick.

The Nissen hut where the briefing was taking place was crowded. The air was hazy with cigarette smoke, buzzing with the sound of nervous chatter. This was to be a big one tonight – maximum effort was called for. There would probably be as many as six hundred aircraft, all converging on one target, within the space of a few moments. You joked with your friends, but inside wondered how many, "Sorry to inform you . . . " telegrams would be sent out tomorrow.

The chatter died away as the CO with his aides strode up to the raised platform at the front of the room. All heads craned forward as with a sweep of his hand he uncovered a huge map of Europe which stretched right across the end wall. A red tape was pinned to it, one end centred on our base, the other on Nuremburg. As our eyes wandered across the map there was a gasp of released nerves.

Somehow it wasn't so bad when you knew where you were going, but it still looked a long, long way away. A tap came on my shoulder from the gunnery leader as he said: "A gunner has reported sick so I am putting you with them tonight. It's their first trip so keep your eyes open." He flew the easy trips himself. I can't say that I blamed him.

Hours later, after a 'ready to die' breakfast of bacon and eggs, we stood shivering in the cold of very early morning. The usually familiar and friendly shape of our Lancaster loomed dark and rather sinister in the faint light from the ground crew's hut. Built from packing cases, it was still stamped with stencilled destination marks that an enterprising fitter had borrowed from an American air base down the road. The crew bus, having disgorged us from its warm interior, scuttled away like a black bug to drop other crews at similar dispersal points.

To a stranger we must have looked a wild bunch of youngsters, not one of us older than twenty-two, the youngest being myself, a mere eighteen years of age. We were dressed in an assortment of football shirts, lucky scarves and masses of flying clothing on top of which we wore 'Mae West' flotation jackets and parachute harnesses, with thermos flasks of coffee and bags of sandwiches to one side, our pockets crammed with sweets, chewing gum, and all the little extras that a kindly welfare officer could coax from central stores.

It was one of my pet intentions, which I never fulfilled, that if I was ever so unfortunate as to be shot down, to try my best to walk into either Spain or Sweden, which were both neutral countries. Some of my friends had done this and advised everybody to head for Sweden, where the authorities provided you with a first class hotel, civilian clothes, a certain amount of personal freedom, and even girlfriends to show you all the sights of the town.

Sweden was obviously friendly towards England, for they provided all the comforts of home and more. Eventually, after a few months wait, you were flown back to England in the bomb bays of a Mosquito aircraft. With this in mind, I always carried, tied to my parachute harness, a side pack, containing food, clothing, a .38 revolver and one hundred rounds of ammunition. I suppose my motto was the same as the Boy Scout's, 'Be prepared'.

A squeal of brakes came as a staff car with hooded lights drew up and the medical officer and padre dashed over to us like bustling shepherds, one issuing 'wakey, wakey' pills, the other a few last words of comfort. A last puff at a cigarette and it was "All inside" the aircraft. A quick equipment check and we were ready to go.

There is a very special smell to an operational aircraft, a bonding together of oil, petrol, oxygen, spent cordite fumes and fear, for that, too, has its own special smell. It is a smell that, once experienced, is never ever forgotten. Even now, years later, memory brings back that strange haunting tang.

Before a raid, there was always complete radio silence to give no clue to the enemy as to our intentions, for hundreds of German operators monitored all the radio frequencies for the slightest clue to our target for tonight.

Our signal to go took the form of a bright green Very light that now spluttered and soared high above the airfield. The raid was on. Our aircraft's engines are started up one by one, and as they are tested by taking them up to peak revs, they enclose everyone in a private world of solid noise.

With a lurch of released brakes we trundle round to take off, our only guides, the small blue Drem lights that signal the width of the perimeter track. We taxi to the end of the runway, a queue of fifteen giants behind us, all ready for the word "Go!" This is the time when everyone experiences the churning of stomach nerves.

Too late to worry; there goes a short flash of green light from an Aldis lamp as the aircraft controller gives our pilot the signal to "Go!" Engines roar in protest; there's a last wave from the CO and the small group of well-wishers, dimly illuminated by car headlights at the end of the runway. We roar away into the pitch black night. After what seems an eternity, the tail lifts, the end of the runway is cleared, and we lumber away into the night. "Crossing the English coast now," came the voice of the navigator over the intercom.

You look down and see nothing, only pitch darkness. Steadily we climb. It gets colder. I give a quick burst from my guns to make sure they haven't frozen solid. There is a long icicle forming from my oxygen mask. The coldest we ever recorded was fifty-six degrees below zero, and believe me, that's cold!

Now it is a question of searching the skies until your eyes hurt, watching for the slightest movement. It is possible to stare at a star until you are certain it is coming towards you.

Enemy coast ahead and little twinkles of light in the sky show you are not the first to arrive. You can smell the flak, or imagine you can, and for the next five hours you can expect anything to happen, any minute, any second. The tension mounts as we weave and dodge to escape the probing enemy searchlights. The flak gunners are busy as a fiery stream heads earthwards. There will be more empty chairs in some mess dining room tomorrow. Two or three hours later the scene was set, the actors in their places, as we beam in towards the group of searchlights, coned like bright silver pencils over the target, not for our benefit, but as a guide to the German fighters.

A rear turret is a lonely and cold place at the best of times, but with the perspex protection cut away to give better visibility there's no finer view in all the world.

The backcloth to the experience that would change my life was in place. It was like a scene from Dante's *Inferno*. The clouds far below heaved and billowed from massive explosions on the ground. A gap in the cloud cover to one side reveals thousands of burning incendiary bombs glowing like a deadly golden carpet on the ground.

The tang of spent cordite stung my nostrils and the sound of tearing metal came as exploding flak particles slash their way into the vitals of our aircraft, coupled to the banshee-like howl of our four Merlin engines under full power as our heavily overladen aircraft lurches through the tormented searchlight-lit sky. Torches of aircraft on fire spin lazily earthwards; some of them to erupt into huge fireballs as their bomb loads explode. Being burnt alive is just one of the many hazards that faced a member of aircrew.

The sky is peppered by the twinkling of exploding anti-aircraft shells and the black puffs of smoke they leave behind them. Long snakes of bright tracer shells whip menacingly past our wing tips, showing that night fighters were on the prowl and intent on someone's destruction. I hoped it was not us.

The blue beam of a dreaded radar controlled master searchlight suddenly catches us in its beam. Within seconds, three other searchlights swing round in perfect unison and they also cone us in their beams. We were lit up like a Christmas tree, vulnerable and unprotected, an easy target for every night fighter in the vicinity. With one hand clamped over my eyes to partially shield them from the glare of the beams, I fire down the beams and am lucky enough to extinguish two of them.

In this moment of extreme tension and fear the bomb aimer's voice crackled over the intercom: "Close the bomb doors. We are going round again. We have missed the aiming point." Their very first trip and the crew were keen to have it perfect. Fear held me in its icy grip as any second I expected to feel and hear the thud of our cargo of death exploding.

It would be hard to find a more incongruous introduction to the completely opposite world of perfect peace and calmness that one usually associates with my work of healing. Statistics we were unaware of at the time said that an air gunner's life in action was numbered in hours –and that we had only three chances in eleven of finishing a tour of operations in one piece. It was a common event to hear of the ground crew having to wash out parts of a friend's body from the wreckage of a gun turret with a pressure hose. Is it any wonder we lived our non-flying lives to the full. I was a mere lad of eighteen summers. The pulse of life ran swift in my veins. And, oh, I did want to live.

Fear and terror proved to be the catalyst in opening my mind to the infinite, for if prayer is a cry from the heart then I, with eyes clamped tightly shut, prayed as I have never done before. That call for help reached through the barriers of all physical reason.

My prayer of sheer desperation was answered in a flash. The composition of this world of time and space were torn apart when in that lonely gun turret, what I can only describe as a great white light of pure spiritual energy poured through my whole being, filling me to overflowing in an instant with both a calmness and a peace that were breathtaking in their intensity.

It was exactly as though a door in my mind had been opened. In that perfect state I could both 'feel' and 'see' the comforting presence of a great soul dressed in a garb of purest white. His kind and gentle voice rang through my mind as he said: "You are alright, my son, for *I* am with you!" Every one of my fears vanished immediately!

Time seemed to be in a complete state of suspension, for in those minutes or seconds – and I cannot tell you which – my life was changed and I would never look at things in the same light ever again. The descriptive power of words are useless to describe the full impact of that encounter.

The flight home to our base in England is comparatively uneventful, but on examining our aircraft later we find that there is much structural damage, with many large holes in the fuselage and wings caused by the intense flak barrage. Some of the shell particles had gone right through the bomb bays, and at such an angle that some of them must have hit our bomb load. Why had the bombs failed to explode?

In the months ahead, I was to face many similar situations with a considerably diminished fear of death, but it did leave me with a brain full of unanswered questions. In retrospect, I could well imagine such a powerful revelation happening to an ascetic holy man or an aspiring saint, but not to a scared, silly lad with knocking knees, perched on the lip of eternity, whose greatest need of the moment was the very immediate one of survival.

After such a 'slit trench conversion', many other people would have rushed in an application to join some church ministry, but we Yorkshire people are made of sterner stuff than that. We tend to make the original Doubting Thomas sound like a religious maniac.

My traumatic experience was kept well hidden in the secret depths of my mind. I never discussed it or argued about it even with my closest friends, partly from fear of ridicule. Who could – or would – understand? The nearest I ever came to asking advice about it was a tentative feeler I put out to the station chaplain. The questions I asked him about inexplicable happenings were answered with a snort blown through his huge handle-bar moustache. He was a nice, kind person who had flown as an illegal passenger on many operations over Germany for he loved flying. His words were brief and hasty. "Don't try and dig too deep my boy," he said, and off he snarled up the road on his motor-cycle combination with his latest WAAF girlfriend huddled fearfully in the sidecar, leaving behind a cloud of putrid blue smoke and myself as puzzled as ever.

It did leave me with an inner unsettlement that knew little fulfilment until my path in life led me into the field of healing. The span of time since that event is now nearly fifty years. In that time, I have progressed from being an individual with quite literally no knowledge of the processes of sickness – and with even less knowledge of how to cure that illness – to my present position of being one of the world's leading healers, who has over the last forty years of practice treated in the region of one hundred and fifty thousand patients!

Chapter Two

THE EARLY YEARS

THE year was 1945 when a grotesque mushroom-shaped cloud of deadly radioactive dust formed over Hiroshima. My personal war ground to a sudden halt.

On my return to civilian life, like many others, I quickly found that air gunners were a glut on the market, and that my skills at shooting down enemy aircraft had no place in this post war era.

I was horrified to find that the standard pattern of civilian life had changed rapidly, from the universal friendship formed from the shared dangers of wartime, to a completely selfish 'dog eat dog' attitude of "Blow you Jack, I am fireproof." I thought of the charred remains of my friends scattered over the length and breadth of Europe and wondered for what use had been their supreme sacrifice.

In those days just after the war, I was like a lost soul. I found great difficulty in gaining any orientation as to what to do in my new life as a civilian, for I had no aims that could match in any degree the exciting life of being a member of aircrew.

Poverty settled itself around me like an old friend, and proved to be a constant companion for many years to come. This period of my life would have been so much easier if my father's name had been Rothschild for by the time I was discharged from the RAF all the choice jobs had gone. I had no alternative but to take anything that was offered in the way of work. This resulted in working with a pick and shovel and doing a series of menial labouring jobs. The only thing I can say in mitigation is that this hard work did strengthen and develop my body muscles, and kept me at a peak of fitness.

After searching for months, I eventually managed to find work assembling the bell punches that bus conductors use. I was told by the factory manager it was highly skilled work and would take at least six months to learn even the rudiments of the job. In actual fact, after years spent stripping and assembling .303 Browning machine guns, often wearing gloves and in the pitch dark, it took me only an hour or so to learn and perfect the relatively simple assembly and fitting of these machines.

My working conditions were not the best, for the work-bench provided for me was directly in front of a large factory clock. To make matters even worse than they were, the clock also had a second sweep finger so not only could I watch the hours and minutes slowly go by, but if I was so inclined, could even count the seconds.

To overcome boredom and stop myself going insane by the sight of the seconds ticking away, I worked like a man possessed, and churned these silly machines out by the dozen. Within a matter of days I was called into the manager's office, where I was told in no uncertain terms that I must restrict myself to making just one single bell punch a day. They couldn't fault the precision of my work, but it appeared that the trade union were complaining at the speed of my assembly. So instead of being offered a promotion at my enterprise I was given the ultimatum, delivered with an ugly scowl. "Cut down your work or you are sacked!" This was followed by the cutting words, "We were hard at work on munitions, while you were away at the war enjoying yourself." I opted for the sack.

I didn't know it at the time, but I had already started on my apprenticeship of healing, for learning about people who are at different levels of soul evolvement is an essential quality if it is intended by the fates for you to treat tens of thousands of patients in the future, as I was.

At that time I was so naive I always imagined everybody thought and had the same values in life as myself. I was certainly in for a rude awakening! Over the next few years I was to know dire poverty, plus the experience of having to endure physical pain, for pain and its removal was to prove to be my main avenue of healing. I realise now that to appreciate pain in others it is essential you have some practical experience of suffering yourself.

I have faced many seemingly intolerable situations and overcome them in a life that has never been easy, gaining with each situation overcome, a greater mental strength. Name me any one of the painful situations that afflict mortals and I can probably say, "Yes, I too have experienced something similar."

Pain came to me in abundance. My list of bone breakages reads like the morning report of the casualty department at any hospital, for if anything the guardians that control my life are thorough.

It reads as follows: broken nose, arms three times, one wrist, fracture of the spine, broken leg and Potts fracture of the ankle, broken toes, three broken ribs, perforated lung and a puncture of the pleural cavity, broken collar bone and twenty-six pieces of bone that had to be removed from a badly smashed elbow.

The Yogis say that until you can control your body it is impossible to control your mind. I discovered that my tuition into the control of my mind had gone further than I had any idea, and that I had gained sub-consciously the faculty to be able to switch off pain.

A very bad landing when I was hang gliding resulted in smashing an ankle and breaking my leg in two places. The doctor at the hospital to which I was carried by friends said I would need a general anaesthetic while he set it in plaster and then plated and screwed the ankle together. In his opinion, "The pain would be too great for anyone to bear."

As I listened to him the inner voice spoke in my mind saying, "Yes, you can." The extent of my trust in my intuition was in for its testing time.

I told the doctor that on no account would I have my ankle plated and screws inserted as I had a good healing body, and I thought I had the ability to cut out pain. At that point, I did not know for certain if I could or not, but what is the use of having beliefs if you don't use them?

29

Still flying forty-six years on, though slightly smaller than a Lancaster.

He replied: "I have heard of such things, but never experienced them personally. I will give you a few moments to prepare your mind."

The doctor returned with a bundle of my X-ray plates, laid me on the table, held my foot against his chest and told me which way to turn my body until all the bones met. Next he proceeded to plaster my leg in that position, and I did not feel the slightest pain or discomfort.

I was shown the God-like position that some medical specialists think they hold and of how professional jealousy raises its ugly head in all manner of disciplines when I reported to my local hospital a few days later. The specialist there insisted on removing the plaster from my leg and foot and putting a new one on, saying in reference to the doctor who had put it on me in the first place, "Oh, that would be just some common little house doctor, with limited practical experience."

Being unable to drive with this huge pot cast on my leg – it went right up into my groin – I became so frustrated that after three days I used a hacksaw to cut it off above the knee, much to the horror of a friend who was a matron at the local hospital. "There is no way that leg can heal if you are moving it all the time," she told me. I knew, though, that it was already at least partially healed.

Five weeks later, the night before I had to return to the hospital for the doctor's verdict, she came and plastered the portion of the cast that I had cut off back together because, as she said, "The doctor will be offended".

On keeping my appointment with the doctor, he said to me,"We will cut off the

30

plaster, and X-ray your leg, then put on another plaster for a further six weeks". "Do you suppose it could have healed?" I asked him. "Not one chance in fifty," he replied. He was quite mortified when after the X-rays were taken he had to admit the leg *was* healed perfectly and I could walk on it at once with no pain.

Combine pain with poverty and you have a double situation to overcome. I badly smashed my elbow and at that time simply could not afford to be off work. It is not easy to drive a fully loaded, eight wheeled lorry with one arm – and yet that is exactly what I did. I took my young son with me to move the gear lever for me while we drove all round Scotland. By the end of the week I could use my arm freely again and I had no pain.

This ability to cut off pain came in very handy when I fractured a vertebra in my spine caused by a two hundred foot crash when I was caught in a 'curl over' of air while attempting to land on the top of some high cliffs in my hang glider.

At the exact moment I lined the glider up for my landing, a squall of snow and gale force wind sprang up. The wing became inverted by the down pressure, and I was literally slammed into the ground from this great height.

It was great relief when I found I could wiggle my toes and fingers for I knew then I had not snapped my spinal cord. I had some of my flying friends carry me over to nearby goal posts and hang me by the arms from the cross bar. I then asked three of them to pull down on my legs to try and move everything back into position, a sort of primitive traction. There was a sound of breaking timber and the goal posts collapsed, throwing us all into a heap of bodies on the ground. I was quietly sick.

I refused to go into hospital, for I knew that the medical way would consist of weeks confined to bed. I had the responsibility towards hundreds of patients booked in for healing in the days ahead.

My friends drove me home and carried me up to bed. The next day – a Sunday – it took me several hours to prise myself out of bed. My back was in constant spasm. I had bruises all over my body. With even the slightest movement I could feel the bones in my fractured vertebra touch and send spasms of pain shooting throughout my body.

I was, however, rather apprehensive as to whether I could endure the actual pain of movement whilst treating people. I was carried into the clinic by some friends and treated patients out of a wheel-chair loaned from an ex-patient. I made the lovely discovery that while I was treating people I had no pain at all. It took about six weeks for the spine to heal itself to a point where I had only a little pain whilst walking. By sheer determination and mind control I was able to carry on healing without having a single day away from my work.

With my usual impatience – and going directly against the mentally given advice of my spiritual guardians – I visited a well-known healer in London for what I hoped would be an immediate and full cure. Much to my disappointment I found the man to be completely useless. His 'treatment' consisted of rubbing my back three times in a casual manner and then proclaiming I was cured. He told me I had worn two discs out and that *he* had made me two new ones that would be fully grown in two days time. He made it sound that healing was just like growing Brussel sprouts.

In fact, there was not the slightest improvement in my condition. All my senses screamed out that the man had no power, only talk, and that if he ever had the gift, he had most certainly lost it. He then made the most arrogant statement I have ever heard a healer speak, on hearing that I was a developing healer myself.

"Oh," he said "There will be many who you can't help. When they come to you for healing, empty your mind and think of me and *my power will heal them*." There was no mention of the chap upstairs.

Perhaps this was another experience to point out just how fallible some people are who try to take up healing for the wrong reasons. The memory of this episode did stand me in good stead, for it strengthened in me the resolve never, ever, to promise a cure. At times that can be a temptation, especially when you have gained good results with similar conditions previously. It is far better to back-pedal and let the results of your efforts speak for themselves.

Although I have had to suffer pain, in moments of great danger help has always come to me and saved my life. One situation that was potentially lethal was when I was hang gliding from the top of some very high cliffs on the West coast. So great was the force of the wind on take off that the glider was blown backwards and flew over a huge high wall. It was undamaged, whilst I, who was dangling underneath, was hurled into it with such violence that the seat on which I was sat was smashed into smithereens. To give you an idea of how great was the impact, the shape of my body was actually deeply impressed in the wall.

The outcome was a revelation, for my body bore not the slightest bruise or cut. Nor had I any discomfort afterwards, which bears out the old saying. 'It's not *what* you know, but *who* you know that matters.'

In my case, it is the self-same evolved soul who first came to me all those years before over Germany. This wise soul is my mentor; he guides my pathway through life. Perhaps the nicest thing of all to me is that he is my best pal.

Thank goodness the powers that be gave me a good, self- repairing body, for I was once squashed between two lorries which broke my wrist, clavical, and several ribs, one of which punctured the pleural cavity of my lung, the base of which filled with blood. The consultant at the hospital wanted to operate to drain the cavity of the blood, but after a great deal of persuasion, he agreed to postpone the operation for a few weeks.

I went back to see him, having in the interim period, sought healing for myself, via myself. After a thorough examination he confirmed that my lung was now clear. "How do you explain that?" I asked him. He answered: "You have a remarkable self-healing body. Think yourself a very lucky man."

Previous to my 'Slit trench conversion' when I was on operations in the RAF, my childhood had been pretty normal, except for certain awarenesses, inner feelings and unplaceable faint memories which I had from infancy. These never seemed to bear any relation to the conduct of this physical world. Only in later life when I had developed my gift of healing fully did it strike home to me that those awarenesses were actually memories of previous lives and pre-birth life in the world of spirit. These three separate memories that I have, are static, for I have never been able to extend or gain further information about them.

In that waiting period just after the war, when I had no idea where life would take me, a strange twist of fate turned my pathway into the field of healing. My father was in hospital dying, or so we were told by doctors. He had only been given a short time to live, a matter of weeks at the most. As a last resort he was taken down south to the village of Shere in Surrey to visit a famous healer called

Harry Edwards. The results of this man's treatment on my father were remarkable – and he lived another twenty years in very good health, walking up to ten miles a day, most days, over the wild Yorkshire moors that were so dear to his heart.

I was amazed at this apparent miracle which overrode every medical expectancy. On meeting Mr Edwards, he told me that like himself, I had the potential of a great gift of healing, but time and patience would be required to develop it to the full. How right he was!

If this is to be a true narrative of the healing effort, I must make the reader aware of the other side of the coin.

In any system that is based on natural talent, be it music, painting or healing, there will always be attracted to it those with no calling to the art, who substitute talk for action, like the saying, 'There are those who can, and those who think they can and can't and those who just talk about it.' To put it another way, 'Many are called, but only a few are chosen.'

Everything connected with the field of the psychic is wide open to entry by both those who are self-deluded and others who are intentionally unscrupulous and without principles. The quagmire of half truths issued by these people is difficult for a stranger to healing to interpret. Healing is often presented in an unnatural way that bears little resemblance to the spiritual benefits which are so readily available to sick people through a mature and sincere healer.

Fortunately, this sort of person is in a minority. I met several of these types in my searchings for the truth who had infiltrated many church healing groups, healing organisations and psychic societies. In those early days I was looking desperately for a greater insight into healing and kindred subjects. In no way was I impressed by what I saw. Rituals were enacted solely to impress the patient and unproveable explanations given like, "This condition is a karmic debt," to explain the patients non-recovery.

By this time I had developed the ability to gain an accurate diagnosis of someone's illness, so was able to have a counter check on what patients were wrongly being informed concerning their illness. In many cases these developing healers made a quite clever mental yo-yo action that immediately absolved them from all responsibility in their own minds for the outcome of any diagnosis or healing treatment given.

This was done in such a subtle way by passing the buck, saying, "My spiritual guide will now diagnose your sick condition." The theatrically-given diognosis that followed was not only completely incorrect but unconsciously very funny.

I remember one lady with a shoulder pain being told by a developing healer, with a dead pan face and in a thick foreign accent, that the condition was caused by a floating kidney!

Many of these diagnosis that I overheard, showed a complete lack of knowledge of the human anatomy. I found it disturbing that many patients were told not outright, but by implication, that they had various sorts of growths, trading on fear that would keep them attending for year's of healing. There is nothing easier to cure than an illness the patient does not have.

The most amazing aspect of this behaviour to me was, that some quite intelligent and educated people accepted everything they were told by these healing tricksters without questioning the rationality of statements. Not only check, but double check anything you are told that taints of this trading on fear.

Use your doctor by asking his opinion of the diagnosis. He, too, may be hopelessly wrong, but if both diagnoses concur there is a strong possibility of it being right.

In my searchings I found no one single person who could measure up to the results concerning the cures through healing that Harry Edwards gained practically all the time.

I remember once watching Mr Edwards give a demonstration to an audience of several thousand people in London's Albert Hall. He gave a wonderful and competent display of healing's wonders, which included gaining full mobility for some patients who had suffered with great pain and locked-up joints for years.

Behind him as he worked were about two hundred people dressed in white coats who classified themselves and were registered by some organisation or other as 'Healers'. Such was their amazement at the results of Mr Edwards healing efforts that they clapped their hands and cheered at each improvement.

It was obvious to me that this back up of healers had never in their experience been able to give a patient the sort of immediate benefit from healing that he was showing them. I realise now, after many year's experience, every case I observed at that meeting was a quite normal event in the removal of illness by spiritual means.

I recognised that all these things I had observed were possible: it was the *how* part that eluded myself and others, if what I had witnessed was anything to go by.

I found that many patients I questioned closely had been attending healing meetings, for years in some cases, with no cure at the end of it all. It was obvious that these patients were being given peace and an inner calmness, but the illness was not being cured, except for the odd one or two who had ailments of an hysterical origin, caused by them being in a constant state of ill ease and tension.

I found it interesting that most of these male 'healers' were of a similar physical type. They were usually of a short and stocky build, blue eyed and with an abundance of head hair. Even their fingernails grew quickly, and their glands certainly worked overtime. In general terms, it could be said they were healthy specimens of humanity, with a superabundance of personal life force they had the ability to pass on to others in a form we understand as magnetic healing. This energy, known by the Yogas as Prana, is limited in its curative effect and was certainly not the level of healing I was searching for, since by now, I knew that far greater things were possible.

There was no doubt about the sincerity of these 'healers' or their keenness to help sick people. Their only limiting factor was the inability to contact the higher stratas of the spirit world, the only place whence healing, in its purest form, emanates.

Perhaps these writings will encourage some to search deeper and thereby expand their horizons for the only test of any healer is this; does his gift cure people of illness?

All healings and all cures, whatever it be termed by the person who practises the art, comes about from the transfer of a health-giving energy via the healer to the patient. We must accept the fact that there are many levels that could be accepted as healing energy, ranging from the highly spiritual right down to the common life force that I have just described, something all healthy people carry with them. It is on this low, unevolved level, in which the healer is giving of his own vital energies from that I have known a reverse action of healing take place in which the healer can actually draw vital energies from the patient. After the treatment, the healer literally blooms: their eyes sparkle, colour comes to their cheeks and they feel great in themselves. On the other hand, the poor patient looks wan, drawn, feels tired out and exhausted. Of course, there is no betterment in their sick condition.

I hasten to add that none of this reverse energy transference is deliberate for the healer's motives are of the best, yet it is certain that this action often takes place with a healer whose gift is in an undeveloped state. If this happens to you as a patient, then for goodness sake stop attending and try a healer with a more advanced and developed gift.

The golden rule regarding healing is that if a healer is going to be able to help you, there should be an *immediate* improvement in your illness on that first treatment.

Regarding myself, the gift has matured over the years of practice to its exciting new development in which often there is no need even to touch the patient. I must always qualify such a statement regarding people and that is, providing they are receptive. From my experience, I can say it is only one or two in a hundred that are totally closed to healing. It is a funny sensation to me when I touch one of these 'closed' persons, for it is exactly as though there is nobody in there. This new advancement of the gift, fills me with awe, wonder and excitement. I am like a person who has received all his birthdays on one day, for nowadays I can often sit several feet away from a client and mentally direct healing energies to the patient's body. More often than not gaining an immediate freeing from pain, which can and is, verifiable by X-rays. Bones move back into their rightful position, trapped nerves are freed and inflammation reduced within seconds – all without physical contact. A small amount of soreness may persist after the treatment for a few days until all the inflammation has died down completely.

It is no wonder that some patients who are deeply immersed in the world of matter find this a completely baffling process, but they have to admit, often reluctantly, that their pains have gone and their skeletal balance rearranged.

Healing of this nature is a completely new experience to most people. Especially if they are worldly individuals. I find it impossible to give explanations they would or could understand.

In actual fact, what I am doing is directing my spiritual helpers, by my mind, asking them to send spiritual energies to the patient's spirit bodies. In the state of altered awareness in which I administer healing, I can 'see' both the patients' spirit and physical bodies in my inner mind. The physical body responds immediately to treatment of the spirit body. Experiencing this has answered a lot of my own questions.

The knowledge that has been taught me over the years of healing practice as to the exact root cause of many illnesses and pains – and the precise location of literally thousands of body nerves that can cause pain and distress in a patient's body – now comes into its own. Much of the special knowledge of the nervous system I have gained over the years is unknown to medical science. Were I to give a detailed account of everything I have learnt regarding the position of these pain-inducing nerves, it would prove to be useless without the healing energy. Also much of it would be unacceptable to medicine in general as it would be contrary to its accepted beliefs and teachings.

It is as though all those years of healing have been with the aim of developing in myself this present application of healing. It will be interesting to see how far it does develop in my remaining years.

The applying of healing energy in this special way is, of course, a genuine example of mind-over-matter, spirit mind over physical matter. I could quote many instances, where this method has worked from a great distance away, as by letter or over the telephone, for instance.

The directive is mine, but the actual moving and freeing of nerves is done by my spiritual helpers, who are tuned into my every thought when I am working. This new offshoot of applying healing is something that could be demonstrated in front of healing's greatest critics – and they are plenty of those – and it would be impossible for them to deny or explain the wonderful results gained by this form of healing, without accepting the reason why –for there is no alternative explanation – other than the source of healing must lie outside this physical world!

This proving to the world would involve publicity – which I, shrink from. Therefore what is now a rare gift, should be bestowed on promising developing healers in the future and will probably prove to be the format of most healing.

Possibly the most difficult thing for a potential healer to accept: is the fact that in no way does *he* heal. His task is to direct the healing energy to the patient. In other words he is the middleman, but I hasten to add a very essential part of the healing process.

If a healer grows such an enlarged cranium and begins to think that he is the main source of the energy of healing and its effects, and then becomes egotistical and precious about himself, then he puts severe limitations on any healing ever taking place. It has been proved to me beyond any shadow of doubt that each of us has a spirit body *now*. Why? Simply because I can see it.

My first patient was my mother. I treated her for a two-fold reason. The first was out of my deep love for her and my distress at seeing her in constant pain. The second reason was curiosity in myself, to see if I could actually gain help for someone, for at this period I had grave doubts about having any ability to heal. My mother had been crippled for years with intense pain in her knees. Told by doctors she had osteoarthritis, there was nothing they could do to help her beyond issuing pain-killing drugs.

In Mum's case, the healing was practically instant, for after receiving it she was able to return to her great love of ballroom dancing. The thing I found very strange was that her knees, which were very swollen and grated with the slightest movement, went down very little in size, but Mum was able to move them easily, with no pain. The grating noise disappeared completely. The only valid conclusion I could reach to explain this effect was that the adhesions causing the pain had been removed from the *inside* of the knees just enough to give her freedom from pain and full mobility, but the cosmetic appearance of her knees had been completely ignored.

During this period of developing my various spiritual gifts, it was as though I was led by the hand like a child by my spirit guardians and shown the wonders of a non-physical universe. I was also shown many of the things that were possible by the correct application of the mind. As I explained before, at this period I suffered great hardships on account of severe poverty. I would accept that possibly I found a form of escapism from the reality of life in these excursions of the mind, so my poverty had a purpose.

I would often sit with my mother in deep meditation. Many aspect, of physical mediumship began to manifest themselves, including transfiguration in which the medium's features change to that of the communicator.

It was in this period that I first heard another spiritual soul speak in my mind. A seer I was visiting said to me: "There is a person with you whom I can see quite clearly. It must be the soul of a Turk for he is wearing a bright red fez on his head." I heard a voice so loud it was like somebody shouting inside a bell. There was all the scorn and derision in the world in his voice as he spoke these words; "I am *not* a Turk. I am an Armenian."

Later, after looking the matter up in reference books, I found that Armenia was conquered by Turkey with much bloodshed. Indeed there has been bad blood between the two countries for centuries.

During this period of learning, I encountered many souls who had left their bodies long ago. One particular personality channelled my thoughts into many obscure subjects and arguments. He educated me in the art of discernment of the truth, the half truths and the downright wishful thinking of people's statements – both verbal and written – which was to prove invaluable in the years ahead.

This guide first came into my line of inner sight when I was in a state of deep meditation. Dressed in Eastern robes, with facial features that were obviously of an oriental origin, his whole bearing and stance were not the sort of figure that would have sprung to my mind if asked to visualise a Chinese person for he was tall and well built.

The first time he appeared in my consciousness I thought with my usual disbelief that this was a product of my own imagination. To test whether or not this was true, I asked the soul his name. With no hesitation whatsoever he gave me his full name, title and the province where he had lived in Northern China. Not only did I hear his words, but I was also told how his name was spelt. After further research, I found full confirmation in a Chinese-English dictionary. His name spelt that certain way meant 'disciple of Confucius'. The middle name he gave me was the Chinese for 'the' whilst the last name was the same as our Harry, Bill, or Jack. I also discovered that the inhabitants of Northern China are taller and of a bigger general build than in the Southern provinces. My imagination could not possibly have dreamed all that up, so I had to accept his reality.

I discovered that there is a certain 'feel' to a soul. It is impossible to describe in words, but this 'feel' gives a true indication of that particular soul's spiritual evolvement and advancement, or lack of it. It is impossible to fake.

Lots of remarkable experiences occurred to me over those formative years that I still consider very precious for those memories are a constant reassurance to my beliefs, especially in the troublesome moments we all go through at times.

Being blessed with an active inquisitive mind, I pursued many avenues of mental exploration, partly out of curiosity and partly searching for a greater understanding of healing. Many times I came to a dead end, being informed quietly but firmly by my advisers; "This much you may know and no more. The knowledge you seek is denied while you live in a physical body."

37

I found there were other ways of gaining knowledge of healing. For instance, if I could not obtain a result with a certain sick condition, I would take a patient down to see Harry Edwards, who would often treat them with his hands over mine. Not always was he able to gain a result with these patients. Looking back, I know now that many of them had huge mental blocks against receiving either help or healing, but, in every case I brought back the knowledge on a subconscious level of how to treat and achieve results with that particular ailment. Later as the gift matured in me, I found that I could obtain healing knowledge just by observing Mr Edwards treating a patient, for I felt a great affinity with him.

Thank you Harry Edwards. I shall always be grateful to you for all your help and encouragement. I should think he is having a well earned rest, for his physical body died some years ago after a very full lifetime of dedicated service.

I have seen him just the once since his body died. I was treating a patient at the time when suddenly he appeared in front of me as large and as clear as life. He gave me a big smile and just said; "I wish I had known you better laddie. Carry on with the good work." Then he vanished.

There is a very special perfume of no earthly origin that I have been aware of many times. It is one that is impossible to describe fully. It's as if all the scents of the world's flowers have been mixed into one essence. Some who come for healing have commented on this fragrance being all around my person home while other patients do not sense it at all. I have known yet others carry this spirit perfume home on their clothing after receiving healing . . . and receive questioning looks from their partners.

These fragrances of the spirit world were first shown to me years ago. At the time, I was travelling with a companion in a car. Suddenly, it was filled with a heady perfume of Lily of the Valley flowers. It was so strong that I pulled the car into the side of the road and stopped. The smell lasted for several moments. Then as suddenly as it had arrived, it disappeared.

Neither of us could give any explanation for this visitation until we arrived at my friend's home, to be met with the news from his wife that she had just received a phone call from Ireland to tell of his brother's death in an accident . . . at the exact moment we experienced the perfume.

All manner of healing phenomena have been shown to me over my years of practice including psychic surgery, which to an unbeliever sounds a ridiculous affair. The first time I had experience of this was when I was taking my assistant home late one night after we had finished the clinic.

It had been raining and the roads were slippery and dark. Suddenly, a car swerved right across our path. I had no time to even touch the brakes and we slammed straight into it. Luckily nobody was badly injured except for my assistant, who received a nasty looking gash which was bleeding badly. This was caused by her knee violently hitting the dashboard. I immediately applied healing to the injury – and within a few moments the flow of blood had been staunched. Further treatment was given later that evening at the girl's home and this took away all the pain. Upon examination next morning, we found there was a neat and precise row of indentations exactly like stitch marks on either side of the gash. The skin tear was fully healed and she had no more trouble with the knee, but carried those psychic stitch marks for years afterwards.

Since then it has become a fairly regular occurrence but applied now with a greater finesse, with patients commenting on having a faint red line around the affected part which fades away to nothing within a few days and with no more trouble from the previously diseased part.

The young assistant had a great soul maturity and a strong natural gift of healing. She was brought by my spiritual helpers to aid me through a difficult period of learning and I shall always be indebted for her help and loyalty. "She was witness to an example of physical mediumship which showed the lengths that the source of healing will go to in its efforts to return people back to health. Incidentally, what I am about to relate has only happened the once.

Many years ago, a patient and her daughter came to see me for the healing of severe arthritis that was affecting every joint in the mother's body. She told me; "I lost my husband about two years previously with a heart attack. The shock of losing him has triggered off the arthritis." There was only a small improvement in her condition with healing so I was beginning to despair of summoning full help for her illness. Time after time she brought up the subject of, "if I could only see my husband again, I am sure I would be cured." According to the lady, they had shared this wonderful love affair and worshipped each other. She was certainly in for a shock. I, on my part, refused even to contemplate giving her such a sitting and became very annoyed over the matter for I felt that what she had in mind, had nothing to do with my work of healing.

This night in particular my assistant had just gone to make me a cup of tea. Whilst she was out, I was told mentally to sit down in a chair and compose myself. I then felt the build-up around me of an energy field and what could only have been ectoplasm. To me, it felt as though I was wearing a mask and my body felt encased in this energy. I then allowed the lady's husband to enter my mind.

My assistant came back with the tea – and was so shocked when she saw this stranger in my chair that she promptly dropped it all over the floor. On my part, I found the experience a very strange and novel one, for I could hear the voice of the lady's husband coming out of my mouth, and listened with interest to every word he spoke.

Here was no great love affair for he played 'holy war' with her. He told her of how selfish she was and always had been and that her health problem was caused by sheer guilt on her part. The husband gave her three months to mend her ways and take up a completely new attitude to life, otherwise she would be in a crippled state for the rest of her days. He left my body with just a curt, "Thank you."

Both the mother and daughter were thrilled at speaking to the husband. I lost touch with the patient after that, so have no idea of what the eventual outcome was.

There has been a continuous flow, spread over the years, of tuition and information regarding healing by my guardians. The general trend contained in their conversations with me was to the effect that I had to show great patience and allow my life's plan to work itself out without any haste, for they were building my future as a healer on firm foundations that would last the rest of my physical life.

I was also told I would from time to time gripe and moan at my lot in life, but that would not make the slightest difference to my path, for I had chosen this particular one long before I was born.

Looking backwards down the years, I can see that all their predictions have come true. It is only now that the reasons make complete sense to me. It was engineered in such a way, to enable me to stabilise my whole being so I would never abuse or misuse the higher energies of spirituality that would come to me in abundance at a later date, that date to be determined by how I passed these tests of life.

Another person put it in a slightly different way when I was holding a clinic at the home of a dear friend of mine who is a rabbi. He came into the room where I had been treating patients, grinning all over his face.

At the time I was just having a five minute break after treating three Jewish people. I asked him, "Do tell me what you find so funny?" It took him a few moments to control himself before he could tell me, saying, "You have just treated three of my race very successfully but they have been having a real argument outside in the hall."

One of them said, "How come this gentile has a wonderful gift of healing bestowed on him by the Almighty and we, who are of the chosen race, haven't?"

His companion answered him by saying; "Well, how do you think we would behave if we were given such a wonderful gift? We would develop a head so big it wouldn't go through the front door." The third person then said in a thoughtful voice, "Oh, I see what you mean."

If you have the potential to be a healer and are searching for ways to develop your gift, I can tell you from my own experience that reading books will *not* gain you entry into any of healing's wonders. It is, however, reassuring to you to know what is possible by a fully developed healer, for what one person can do another can follow.

I trod that same pathway of yearning for more and more knowledge. The local library assistant was helpful and guided me to the section devoted to healing and kindred subjects. There were row upon row of such books and I read them all like a man inspired. I learned of Christian science healing, divine healing, faith healing, spirit healing, magnetic healing, psychic healing, contact healing, absent healing and positive healing. Most of them were beyond my understanding, consequently, I finished up more confused than when I started reading up on the subject. I read of forces called odic, of auras, of spirits, and of etheric bodies. The word 'esoteric' had me puzzled, for at that time I had a notion it meant a good night out on the Continent!

My head reeled at so many apparently conflicting views. That is why this book is written in such a simple manner, for one such as this could have helped me greatly in my search.

Great patience is needed for spiritual knowledge to percolate through to your physical mind. Like many other people with a partially developed gift, at times in the past I have grown impatient at what I thought to be my lack of progress. I have then taken an initiative directly against the advice of my spiritual advisers. Invariably, it has turned out to be a complete failure.

The first time I went against their advice was when I desperately wanted to use my new-found gift of healing on a larger scale, for I felt it would be the only way I would find any fulfilment in life. I raised all the cash I could and took a three-month lease on premises with a view to opening a healing sanctuary. It was simply not meant to be, for I came head-first against bureaucracy and closed without opening! I was refused planning permission and ojections from nearby churches and local authorities proved to be insurmountable. The forces of chaos were certainly hard at work against me.

Not satisfied with that fiasco – and again, against my intuitive inner voice's warning – I did a repeat performance. I was even more impatient to enter what I imagined to be the perfect world of a full-time healer and once more decided in my own impetuous way that I knew better than my instincts. I felt certain I would be fully supported in my efforts by the forces of love that administer healing.

In my innocence I thought that this fact alone would force the issue in my favour. I placed an advert in the *Yorkshire Post* to the effect that I was prepared to visit and give healing to sick people in their own homes, adding that if there was no cure, there would be no charge. My rose tinted glasses were certainly in full operation since I was snowed under with the replies and worked myself nearly silly trying my best for them. Through snow, hail, rain and gale, at all hours of the night and day, I struggled around to see patients, dogged and determined.

The end result was a revelation to me for after six months of solid effort, I had not a penny in the world to show for it and was in despair. There had been scores of quite wonderful and unusual cures, but only a handful of patients had the gratitude to help me by payment. Some who had been cured of long-standing ailments agreed their conditions had been cured and had the cheek and rudeness to turn round to me and say that they would have become better anyway!

My whole being was filled with total disillusionment and sadness; my world felt shattered. My inner voice told me: "We told you. Why will you not listen to good advice? Our only aim is for you to spread God's love. We will look after your welfare. You are so headstrong we would never give you any advice that would cause you harm or distress. Your greatest need is not to learn about healing, but to learn about people." Since that episode, I have always followed any advice that my advisers have given me. They have never let me down.

The moment I had been eagerly awaiting came. I was told mentally, "The time is *now*." My friends immediately rose up in mass protest and gave me dire warnings as to what a fool I was. I was told by them that the spiritual adventure I contemplated was doomed, like the rest of my previous efforts, to failure. I elected to follow my inner voice, plunged myself heavily in to debt, and had a go. As a true test of faith I would recommend it to anyone. If I had known the full measure of moral courage needed and the sheer determination I would have to show in the next few years, I can assure you I would have viewed the future a lot more apprehensively. I had passed the tests of life with flying colours.

Readers of a scientific mind will be interested in the following. Physical changes take place in a healer's body as the gift develops. The nerve centres, or chakras, used by spirit to receive and transmit healing energy to the patient become enlarged with continual use, especially the solar plexus chakra, which in my case has developed in size to about two feet by one and a half feet. When I am working, this area emits an icy power and is cold to the touch. There is also a place between my shoulder blades from which an icy draught blows outwards. I find it uncomfortable if somebody places a hand in this area.

Around my body is an energy field that can be felt by any sensitive person from several feet away. Those of a scientific leaning who have tested me in the past, say there is evidence of a strong electrical field varying from a quarter of a volt to nearly a volt, extending several feet outwards from my body. When they have connected me to a oscilloscope, there is a powerful sine wave pattern recorded. Sometimes if somebody is recording on a cassette when I am healing, there is evidence of a powerful signal exactly the same as if one were close to a powerful radio transmitter. These are the limits of evidence I can produce of a scientific nature, bar the most important one, the disappearance of illness in the patient. The energy of life around a healer when he is working is visible to the sight, for if viewed against a dark background it can be seen as a haze all around the healer's body. I always receive the same stock, rather sulky reply from scientists They say on leaving, "You have something special, but it does not appear to belong to known physics." This does seem to annoy them!

Chapter Three

MY HEALING MISSION TO ISRAEL

ISRAEL is a land steeped in historical happenings. Even the fiercest critic of Judaism would acknowledge the fact that the barren desert has been made to bloom by the application of grim determination and, sheer hard work.

It is an old and fascinating country, in which many religions have their foundations. Israel walks hand in hand with biblical history. It was also a land ordained by destiny to which I should take my gift of healing. It is a long way from the dirty and dull streets of Bradford to this land of sunshine.

Read of the complicated ways that are used by the fates, who are in total control of my life, to bring to fruition their plans for gaining spiritual help for those that suffer.

My entry into Israel was through a patient who made a miraculous recovery from a serious illness. Just that single healing was the start of six healing missions into that country, culminating in bringing health to thousands of people. Many of those who were cured had been in intense pain and distress since the last world war, when a large proportion of them were incarcerated in concentration camps, and who had barely escaped with their lives.

To those brave, lovely people, who bore their pains with such patience and fortitude, my visits were like an answer to a prayer. I, in turn, still consider it a great privilege to have been the one chosen to bring help to them.

There is a minority of private doctors in Israel who, devoid of all human feelings, traded on the fact that Jewish people in general have a great fear of ill health. Many of these doctors were so incompetent that completely wrong diagnosis were regularly given, thereby making any treatment useless, plus placebos, weird medicines and non-effective drugs that were prescribed, knowing they were of no medicinal value for that patient. To them I say, "Shame on you." Many of the old time 'snake oil' salesmen in the middle West of America had more compassion. This handful of doctors had many money-making antics, including subjecting many patients to painful and completely unnecessary surgical operations. All this, costing money, of which many patients were desperately short. One day such practitioners will have to answer to the Almighty for the sheer greed in bleeding their own people.

Such is the political influence of some of these undedicated medics in Israel, that on my last visit I was arrested as I arrived at Ben Gurion Airport on a trumped up charge . . . and slammed straight into a police cell!

I was then subjected to the indignity of a body search by soldiers and told I was

43

suspected of being a spy for the Arabs and therefore I was considered a high security risk. Within minutes of this happening, they tried to place me on the next flight back to England. Luckily there wasn't a single seat spare on the plane, otherwise I would not have been able to finish my healing mission.

The humiliation and shock to my system was to say the least shattering, for within a few short moments I descended from the high peak of sheer joy and inner elation at the anticipation of helping hundreds of patients that had been booked in for me to treat, down to the utter rejection of having a .45 automatic pistol stuck in my ribs and being told I was under arrest.

Dismay turned to anger as my short fused temper threatened to blow. What a way to repay all the good work my gift of healing had been instrumental in gaining for so many people in this country!

It was at this point the inner voice spoke in my mind, saying; "Be still, my son. All will be well." My indignation subsided. I was then placed in a cell under the watchful eye of two armed guards to await the next plane back to England.

My prospects looked grim for I was dressed only in shirt, trousers and sandals, with no luggage . . . and it was winter back in England. I had not a single penny on me as I left all my money in the safe custody of my lady, who was nearly demented with worry for me, having been told untruthfully that I was already on an aircraft 'en route' back to the United Kingdom.

Waiting patiently in the police cell, I basked in the warmth of spiritual energies that seemed to encase me in a safe protective blanket and awaited whatever fate had in store for me. A great peaceful stillness settled over me and I grew inwardly quiet to such an extent that I fell soundly asleep.

When I eventually awoke, the atmosphere in the police station had changed completely from one of downright hostility and suspicion, to that of definite friendliness.

My guards even brought me a mug of tea. One of them who spoke good English came over and conversed with me. We had a long conversation about my work of healing. It became obvious from what he said that he knew exactly who I was and the reasons why I was in Israel.

He then asked me if I would be willing to treat both himself and his friend as they had both been troubled with very painful spinal conditions for some years. I agreed, and proceeded to treat them. I was able to cure both their conditions within the space of a few short moments, much to their obvious astonishment.

My internment continued for several more hours, until the organiser of my mission to Israel appeared. He was both flustered and apologetic, bringing with him the necessary clearance papers to gain my freedom. He told me it had taken the full weight of the Minister of the Interior and the co-operation of two Senators who he knew, to gain my freedom.

It was obvious that many strings had been pulled and palms greased, in a vain attempt to stop me healing. The actual truth did not emerge until several months later when I received a letter from some patients I had cured.

The reason given for my arrest was, I cured so many sick people that certain medical doctors had been treating unsuccessfully for years. It was these doctors, who were so frightened of losing a fat, easy living, that they had conjured up the false charge against me in an attempt to stop me healing.

So much for the dedication and vocation of some doctors! This ugly section of

44

the medical profession is in a distinct minority for I did meet many dedicated medical personnel in hospitals and was able to treat a number of them with great success. They could not assimilate my ideas on sickness and health, which I suppose is quite natural in view of the fact that many of my theories were directly opposed to those they had been taught at medical school. However, they had to admit the total success of my healing, even if they couldn't understand its workings.

I think that what impressed them mostly was the energy field that is all around my body when I am giving healing, which, as already explained, can be felt from several feet away.

The aftermath to this strange story was that over the following two weeks I was able to treat several hundred people, with the usual good results. I was warned to keep a quiet profile during this visit. At times, I gained the uncomfortable feeling of being spied upon, fully expecting that other efforts would be made to stop me administering healing. The powers of goodness must have all their work cut out to frustrate those of chaos.

It is highly probable that a lesser person would have said "That's it!" and taken his bat home, hurt and disgusted at such treatment. I did, however, say to a highly placed official when I was leaving the airport; "The only way I will return to Israel will be at the written request of your government. Healing at a level of success not seen for centuries was offered to your people by the Almighty. Some of your own people rejected it, exactly as they did in the past. I am going home to England. It's up to your people to muse over what has happened, through the gift of a Gentile from England." Incidently, I now have that permission.

For those who think being a healer is a certain pathway to great riches, it may be of interest to know that on only one occasion were we 'in pocket' through our work in Israel, and then it was only minimal. I hasten to add, though, that the experiences I went through and all the love and affection that was literally showered on me, plus the wonderful benefits gained for my patients, far outweighed any monetary considerations.

At the start of this chapter I mentioned a 'Miracle of healing' that instigated my missions to this land. I am very chary of using such a word, for in my opinion, healing must honour the boundaries of nature's laws. But on this occasion I think that what follows did fall into the category of the miraculous.

They say that God works in mysterious ways, and none can be more mysterious than on this occasion. The patient concerned was a very religious person, belonging to the Lubavitch Sect of Judaism, who in everyday life was a diamond dealer. On a routine business trip to New York, he suddenly developed severe sugar diabetes. One of the side effects of the illness in his case, was to render him practically blind. The dealer was rushed into a famous New Jersey hospital, where for many weeks hospital doctors tried desperately to stabilise his blood sugar level with massive dozes of insulin, all to no effect. Finally, after all their efforts came to nothing, he was discharged and advised to make his way home to Israel.

The headquarters of his particular sect of Judaism are in New York under the control of Rabbi Schneerson, whose father-in-law started the organisation after arriving from Russia many years ago.

The patient arranged for a personal audience with Rabbi Schneerson, who has a great reputation for having 'gifts of the spirit' himself, to ask his advice on this serious health problem. The rabbi's advice was: "On your way home to Israel, stop off in England and visit Don Greenbank at his home in Yorkshire, and he will cure you."

It was such a direct and forthright statement, no ifs, no perhaps, no maybe, but he will cure you. He was right.

The patient duly arrived in England and came to attend me for healing. Within a few moments he had recovered his sight to such an extent that his thick lensed spectacles were no longer of any use to him for he could see much better without them.

The next morning, he rang me from Heathrow Airport to say that he had gained even further improvement in his sight, and that he was filled to overflowing with a wonderful sense of inner peace. He flew home to Israel and was admitted at once to the Tella Shamir Hospital in Tel Aviv where intensive medical tests were carried out. Doctors were unable to find the slightest trace of diabetes.

The aftermath of this was, that the hospital in Israel telephoned the hospital in New Jersey, and a huge row developed. The Israeli hospital commented, "We are rather surprised that you, with all your sophisticated equipment, wrongly diagnosed this patient as having sugar diabetes." They were, however, unable to say what in their opinion, had been wrong with the patient.

The hospital thought of it as a feather in their cap, being able to rebuke a famous American hospital, but I rather suspect that there had been occasions in the past when it was the other way round. The patient, as usual – which never ceases to amaze me – dare not mention to doctors that he had been to see me and received healing. The diamond dealer did, however, tell all his friends and acquaintances. The response from them was so great that within a very short space of time he contacted myself with an invitation to Israel, producing a list of several hundred people who wished to receive healing. That figure was to rapidly grow into thousands as the cures flooded out from under my hands.

The very first healing treatment in this strange land was a most dramatic one. I was taken to a settlement situated just outside Jerusalem where I gave healing to a little girl of eight years of age who had been totally deaf in one ear since birth.

Her healing would set the pattern for all my future work in this country for she was completely cured within the space of a few seconds. After healing, she had perfect hearing for the first time in her young life. In fact, her hearing in the once totally deaf ear became so acute she could hear the ticking of a lady's small wrist-watch quite clearly. Word travels quickly around rural communities in Israel and within a matter of hours we were inundated with requests for healing's help. The Four Seasons Hotel in Natanya began to resemble a hospital, with patients waiting in long lines for treatment, filling the corridors and even the hotel reception area. Finally to accommodate them all, we had to move into one of the large penthouse suites.

On one occasion I was forced to smile as I was deeply immersed in treating patients when the interpreter came dashing into the room. She was pale faced and trembling like a leaf. "Protect me please. I think it's the Devil himself at the door," she shouted at me, obviously scared out of her wits. I dashed to the door and found an angry little paunchy man, who was loosely dressed in a bright scarlet dressing gown covered in astrological signs. He had come to complain at the noise caused by the waiting patients queuing in the hallway outside his suite. There was no appeasing him for he was not a nice person. Later, he tried his level best to have us thrown out of the hotel. This was all to no avail for the manager had been treated and cured by myself just the previous day, of a long standing complaint.

It was obvious the hotel had never seen anything like it before as a stream of patients became a flood. They included soldiers who had been wounded in the war, workers from distant settlements, very orthodox rebbies (leaders of sects), biblical students, farm workers, artists and artisans, and brutalised victims of the concentration camps, in fact every possible type of person you could ever imagine flocked for healing.

It was such a heart-warming experience to be able to relieve people of pain they had suffered for the last thirty or forty years. Many carried tattoo marks on their forearms, placed there in the death camps.

One sad case was an old lady, well into her eighties, who for years had been forced to take massive daily doses of pain-killing drugs to ease her pain which had been caused by having her back smashed in by a rifle butt in a wartime prison camp.

I thank God that not only was healing able to remove all the pain from her spine and make her body fully mobile again, but healing was also given to her mind. The old lady gained a completely new outlook on life and as a result slept peacefully every night after the healing. Later she told me that all those hurtful memories which had haunted and scarred her mind had now gone. She could hardly remember those terrible years of imprisonment when her family had all been killed, one by one, until only herself was left.

In Israel, being a very religious country, all the settlements and kibbutz are closed on the Shabbat, (sunset Friday to sunset Saturday), yet so acceptable was my work of healing that we were given special dispensation to visit these places and give healing, a thing unheard of previously.

We were forced to smile at some of those first patients, who in many instances turned out to be rebbies. A lot were not really ill. I could tell this instantly from my awarenesses, and I told them so. They had really come for healing to test myself and my motives, not without cause, as was explained to me later, for there has been many false 'miracle workers' enter the country, sailing under the banner of religion.

Having passed the tests with flying colours, for these rebbies were witness to many spectacular cures – they went back to their flocks and spread the word that they could safely come to me for help, as I was 'an honest man!'

Under the constant pressure of treating so many people, my days and nights were filled with all manner of strange and inexplicable happenings. This had the effect of making all my senses more acute, so much so that at times I thought my mind would blow under the pressure. It felt as though I was like a highly tuned musical instrument. I lost my appetite completely for my body no longer felt the need for food. Possibly this was because there was a constant flow of healing energy through me. I did, however, feel the need to drink large amounts of liquids. In some way, this was used in the healing effort.

You have probably heard of the 'gift of tongues'. Well, I have experienced this curious phenomenon many times, not the gibberish that one usually associates with this term, but a complete and full understanding of a foreign language.

The first time this happened to me was after I had been working intensely for several hours, in an hotel in Tel Aviv. A man came for healing – it turned out that he was a biblical scholar from Jerusalem – who didn't speak a single word of English. At that time I must have been in a greatly altered state of consciousness, for to me it was like a reunion with a brother after many years apart. The feeling was mutual, and we embraced as if we were family. We then proceeded to have a long and involved conversation in classical Hebrew, the ancient language of the Bible.

The interpreter was stunned, since she could not understand a single word we were speaking to each other. On my part, I just accepted the fact that I could understand every word that was spoken, both by him and myself. Then I treated his sickness and put it right. We embraced like brothers, and he went on his way with a smile.

Only later did I find out from the translator that I had been speaking this strange tongue. Another odd aspect of this encounter was that everybody who was in the room, swore he was an old man with a long white beard while I 'saw' him as a young man, at the most in his early thirties.

This was another mysterious example of God in action. Probably in one of the nicest ways I have ever seen, was what happened to a patient I treated. His story began when he was in America studying at a theological college. It appeared he had suffered from multiple sclerosis for a number of years. The condition became so advanced he could only walk with great difficulty, and only then with the aid of two walking sticks.

One day, at study in the USA, he had a strange overpowering urge to return to Israel. Following this mental directive, he caught the first available plane though he still had no idea why he had to go home. Three days later he had another overpowering urge to return to his old college in Jerusalem. I, on my part, had been taken to the self-same college that morning to treat the principal, who, strangely enough, was also suffering from multiple sclerosis. The condition of the principal was too far advanced to be able to acquire a great deal of help, as it was obvious he was in the terminal stages of the illness and had only a short time to live. In point of fact, he died two days later, exactly as my intuition told me.

We were on our way out of the college when we met the man who had just returned from America. My companion had known him for a number of years. He was in a sorry state, dragging his feet along and only able to walk very slowly and with great difficulty. When I was introduced to him and he was told I was the English healer, he begged me to treat him, as the reason for his visit home was then becoming obvious.

We re-entered the college and found a quiet room where I could heal him. He responded well and within a few moments regained a lot of the lost feeling in his limbs. His balance also improved and he was able to walk out of the college gates with ease, his bearing becoming erect, where previously he had been bent like an old man. Moreover, he was able to walk with the aid of just one walking stick, using it merely as a balancing aid.

We heard much later that a most exciting thing happened to him and his wife. After seventeen years of marriage they still had no family. Six weeks after I treated him, his wife became pregnant – and later delivered a fine, healthy son, something they had prayed for years to happen. Their prayers were answered in the most unexpected way. He told me of one thing they had learned from me, "That God works through people."

There are some things about Israel I find very disturbing to my mental state. My acute senses tell me of mighty natural energies nearly out of control. That is why I can never visualise a state of peace existing for very long in this land. There is such a climate of what I can only term 'an unrest of the earth.'

It has nothing to do with the people, but everything with the land itself for there are certain parts of this country that disturb me like nothing else I have ever encountered anywhere before. It is as though there are raw primaeval energies contained in the very earth itself. I cannot explain it any deeper than that. All I know is that, when I visit these places I have an uncomfortable feeling inwardly, and the hackles rise on the back of my neck. Full understanding of these forces is not possible as they lie well beyond any form of human comprehension. These energies feel neither good nor bad: they are strictly neutral in character. Perhaps the best description would be that, to my acute senses they seem to be alien energies, ones that do not appear to originate on this planet. Now work that one out?

Other areas of Israel are a direct opposite in that they exude a feeling of perfect peace and tranquillity and I could quite cheerfully live there. For instance, there are parts in the Galilee where the spiritual peace was so strong, it made the whole act of healing an easier than usual affair.

Many sensitives who have also visited these regions have confirmed my opinion. I have heard it described as 'natural forces in conflict' or 'mighty forces of love and strong, energies of chaos in an age-old struggle for supremacy.'

Everything there seems to my senses to be exaggerated and larger than life, more so than any other place I have encountered on this globe. Perhaps as well as the alien element, there is the fact that over the centuries there has been so much bloodshed in some of these places that the very stones themselves are steeped in gore and impressed with pain. This is bound to have a depressing and disturbing effect on any sensitive.

The involved nature of my ministry of healing and the organisation and work in its administration from the after life, must be breathtaking and colossal in both its conception, and actual operation. All this work just to enable me to be the front man in bringing back health to the suffering.

The involved nature of healing was shown to me once again when I was giving treatment in a private house in Begni Brack, which is a suburb of Tel Aviv.

From what I saw, it would appear that people of this world, both those still living in bodies and those who have left theirs, are being gradually educated into this method of gaining health from the Heavenly Kingdom.

For several hours I had been treating patients. The room where I was working was literally alive and bouncing with healing energy. I was deeply engrossed in treating a patient. Have you ever had the feeling that somebody was watching you closely? The effect is to make you feel rather uncomfortable. Well, that was exactly the sensation that I felt.

Glancing upwards, I had the shock of my life when I saw that the upper part of the room had taken on the appearance of an operating theatre in a teaching hospital, one where student doctors can sit above and study the art of surgery. Deeply engrossed and staring down at me and the healing scene, were dozens of people dressed in all different kinds of fur headgear, similar to that worn on special occasions by the very religious orders of Judaism.

I became so fascinated and engrossed in the scene above me that I lost my concentration with the patient. As a result, the healing process began to falter. The next instant I heard the voice of my spiritual guardian speaking in my mind. In his familiar deep, yet soft voice he said: "Ignore them, my son. They are merely here to receive instruction." With those words, the scene above faded from my awareness and I was once more able to give my full attention to the patient I was treating, with the usual fulfilling result.

I did not receive any further explanation as to the 'how and why', of what I had just been witness to, the implication being that I should mind my own business and perform to the very best of my ability the job I had been brought to Israel to perform. That task was to act as a channel for healing, and that I must realise by now that the whole venture was divinely inspired and of such complication it would be beyond my understanding.

I was told later by a rabbi I enquired of that some of the clothing and ornaments of apparel I described to him as being worn by the souls that were watching this particular healing, belonged to sects that had died out and which had no followers in this day and age. In Judaism there are many divisions of religious opinion, mainly because the Torah, or the five main Holy books of Hebrew law written down by Moses, around which it revolves, is not a set of inflexible laws.

While all Jewish people should follow the basic pattern laid down in the Torah, the books of Holy scripture are very loosely put together. As a result of this, many aspects of theology are wide open to differing rabbinical interpretation on many small issues, with greater individual emphasis being placed on some matters more than others. Over the centuries this has resulted in different sects being formed, similar in many respects to the many divisions of opinion that exist in Christianity.

Another interesting point regarding my healing is that the longer I am working, then the 'higher' I become mentally, and the more energy comes through me for the patient's benefit. I never seem to tire and my senses become ever more acute. In this refined state it is quite usual to become aware of things that are outside my normal spectrum of observation.

This alteration to my conscious state, often results in myself not having the slightest idea what has happened during the healing, for this particular 'high' state carries no memory. The only way I am able to write this book is that my mind has been opened by my spiritual guardians to allow the return of memories and so relate these writings. In the clinic here in Yorkshire, when a person walks out after treatment, so my memory of them goes with them. Although I feel quite natural and speak normally, all the time I am transmitting healing I must be in an altered mental state.

Later I am often told by patients of the puzzling things that have happened inside their bodies while receiving healing. When in this euphoric state, it is quite usual for me to experience crystal-clear, inspirational mental flashes, whereby I can tell the patient with certainty of factors contributing to their sick condition.

On my many trips around Israel, I found it distressing to see the treatment of most religious places of interest, be it Jewish, Christian, or Muslim. So if you ever have an opportunity to visit the country, be prepared for a shock. Instead of leaving these sites in a natural condition, the various powers that be have covered these venerated sites with often grotesque buildings of a pseudo-churchy character. That would be bad enough in itself, but to make matters worse, in many instances, possibly to keep out intruders, the perimeter walls have been covered with either rolls of barbed wire or shards of broken glass set in cement. It is purely a personal thing, but I wish they wouldn't.

Before going to Israel, the identity of that special soul who first came to me in wartime on that cold winter's night over Germany so long ago now, was still a complete mystery to me. He had exasperated me so many times in his refusal to give me any information as to who he was or rather who he had been when he lived in a body. Time after time he answered me in the same way, saying, "names belong only to the physical world of matter and are of no importance. There are 'fibbers' on the lower planes of spirit life just as there are on the earth plane. If any soul ever contacts you through your awarenesses and tries to impress you with his previous earthly calling, then sadly he has progressed very little up the ladder of spiritual progression. Any statements he makes to you should be viewed with a strong measure of caution."

It was only after many years that this veil of secrecy was partially lifted, and that only came about by the remotest of chances, or was it intended?

In England, by sheer coincidence I met a lady who had travelled the world over with her calling, she was a lecturer on spiritual matters, in Yorkshire on a flying visit. By mere chance I happened to be at the home of some friends where she was staying.

We shook hands and had a general conversation regarding her work. Suddenly, out of the blue, she said to me, "Do you know a soul from the far side of life who had a long white beard?" I nodded my head in reply. She then said, "Well, I have brought you his picture. It's an icon, and very old. I have had it for years, but as soon as I met you, I knew it was intended for you." With no more ado, she produced the icon, which was obviously very ancient. My heart sank, since it bore no resemblance to the person I had seen in my mind's eye for all those years. Then my mentor's voice filtered into my mind, saying, "Don't worry. It is only an artist's impression, but it will be useful to you for it carries good energies." The lady continued, "I have no idea who the painting depicts, but it is certainly intended for you."

Some time later, a Roman Catholic priest came for healing. Out of curiosity I mentioned the icon, and asked him if he knew who the person painted on it was. "Of course I do," he replied. "That is a painting of Saint Jerome." I then asked him to tell me all he could regarding the saint.

"Well," said the priest, "He was quite a character, a rebel against the system, and very intellectual. In fact, he was the first person to translate the Bible from the Hebrew into Greek and Latin. It appears that he went to live in the Vatican in Rome, but became so appalled at what was happening in what should have been a Holy City, that he took himself off to Bethlehem with two assistants and two sisters to care for his needs. They lived together in a cave near to where Jesus is said to have been born. He kept a lion as a pet, he and his assistants ran a

51

hospice for travellers and pilgrims."

(Saint Jerome – his full name was Sophronius Eusebius Hieronymus – he retired to the Syrian desert after having a vision and devoted himself to a mastery of Hebrew. In AD 370, he was ordained at Antioch. Later in AD 385, he settled in Bethlehem. His body died on 20th September, AD 420.

This answered some of my questions, but full confirmation did not come to me until some time later when I visited Israel for the first time. On visiting Saint Jerome's former home, we found that a convent had been built on the ground above the cave where he once lived. Right in the middle of the courtyard stood a statue of the saint. Confirmation was immediate, for this was indeed the person who I had 'seen' in my mind's eye for all those years.

Going down into the cave where he once lived, I asked some friends to take a photograph of me there. I requested they left me for a few moments while I sought attunement, then to return and take a second photograph. The results when we had the film printed were astonishing. The first picture was quite normal yet the second taken a few moments later from the same position, shows a complete transformation of my features. Indeed it looked like a completely different person, with definite signs of ectoplasm around my shoulders and my face, taking on the features of Saint Jerome.

Returning to the icon, it proved to be in itself a tremendous source of healing energy. It always exuded a soothing, healing coldness which had the quality of removing inflammation from a patient's sick condition. If a person was in deep trouble with a serious illness, I would often feel impressed to lend the icon to them, on the understanding that it would be returned to me when the illness had gone.

I carried on with this practice for a number of years. A great many patients gained wonderful cures until I finally loaned it to a person who I knew was in the terminal stages of an illness. Whilst not expecting a cure for this patient, I hoped it would make her passing easier and more peaceful. That was the last time I saw the icon. Neither did I hear from this person's family. I hope that the power contained within this lovely object is still being used to help sick people. If it is not and somebody reading this account knows of its whereabouts, please return it, as I have good uses for it.

It was one of my life's greatest pleasures in Israel to treat many children for a variety of ailments. It warmed my heart, as when they were speaking of me they called me "Do-Do-Dan," which means Uncle Don in Hebrew.

Earlier I spoke of the forces of goodness and those of chaos that abound in Israel. Some friends who accompanied me on one of my visits had first hand experience of this force of chaos. Do not gain the impression they were airy fairy gullible folk, since they are down-to-earth Yorkshire business people. They are, however, very sensitive to healing, for both they and their animals have received cures on a number of occasions over the years of our friendship. Moreover they have witnessed thousands of cures as observers in my clinic.

I have emphasised these facts to show they are quite normal, and in no way neurotic. The night in question, after an exhausting day watching me heal and dealing with patients, we all went back to the hotel, had our evening meal and after a short stroll, retired to bed for the night. My friends told me they fell asleep at once, but were awakened in the middle of the night by an ice cold presence that filled the whole apartment. Also present was an intense feeling of what they could only describe as sheer evil.

My friends felt all alone and unprotected; they clung to each other and prayed desperately for divine help. After what seemed to them like an eternity, the cold and hateful feeling gradually subsided. They were too disturbed to sleep and just clung to each other until the dawn broke. As sunshine flooded their apartment, everything at first glance appeared normal, until they noticed that of the many vases of flowers in the room, not a single bloom had survived. They all lay wilted or dead.

My friends were shaken to the core of their beings. It was a great relief to them when my mission finished and we all flew home to England. Their troubles, however, were not at an end for strange and inexplicable happenings occurred in their home.

The effects of these experiences touched them both deeply. Later the husband had what can only be termed as a nervous breakdown. Even to this day, years after these experiences, he finds it very difficult to talk about the matter without becoming extremely upset. Such are the dreadful effects that the forces of chaos work on good people!

I am well used to attacks by the forces of evil, but in my case, I am spiritually well protected by the forces of love. Having spent half a lifetime in constant battle with these dark forces who delight in destroying good works and high ideals – and subjecting decent well intentioned people to abuse, in an attempt to destroy their principles, I can speak with authority.

It applies to every person who tries to do a good deed or perform a generous act. Then trouble will roll in within a short time in an attempt to try and dissuade you into never doing a similar thing ever again.

On the other hand if you do anything bad, unsavoury or unkind, I can assure you that not a single thing will stand in your way and the going will be easy. Look back through your memories and you will find that I am right. Somewhere I read the cynical remark that 'no good deed goes unpunished.'

It is a good thing there is a compensating force of goodness which holds a balance against these evil energies. Both my lady and myself experienced the following good influence. For want of a better term, I shall call the presence 'the spirit of Israel'.

My lady and I were in different rooms at the time, but we both heard and felt its presence simultaneously. Then a mighty voice boomed out in our minds. It said; "My people are your people. Your people are my people. My people need your help."

With this statement the presence left us, leaving behind a great sense of perfect peace and an inner reassurance that all our efforts to help the sick in Israel was recognised in high places.

Such visionary experiences – often a by product of the healing experience – are not as frequent as I would like. Perhaps this is mainly because my role in life says I must keep both feet planted solidly on the ground and make healing acceptable to everyone, but thank goodness they do happen.

Of all such events I have experienced over the years of healing, the one that had the greatest impact on me, and whose memory is as clear today as then, occurred very early one morning.

The dawn was just breaking on the Sea of Galilee. The sun had not yet risen. I remember clearly there was not even a ripple on the water. A heavy mist rolled down from the hills and formed a soft curtain across the sea. It was an unreal scene as I walked into the water up to my neck. In a state of meditation I drank in the breathtaking scene of peace, total calmness and inactivity, for nothing moved. Even the cry of the birds was hushed and muted. In the distance the Golan Heights made an impressive backdrop to this tranquil scene of perfect peace. It was at that moment that my vision happened. Moving slowly towards me through the mists, on the surface of the water, was the figure of a man with a brilliant radiance all round his outline.

The divine light issuing from him was so bright I was unable to distinguish any of his features. I basked in the glow of the purifying spiritual radiance that flowed from him in waves of pure love. The most startling thing that stands out in my memory was his hair, which was smooth, with a luminous shine to it. Going right down to his shoulders, it gleamed strongly in the light that shone around him. Its colour was a curious mixture of dark brown and russet. I have seen that colour only rarely, like the sun shining on a horse's coat after it has just been curry combed. Not a word was spoken, for they were unnecessary. Finally with a hand raised to me in a blessing, the figure faded from my sight, leaving me elated and overwhelmed.

I have no idea how long this wonderful encounter lasted, for time seemed to be in a state of suspension.

Words are a poor substitute to the actual human experience of such a soul-touching event. It is happenings of this nature which give birth to the all powerful knowing faith and practical beliefs that are essential for one to be able to face and overcome the problems, derision and envious scorn, that the world of matter frequently throws at those who have gifts of the spirit.

I am certain that my role in life is not one of being a superman for I am in my own mind a very ordinary person, who is shy and retiring in my inner nature and mind, with all the faults that this human condition is prone to and who, at times, feels totally unfitted for the role that fate has allocated me to play.

I probably would be like anyone else in normal circumstances, without having this ability to tune into the Holy Spirit. A transformation takes place when I am attuned and acting as transmitter for the healing energy. In an instant, I become a completely different person with a powerful charisma and a gift that feels capable of raking the very heavens themselves in its efforts to gain help for patients.

Like most people, I do at times make self – examinations and wonder who I am in reality. It is for certain, though, that I am performing a task allocated to me long before I was born into this human condition of life.

On one occasion I was taken to treat a patient in the Haddasa Hospital in Jerusalem. The sufferer was a youngish man who was in the terminal stages of an illness caused by a malignant tumour in his brain. Before going into this particular hospital, he had been to America for an operation. On his discharge, the hospital told him he was completely cured, which simply was not true. On his arrival back home in Israel, the illness flared up again. At the point I saw him, he had been in a complete coma for several weeks. To enable me to treat him in privacy, he was wheeled in his bed into the office of the hospital's resident rabbi.

Within a few moments of me beginning to treat him, he opened his eyes wide, smiled broadly and started talking excitably to one corner of the room. The rabbi made a motion with his hand, to the effect that he thought the young man was having delusions.

I rapidly tuned in to the patient's mind and immediately saw exactly what he could see. I was aware of this very imposing soul dressed in a large fur hat that orthodox Jewish men wear on their Shabat. As well as seeing him, I gained a full appreciation of what the situation was all about. I was able to give the resident rabbi a full commentary.

I told him, "This patient is actually talking to the soul of his grandfather, who was a famous rabbi with a very large following in Jerusalem." I then went on to describe, in full detail, the special fur hat that the soul was wearing, which belonged, in that certain shape, to the grandfather's particular sect. The clinching point of identification to the resident rabbi was when I told him that this personality wore a big red, bushy beard.

I went on to tell the rabbi that the grandfather had come for his grandson, and that the boy would be departing his body within the space of two days. In point of fact, he died peacefully in his sleep two days later. The rabbi was astonished. Tapping his head with his finger, he said; "You can 'see'. This is wonderful news. I have heard of such things, but never before encountered it." He then verified that the grandfather *had* been a famous rabbi, and that he *had* worn a big red beard.

Possibly the quickest healing that happened in Israel took place within the space of a few seconds. Rabbi Yossi Rosenstine, probably best known the world over as a painter of Biblical scenes in the surrealist manner, brought his four-year-old son for healing.

The child had been released from hospital that very morning suffering from what was termed an abscess of the lung, a diagnosis that had been confirmed several times previously by X-rays. I sat the little chap on my knee and having identified mentally where the trouble lay, sought healing's help for him.

The healing energy that came for the little one was staggering in its intensity. It came like a bolt from heaven. Immediately I was told via my intuitive senses that the cure was full and complete. My words to the father were; "All the pain has been removed. The abscess is now fully healed. Return to the hospital now and have further X-rays taken and the doctor will give you confirmation that the cure is complete."

The boy confirmed all the pain had gone. His breathing was normal, with none of the rasping sounds he had previously. With a smile of thankfulness the father dashed out with his son and returned within three hours, beaming all over his face. The X-rays and the doctor, *had* confirmed my words . . . all to the utter consternation of the consultant who had examined him only hours earlier that very morning.

The next day, the father returned with a bus load of eager patients he had collected from all the settlements around his home. Every one he brought to me was given great relief.

Israel is full to overflowing with historical religious sites. Some of them have even been duplicated by the slips of historians. Truth grows dim with the passing of the centuries so it is sometimes difficult to know fact from fiction.

There are, for instance, two Golgothas, translated as 'Place of the Skull'. History says that the site of Jesus's crucifixion was overlooked by a large rock bearing a strong similarity in outline to a skull. One of these places is the Church of the Holy Sepulchre, which is shared jointly by three different sects of Christianity, The Greek Orthodox Church, the Armenian Church, and the Roman Catholic Church. I can think of no place more suitable to turn a thinking person *away* from religion.

The church itself has an air of doom and decay. It's priesthood guardians perform their tasks with a totally dedicated materialistic attitude. Everything carries a price tag, from a candle, to a relic or a tour of the tomb where Jesus is said to have laid after being crucified. A horrific, treble life-size effigy of Jesus is arrayed on a huge brass cross. Underneath sat a fat priest avidly counting a huge pile of shekel notes that had been given as offerings by the faithful. Such was his obvious love of money that he was utterly oblivious to anything or anyone. A more incongruous scene one could never imagine. An endless crocodile of people trooped in and out of the church with an air of rapt religious anticipation. They were so absorbed, they did not notice the soot, grime and gloom, or the avaricious looks of greed worn by the church's custodians.

The background music of an endless tape of *Ava Maria* played on a worn cassette player, and the tatty, run down, unwashed entrance, completed a scene that to me, was more reminiscent of Hades than one of God's houses of love.

I remember well that I came out in tears and expressed my horror of the place by saying to my companion, "In my opinion, that place needs burning down to the ground."

The very next day, we visited an official office – and the person in charge asked if we had heard about the mysterious fire that had started in the cellars of the Church of the Holy Sepulchre. My companion shot me a meaningful look and whispered: "You want to keep your mouth shut! *They* listen to you up there!"

The other Golgotha is situated near the bus station in Jerusalem. It was discovered, it is claimed, by General Gordon, famous for his campaign up the River Nile. The gardens have been tastefully laid out and is a lovely place to visit.

We went to the tomb where Jesus was said to have laid and found it contained a strong measure of spiritual peace. For perhaps an hour we sat in the tomb, drinking in the silence and enjoying the feeling of peace and spirituality that it exuded. Leaving, our visit was somewhat marred when, on stepping out of the tomb, my companion was accosted by a lady from a party of American tourists, who asked her, "Is that the loo, honey?"

Later, when looking round the gardens, we found one particular spot where a spiritual energy shot through your whole body from head to toe, and filled you with an inner elation and peace.

Somebody *very* special had stood on that very spot. Such was that person's power, that the fabric of space was still charged two thousand years later.

Being of a curious nature, when I come across these inaccurate recordings of religious history, I usually ask my spiritual mentors for the right answers. Invariably I receive the same, well worn, stock reply, namely: "The answer that you seek, is not available to you while you live in a physical body. The answer would prove of little value or importance to you in the scheme of life."

The special spot we found in the garden tomb.

In India, for instance, in Kashmir town, there is yet another tomb reported to be that of Jesus. This particular tomb is revered by Muslims, Christians, Hindus and members of a large Jewish community. Stories of his preaching and of the many healings that he performed are written in Hindu Sanscrit of that period when he was alive . . . which is *after* the time he was reported crucified.

One such story is that of an Indian prince who, on seeing a person dressed in white robes preaching on a nearby hilltop, called the man to him and asked who he was. The stranger replied: "My name is Jesus. I fled from my own country far away in the East because I was sorely persecuted by my own people."

These stories say that Jesus lived until he was in his eighties, that he married and had a large family. If you are interested, investigate for yourself, but please don't start another holy war in the process for it is of little importance in the final analysis!

In Israel, the physical demands on my strength were enormous. It was quite usual for me to give healing non-stop for ten, eleven, or even twelve hours at a time. The largest number of patients I treated in one day was seventy-eight and that meant seventy-eight good results. The principles under which I work say quite firmly that I have to stay with each patient until I have gained as much help as possible at that particular time. On this occasion, I started healing at eleven in the morning . . . and worked right through non-stop until two the next morning.

Even at that hour there was a large number of people we had to turn away. Some of them followed us back to the hotel where they wished me to continue healing.

Physically impossible, I would agree under normal circumstances, but with the power of love filling you to overflowing, there are no limits to a person's endurance. The only limitation, if any, is myself. However, as soon as the guardians of healing who control the energy cease feeding the power through me, then I have to stop, for without the heavenly power I would be exhausted within the space of a few moments, and nothing would happen for the patient's benefit.

Strangely enough, there was never any dispute over the fact that I was a gentile in a Jewish country. My healing efforts were accepted at all levels of their society, without question, as originating from God.

One has, of course, to feel sorry for a small minority of very orthodox people who were civil enough to me and respected my calling, but who were so arrogant and unswerving in their ideas that life as they live it today is essentially the same as in Biblical times – and those were cruel days.

Some religious people I met were so hard and harsh, completely unswerving in their dedication to the written words of theology, that I found it difficult to understand how they can declare to the world how good and holy they are and of how well versed they are in the scriptures. Yet I have seen with my own eyes some of these modern-day zealots armed to the teeth with Tommy guns. They were only held back with great difficulty by some young soldiers from the un-holy action of blowing a group of unarmed Palestinian Arabs straight to kingdom come. This small section of religious extremists creates an unrest out of all proportion to its numbers. It is an unrest which distresses the rest of the community by creating an atmosphere of unease, distrust, fear and suspicion. The lessons of history have not been learned.

SOME TESTIMONIES FROM ISRAEL

IT is a difficult task to give long lists of testimonials from Israel as most of them are written in Hebrew. Here, however, are just a few of many hundreds.

Yitchock. A general in the Israeli army, now also the Mayor of Bni-Brack. He says, "I was about to go into hospital for an ear operation. There is no need of the operation now. Thank God and Mr Greenbank. I had severe pain, dizziness and vertigo. No pain now and no vertigo!"

Mrs Oshinsky. "I have been suffering from very painful arthritis for the last thirty-five years. Now after healing I am nearly new."

Feuchwargr, Izhah, Samaria. "Thanks a lot for your help. I feel better immediately. With belief in God I will receive even more help." (This person was waiting to go into hospital for open heart surgery. He was told by doctors he had three blocked arteries into his heart. After receiving healing, to test the good effects, he ran up and down eight flights of stairs at top speed in the apartment block where he lived and suffered no ill effects. Before receiving healing, he was forced to stop several times with bad chest pains – and that was just from walking slowly up one flight of stairs. The operation was cancelled as it was no longer necessary, much to the complete puzzlement of the doctors at the hospital!)

T Rodeneimar. "I am one of her ten children. Thank you for helping the nicest and best lady in all the world." (We were able to take away all pain that this lady had suffered for many years. We were also able to make her body fully mobile so she could walk like a young person again.)

Mr Z Golstein, superintendent in charge of the Sheba hospital. "I underwent a heart operation in Cleveland, USA, for the unblocking of arteries. After returning home to Israel, I found I had exactly the same symptoms as before the operation, which, I can tell you, was very painful. I went to Mr Greenbank for his healing. He immediately took away all the symptoms in just one treatment. I feel fine again now.

It always gives me a great upliftment to gain help for children. Particularly impressive was the healing of the following patient who was just seven years of age. He walked into the room with great difficulty for he was wearing two callipers, one was so constructed that it was impossible for him to straighten his leg. The medical diagnosis was that his left hip had practically worn out. Doctors told the father that the child must never be allowed to place his foot on the ground. No operation was possible, they assured him, and it was highly likely he would be a cripple for the rest of his life.

Healing was given to him. The results were immediate, for within a few moments it was possible for the child to run around the room with no pain or discomfort.

I felt impressed to tell the father not, on any account to replace the callipers, but to take him back to the hospital the next day for tests and X-rays, which would confirm he was cured. This the parents did. The consultants at the hospital were astounded and could give no rational explanation for the child's return to normality. They confirmed my words that the child's hip and legs were now perfect, and that he was cured.

Bortz Joz. "You are certainly blessed by God. Many thanks for helping me." This is the height of understatement for the patient had been to his doctor, who in turn referred him to an orthopaedic specialist at the hospital. The appointment was for the following week. His symptoms were as follows: pains in the lower back, neck and stomach. Within a few moments, I was able to put these conditions right and take away all the pains. He immediately rang up and cancelled his appointment with the hospital specialist and he has had no more trouble since. I also treated his son, who had helped to carry his father into the room. He was only twenty years old, and had suffered for years with intense pain in both knees. This condition was healed within minutes.

Here are more testimonials translated from the Hebrew. You must excuse the fractured English!

"I cannot find the proper words to thank you for saving my boy from having to go through a most difficult and potentially dangerous operation on his spine. My son and I are very happy. We hope that the Almighty will grant you a long life and much patience long to continue treating people."

"Thank you for helping me. Since the age of four I could not breathe like other people. Now I can. I hope you will help many more in Israel."

"Thank you for helping my daughter. She can now hear out of the ear that previously she could not. This was after doctors said nothing could be done to help her condition."

"For forty years until today I could not straighten my foot due to being wounded in the Second World War. After your healing touch, I can straighten it with no pain or discomfort at all."

"I walked out with no pain at all after receiving your second treatment, with a wonderful feeling inside and no pain at all."

"My concentration camp number is 52732. I was in Auschwitz camp. I have been in pain ever since I was attacked by the Gestapo in 1942. Now I have no pain at all."

"After four years of trouble with my right leg, I could not walk properly. I suddenly find after you treated me that I can now run up a flight of stairs with no trouble or pain at all.'

We have received many letters from Israel confirming the good that was done by healing. Here are extracts from another; "I have just spoken to the grandmother of the little boy whose life you saved. He had a hole in his lungs. Doctors could not help him. When the grandmother heard that doctors could do nothing, she knew help would have to come from another source. She started praying very hard for him and went to ask for help from all the holy places and also visited many rabbi, for their blessings. Today she rang to remind me that you had saved the little boy's life. After receiving healing from you he immediately became well. This was confirmed by doctors.

"I also spoke to the mother of the little girl, who could only crawl and make noises like an animal. She is now talking nicely. Her development is continuous, little by little. She does not say sentences yet, but now she has a good vocabulary and can make herself understood at the kindergarten she has just started to attend. Doctors declared that they could not help her at all; they said she was severely retarded, had suffered brain damage at birth and would never be able to walk, just crawl on the ground.

"After receiving healing from you, she is now walking and talking, and is able to play with other children. Her fits and convulsions have stopped completely. Her mother cannot thank you enough."

Another letter from Israel reads.

"The old rabbi you treated – who is now in his nineties – is well. After being imprisoned in a Soviet concentration camp for many years, the doctors say it is a miracle in itself that he is still holding out. After receiving healing from you, his blood count rose immediately from nine to eleven per cent. Previous to healing, he was taking drugs for lack of salt in his body. Now he no longer needs drugs as he is so well."

"The little boy you treated called Shimsham has shown great improvement in his hearing. The hospital confirmed this after tests proved that his hearing had gone up from four per cent to twenty-one per cent. He can now hear when somebody knocks on the door. Consequently, his father is elated."

"Kalman Rot, who previous to your treatment suffered very much with pain in the legs, had received a different diagnosis from every doctor he saw. One said it was bad circulation, another that it was water in his legs, whilst a third said it was inflammation. Only you were right, Mr Greenbank. As soon as you saw him, you told him it was an out of place vertebra pressing on nerves that go into the legs. As usual, you were right. You instantly released all the trapped nerves causing the pain. Immediately, he could walk with no trouble. He still finds it very hard to accept that his pain has gone for ever after all he has suffered. His mother tells me all his friends are astonished he can walk normally now."

"The doctor you treated, Dr Samra, from the Sheba hospital, has received a complete cure from the knee you healed. Previous to seeing you he had been to all the best professors in Israel – and not a single one was able to help him. The intense pain persisted until he saw the right person, yourself. He is quite astonished and keeps on telling people: 'We doctors spend literally years in the study of illness and medicine. Yet it was spiritual healing that gave me a cure after orthodox medicine could not help'."

"The man you treated for the serious heart condition has received a very big improvement. In his own words, 'I am now a new man.' It really is unbelievable. Where would we all be without our Do-Do Dan, Uncle Don?"

"You have made so many people happy. We are all grateful for your help, given so heartfully. With every patient you treat, you are full of loving care and patience. Mr Greenbank, never forget that when you help a child you are actually assisting three people – the child, the mother and father. You are instigating a new life for all three'."

One particular person you have made very happy is Mrs Stern, who was told her son would have to undergo a four hour operation – it was potentially dangerous – to correct a curvature of the spine. She brought him to see you . . . and within a few moments the spine straightened under your hands! You took away the pains in her back, legs and hands. You cleared Mrs Stern's nasal passages so that now she can breathe properly. Every single person you treated from the village of Bet Mier has received great benefits from your healing along with most of those you saw in Messilot and the majority who came to you in Bni-Back. You have helped so many thousands of people in Israel for without your treatment they would have been in pain for the rest of their days as in most cases doctors were unable to help them. Never forget that if you can help, just one sick child live a normal life, then to the Almighty, it is as if you have helped the entire world."

Chapter Four

LIFE AFTER DEATH; FACT OR FICTION?

SOME idea of how people view important issues completely out of perspective, can be shown by the remarks of a well-known sporting character as he was being interviewed on television. When asked if he thought that a certain football match was a life and death issue, he replied, "Oh, it's far more important than that!"

Every year, half a million people in this country do something quite original. It is a thing that most of them have never done before: their bodies are going to die and stop working.

The apparent finality of this dying business is not easy for people to come to terms with, especially if their lives have been confined solely to worldly affairs.

Many times, I have had the following said to me by patients: "Don, I am frightened of the pressures imposed by modern life and scared stiff at the thought of dying. Please tell me what you have experienced regarding life after the body dies. This is always interposed by the following negativety, "uh . . . if there is such a thing."

They then go on to say: "I am not aware of anything beyond the obvious. I only know what I have been told in churches about the subject. Their explanations just do not make sense to me." To those who asked me – and others who wanted to but were too shy – I shall try my best to give you as much information as I can on this curious phenomenon.

If we were talking about 'Bulls' and 'Bears' on the Stock Market, I would be completely lost, in the same way as if I were asked how to rewire a car's electrical circuit. But as regards the dying business, this lad can speak with great authority!

Of all the issues raised by dying, the most misunderstood is the widespread belief that says, "After your body dies, you become a spirit." This is a complete fallacy. Let me explain why this is so. You cannot become a spirit after your body dies simply because you are one right now, living in a fleshy overcoat you call a body.

It is on this one important point that the whole action of spiritual healing hinges: it is also perhaps the point that creates the greatest controversy regarding healing.

Put aside the popular image of a healer being somebody with 'healing hands' for this is a misnomer. A healer could well earth to a patient through his elbows, feet or shoulders . . . and the healing energy would still flow through him to the individual concerned.

Neither is he a person who practices some strange form of yoga. Nor does he talk people better. For without spiritual power from the next world coming to the patient, not a single person would ever recover from any illness through a healer's ministrations.

So important is this issue that I am going to repeat it so it will fully sink in. The only reason you can receive spiritual healing is because you are a spirit now, but one living in a physical casement we call our body.

The thread that binds us to our physical body is a very fine one at the best of times. It has been described by seers many times throughout history as being a silver cord. It is one of the laws of nature that when a body is no longer a fit receptacle for the spirit, due to age, accident or an organ-destroying disease, then that silver cord pulls apart and snaps. The spirit is instantly released from the confines of this physical life. Many call this dying: perhaps a better word would be rebirth.

I have stressed the following, regarding your body being merely a temporary home for your spirit because only when you have accepted this as a fact, can you put many of life's inconsistencies into perspective. Your body is just a house for your spirit. As such, that physical body is only designed for a certain span of years. This we term our lifetime and may be either a short or long one depending on what task has been allocated to you to perform for your soul's fulfilment.

Besides this fact, body organs do have a tendency to wear out with continual use. No healer or medical man can make it possible for your body to live for ever. Perish the thought!

Think long and carefully on this matter and you will realise that every action regarding the working of your body is an automatic one. Every physical movement you order your body to make comes under the express control of your subconscious mind. You do not have to worry in the slightest about it. Take a step forward, and there's no problem. One leg immediately moves in answer to the request given to your subconscious mind. Every other movement and action responds in the same way under your mind's control. It is exactly like a car being driven along by another driver while you lounge back in the rear seat and enjoy the countryside.

Treat your body with dignity and care, and it will serve you well as a vehicle for your journey through life. If you do this, the real you when you arrive at the the end of your life's journey, should be a much wiser soul than when you started out.

Possibly your next question to me would be, "If what you say is true, why haven't the recognised churches snatched at this issue of the body being a temporary home for the spirit, like a duck to water ?"

I am fully aware that most churches are run like any other commercial enterprise, with profits and accounts. One thing they do not have is sales managers because if they did, the issue of life after death would have been pounced on as their strongest selling point in their game of gaining new converts.

The instigators of the world's religions were quite universal in their insistence that life continued after the death of a person's body. Unfortunately, all we receive from our modern clergy are some rather vague generalities, often couched in soppy, sentimental language, that there is definitely a heaven, a paradise or a land of eternal sunshine beyond the clouds. But – and here comes the Catch 22 –

it is available only if you followed to the letter the teachings of that particular religion. You do not have to have a towering intellect to realise that this twist of the truth is really a form of moral blackmail.

This blank spot of having no relevant information on the afterlife from orthodox churches is due entirely to one little but very important fact: that to preach of a life after death a person must have had some personal experience to endorse their views, otherwise they are flannelling – and I have heard a lot of that over the years.

The majority of churchmen I have met are able to go no further than expounding what they have been taught at their particular theological college.

Such second-hand knowledge can never be of any worth unless you are a sheep, particularly when it is obvious that the greatest mystical experience in the average clergyman's life never goes beyond the completely baffling puzzle of who put the foreign coins on the collection plate last Sunday.

At least one Anglican churchman had insight, to such an extent that he formed a special investigatory committee to search fully into the possibility of life after death. That was Dr Cosmo Lang, when he was Archbishop of Canterbury. The answer took a long time in coming, but when the report eventually arrived from this committee, it was to the effect that not only was there proof, but abundant evidence of a definite existence, with the retention of personal identity, awaiting every person after death.

The publicity from such a wonderful and powerful revelation should have filled the headlines of the nation's newspapers for months ahead, but it didn't. This confirming report must have proved so shocking to the fuddy duddies of the Church of England, that it was deliberately suppressed by this stolid band of diehards and hidden deep within the Church archives, possibly under the heading of, 'too controversial for the masses'. However, it has since been released under the forty year ruling.

Change does not come easily to old established beliefs and dogma. It reminds me very much of a satirical Victorian ditty that expressed a similar attitude 'Bless the squire and his relations, and keep us in our proper stations'. This was to be sung while touching the forelock.

A long time ago when I first started on my quest of finding answers to seemingly unanswerable questions – and this was before I had grasped even partially the geometry of the forces of nature – I asked a question. It is one that must have been asked by every living person at one time or another.

In a state of deep meditation, I asked quite simply, "What happens to the 'I' part of me when my body dies?"

The answer, when it came, could not have come from my own subconscious mind, as at that time, I had no knowledge of the subject to draw upon. Please spend a few moments thinking about the answer that I received for it is simply loaded with wise implications. It came direct from my spiritual guardians and was as follows, **"You evolve through many different consciousnesses and vibrations until you finally blend with the great mass of intelligence that you call God"**. It is all there in that one single sentence, a full and condensed explanation of what life is all about.

The human inhabitants of this world of ours are pretty evenly divided between the ignorant and the sensitive. It has nothing to do with beliefs, but everything to do with soul evolvement. The ignorant ones, who strangely enough can be academically brilliant, are the 'first time in a body' merchants. Consequently, they make every mistake in the book of ethics, sometimes more than once, for they do not learn life's lessons easily.

Have a smile with me as I tell you of a school of thought that is usually linked into a religious context. It brings to the believer a certain smugness as his imagination views the scene of what is in store for him after he draws his last breath. Then tell me which of the two types of people you think he belongs to.

By the way, I have asked for a special dispensation from God to the effect that if people go to heaven, who think they are going to go to heaven, then I don't want to go there. So I have asked him to reserve a little place for me, at the back of beyond, one filled with little children and lots and lots of animals for they too, have souls.

The following is what I call taking out a spiritual insurance policy. See if you can spot some people you know who act in this fashion. To be truthful, I did enjoy writing it.

The belief is that there is a soft plushy life ahead for him after his body dies. All that is necessary to achieve this honoured position is that the following rules should have been observed: that he has attended church, chapel, mosque, synagogue or meeting room regularly, and sat with eyes closed as the chap in the smart frock has prayed over and for him.

That he had gone through the humility of calling himself a sinner, even if he couldn't really quite bring himself to believe it. By these simple actions he thinks he has fulfilled all the spiritual requirements considered necessary for entry into that elevated state we term heaven.

So his earthly life comes to an end. Immediately he is surrounded by a bevy of beautiful angels who, to the sound of celestial music, transport him high up into the sky. He is dumped down with all due deference and ceremony befitting his person. In this lovely place signposted 'The Elysium Planes', he willingly joins the tail end of a queue of select souls waiting to enter heaven proper.

Looking around, he notices that high overhead lots of cheeky-faced, plump little cherubs with puffed out cheeks are playfully blowing the clouds about, exactly like the ones he saw on old charts. The masses of pink candy-floss vapours swirl apart, and our smug friend has arrived.

One could never call the entrance modest for it consists of two huge pillars so big you cannot see the top. On those pillars are hung gates of real pearl. A little to one side stands a blue neon sign that repeatedly flashes out the one word 'Heaven, heaven, heaven.'

A deep American-type voice, like Charlton Heston playing God, booms out, asking each applicant his name and previous occupation on earth.

To one side, the saintly figure of Peter sits on a puff of cloud, worriedly consulting the akashic record of the man in front. Our smug friend is puffed out with confidence. Just wait till his good friend Peter – you can't beat getting on first name terms – reads his record.

In his mind he runs over the spiritual assets that should gain him a good position at the heavenly table of plenty. They included the special prayers he paid for in advance only last week, the masses read on his behalf, that brand new candelabrum he bought for the church – he even received a tax rebate on that –

but that's by the way. Also the monies he left to the cat's home in his will, proving what he had always advocated to his employees in his betting shops: that it pays to hedge your bets.

The reader at this point is allowed to alter the last paragraph to fit in with his particular sect or his religion's spiritual perks. Thank goodness there was a twenty-year time limit on the sins recorded, something about being short of staff in the recording section, or so that slightly tipsy priest had told him. There were just one or two dodgy bits when he first started in business that he would rather forget. Nothing dishonest, mind you, but perhaps what may be considered a little bit of sharp practice here.

A slight tap on his shoulder from one of the heavenly helpers invited him to have a preview of what was in store for him once the preliminaries are over. A quick, sly peep through the gates is permitted.

He was simply staggered. What a wonderful sight met his eye! It was everything he ever imagined it could be and more. Fountains were spraying, fanfares playing and the general mood was one of jollification, truly befitting a favourite son who has at long last come home.

The famous celestial choir were in full throat as each entrant receives a rendering of *There will always be an England, Land of my Fathers, America,* or a rousing chorus of the *Red Flag,* depending on the person's earthly nationality.

For very important, special people – these included politicians, heads of state and church dignitaries, there was a rather loud rendering of *The Entry of the Gladiators.*

Business seemed to be thriving as he viewed a little kiosk just inside the gates, where busy novice angels were dishing out a rather snappy line in see-through nighties, glowing white haloes (as seen on TV), fully feathered wings, and the neatest golden harps you you ever saw. Our smug friend nearly swoons at the thought of what was in store for him. Rather a pity he could not bring his stocks and shares, or the tin box of savings he kept under his bed, for this set-up looked right for a takeover. Still, it does feel great to be good.

Our purist friend sure has a surprise in store for himself.

Shall we leave him in ignorance until his time is up? I know full well that opinions vary greatly as to what the new state of life for the soul will be after our bodies die. If we glance at all the horrific things that are happening in this world at the moment, human beings inflicting pain, misery, and taking the lives of others, it is obvious that some people think there is nothing but total oblivion after the body dies. With that type of thought drenching the mind, there is no need at all to have any qualms about one's personal conduct in this world.

The argument put forward repeatedly by the super materialist cynic is that the whole concept of an afterlife is a pure invention, acting as an imaginative balm to a person's inner self whilst he is alive.

The cynic goes on to state, that nobody has ever come back to say for certain that there *is* an after life.

Well, as usual with cynics, they are completely wrong. Communication with souls who have left their bodies has happened times without number throughout the ages to seers, visionaries and sensitives, and to every race of people this world holds. So strong was the impact of these revelations of the spirit in proving the reality of another life beyond this one, that they taught others. Eventually, the followers of those special people founded the world's religions.

The beliefs of long ago had a common basis in their complete acceptance of a continuation of life after people left their body. For instance, the Vikings hoped for death in battle; they thought this would guarantee them instant entry into Valhalla, that paradise in the sky specially reserved for heroes, even if they did do the odd spot of pillage and rape that is how 'He-men' of that day and age proved themselves.

The North American Red Indian, so-called because the first white settlers thought they had arrived at the continent of India, knew for certain for he talked with eagerness of going to his 'happy hunting grounds.' We must treat his beliefs with respect since he lived a code of life that was in close contact with nature.

The Islamic religion teaches that there is a paradise, but it is male orientated. The teachings of the Hindus informs us that after this body of ours has worn out, and usually after a period of rest, we are reincarnated into either another human body as a baby or even an animal depending on our good or bad showing in this life. I go along with this belief, though I can't say I am enamoured at the thought of coming back as a buck rabbit on Ilkley Moor. However, on reflection, it might just be a bit of all right!

Most Christian sects sternly teach that the day will dawn – deemed Judgement Day – when all the dead shall rise up out of their graves. Until then you sleep soundly. No mention is made of those who are cremated.

Besides this theory being horrific in construction, this fair and green land of ours is going to be rather overcrowded, so I think we can throw that theory in the dustbin as being just plain balmy.

You may well smile a patronising smirk of "How silly can you get?"

The average person is just as guilty of wrapping up myth, mystery, downright wishful thinking and believing his conclusions to be true.

My experience of being used as a receiver of healing energies has brought with it a deep insight into the basic facts of both this life and the one to come after our body dies.

For instance, I don't just think, I *know* that when our bodies wear out, or meet with a serious accident, and as a result stops working, we shall discard them, and that there is neither pain nor the slightest discomfort in the last few seconds of the body dying. It is no more than after a hard day at the office when you come home and take your overcoat off.

We then immediately enter another dimension of life, exactly like a butterfly emerging from a chrysalis, still retaining our personal identity, feelings, and loves, yet facing a life that is more fulfilling and rewarding than the wildest leaps our imagination could offer.

Our terms of reference in this new spirit life, are so completely different in character to this physical condition we are now living at the moment, that there is little understandable description I can offer you which would convey the heights, scope, and freedom available to you in this new life. But it's ever so nice to know it *is* there.

Thought is the operative word, for by the mere act of thinking of a place you will be able to transport yourself there. There will be no barriers to your freedom of travel and expression, only that imposed by your lack of higher spirituality. In other words, certain areas of spiritual life cannot be entered until you have advanced and gained soul maturity.

Before you pooh-pooh this idea as being preposterous, think again. Every unnatural artefact on this world is a product of pure thought; every invention started with an idea; every oil painting becomes a permanent record of the painter's inspiration; every car, ship, aeroplane or household appliance started out as a thought in someone's mind, every piece of music or every work of literature is thought transported into a fact. That inspiration can be played and read over and over again for it will never wear out. In fact, Mary Baker Eddie formed the Christian Science Church based on these concepts.

Most of the events I describe in these writings are based on personal experiences that have happened to myself. If it were possible to link my mind into a television camera in such a way that you could view what I was actually seeing, hearing and appreciating, it would strike home to the reader, and in doing so make the writing of this book completely unnecessary.

As a thinking human being, you have a right to accept or reject anything I say. It will not make any difference to anyone bar yourself, but it can make the act of living a lot happier for you if you can accept my views. Truth is truth. It is impossible to change, and will always be unalterable by a person's particular opinions. I do hope, though, that one day, after you have crossed the barrier between the two worlds – and you will – that you spare me a thought by saying, "You know, that fellow Greenbank was right after all!"

If you are an average person, you're living out there in a world of television, football matches and horse racing. Perhaps you do a job in local government, which I am given to understand can be as boring as watching paint dry or cement set, or you may be in the bustling world of trade, politics, or fashion. It is *you* I want to reach with my words because *you* could well be missing out on what life is all about. Let us revise your ideas on this life and the life to come.

It has been said many times that there are just two certainties in life. One is that we are provided with a physical body and born into this world. The other is that this body of ours will one day wear out and die, returning to the elements, exactly in compliance with the rest of the natural world.

Nature has certain basic laws which say quite definitely that nothing can ever be completely destroyed, only chemical changes are allowed to take place. Therefore, this law applies to man as any other particle of the natural world.

You have a perfect right to ask, "How do you know, Mr Clever Clogs?" It is not just myself for over the years I have taken a census from lots of my patients on out-of-the-body experiences. It is more common than you may think. Most people I enquired of have admitted to at least one instance of having a vision, an unusual happening, a premonition that came true, or an actual sighting. In many cases conversation has occured with souls who have left their bodies and speak from the so-called far side of the grave.

Over the years of my healing practice, I have experienced thousands of events that have drawn back briefly the veil between the two worlds. Perhaps it would be more instructive if I told you about those early years of healing, for I was exactly in the same position as most people reading these words are now.

When I first began delving into the mysteries of healing, as I said before, I read every book I could lay my hands on about the subject. Having no practical experience, I finished up more confused than when I started. Then slowly it dawned on me there is no substitute for personal experience, and that these experiences vary from person to person. I found I was able to open my mind to the infinite. This fact alone allowed good influences to work their will through me to bring back health to the sick.

Although other people's experiences were interesting, healing was such an individualistic affair, there was no one who could show me the actual road I should take to develop my gift to its maximum. I discovered that the only course of action necessary was to follow my own intuition, wherever it led me, for by this time I knew my fate was in safe hands.

Future events were to bear this decision of mine out since the gift gradually matured with time, coupled with the experience gained from treating thousands of patients.

If I wished to sound cloying and rather sickly, I could say that I found the answer to my bewilderment in a state of deep meditation, that in the hidden recesses of my mind I discovered the throbbing pulse of unreasonable hunger that was striving for fulfilment and expression by service to mankind, but it wasn't like that at all.

It was by no means an easy task to find myself. The reflection in the mirror presented nothing extraordinary back to me. I had no great cracks of worry lines, no tossing mane of hair, or the piercing eye of a future Svengali. The only thing that reflection told me was that I was not facially cut out to be a guru, confidence trickster, share pusher, bank manager or win a prize in a beauty competition, and that is all.

As time went by and I practiced my gift, gradually becoming more and more overshadowed by that same loving soul I had first encountered all those years before, by this time, I also knew for certain that my true vocation lay in healing the sick.

The rapport between this soul and myself became so acute and intense that I felt completely overshadowed by him while I was applying healing. There was a constant interchange of thoughts concerning patients' sick condition's between us. I learnt to recognise the different types of people who came to me for help and to 'read' them intuitively. Often the actual cause of their complaints would be given to me so I found I was able to diagnose exactly what illness they were suffering from and generally the cause of that complaint. This was often the complete opposite to that which the patient had been told by orthodox medicine. The patient's often rapid recovery proved my intuition was right.

I found also that I could detect from a single word dropped in casual conversation, that patient's particular mental hang ups, and personal prejudices. Later, this gift was to grow into having the ability to read a person just by touching them. I found I could blend easily with some patients yet others, whose talk was reasonable enough, would make the hair on the back of my neck stand up and I instinctively recoiled from them, for they were putting on an act to the world, and I knew healing was not meant for them.

Even later, this ability developed to the extent that I was able to tell at a touch, the old souls, the ignorant ones and those first-time-in-a-body souls. Often, the last two were the same.

I also became ever more aware of other souls being present when I was giving healing. The outcome of all these things was that my awareness became ever more mature. As a natural consequence, the percentage of cures for patients I was treating sky-rocketed.

Eventually my precious gift reached a stage where I could say with confidence that it was fully developed, and if a cure was not forthcoming I should never blame myself by thinking I was inadequate for the task, as I must confess I have done at times, particularly when I first started healing.

I have been asked so many times, "How do you 'see' spirit forms?"

This is a very difficult question to answer so could I explain it like this? Have you ever walked along a parade of shops. You can look through the window and see the goods inside or, by altering the focus of your eyes, view the reflection of yourself and passers by, if the windows have been cleaned! 'Seeing' spiritual entities is done in exactly the same way, except that you do it with the mind. You alter your mind's focus in a certain way. In this altered state of awareness, you can see all around you, not with the eyes but with the mind.

This attuning to spirit does vary from time to time for I have known occasions when a soul has come to me, starting out as a pinhead of light in my mind that gradually draws nearer and nearer, forming into the features as it draws close, until the face is so clear I can make out every pore of the skin.

At other times, it is a 'knowing', when I can't actually see the soul, but am able to give a perfect description and relay the communication they wish me to pass on . . . without hearing their voice or seeing them. All this relevant information registers in my mind like a ticker tape.

Part of my personality being very logical, I have tried to rationalise the process, but can't. Possibly the communication is on a soul-to-soul basis, from a spirit out of a body to one in a body.

I have been told by my spiritual advisers that in the spirit world, one expresses one's self by a similar thought process. They have also informed me that the spirit world is comprised of many levels so that souls who are unevolved and ignorant are restricted to the lower levels.

Souls who have lived through many life spans – coupled to the good works they have performed in those lives – are able to rise to higher levels of spiritual evolvement on a plane of existence that is a natural just reward for their good works.

Did not a certain person say "In my Father's house are many mansions?" This extension of life in the world of the spirit is a reality of nature located not on some far distant star cluster, but only fractionally away from this physical plane of life, on a much higher frequency. Many people become puzzled over this explanation and ask how is it possible for two things to exist in the same space.

Any scientist will tell you there is no such thing as a solid; neither your body nor the floor on which you are standing. Each object in this world is composed of different molecular patterns in their atomic structure.

Through you, solid person that you think you are, at this very moment are coursing thousands of different electrical signals, radio waves, and television pulses. If there were such a thing as a microscope capable of looking right into the atomic structure of any specimen, we would see a scene of constant activity as electrons, protons and neutrons rush around in an orderly and amazingly fast dance. For it is a fact that everything in this world vibrates at a certain number of cycles per second – you, the chair on which you are sitting, and the fabric of your house.

So the conclusion drawn is, that a solid only appears solid. Television pulses waves, radio waves need a receiver that will accept these signals by lowering their vibrations. There are also various devices that will amplify the strength of that signal so that we can hear and see the transmitted picture on our television screen.

This is all in obeyance with one of nature's laws, which says two objects must be in sympathy to transfer energy. Exactly the same law applies in healing. Three things are needed to make a person well, omit any one of them, and nothing will happen. They are the spiritual source, the healer, and the patient. The whole theory and practice of healing revolves around these facts.

WHO ACTUALLY REGULATES THE ACTION OF HEALING?

The higher realms of spirit life are the source of the actual healing energy. The manipulating of this wonderful energy which has the quality of terminating illness is done by evolved spiritual entities. I guess God's a pretty busy fellow so he delegates.

These administrators of the healing energy, who incidentally have lived through this human condition many times, dispensed with their bodies long ago. Therefore, they all have first hand experience of the many problems that infest the human condition we call life.

The plane of existence they inhabit is as real to them as this physical one is to us, with the added bonus of their being able to operate by the action of using pure thought processes, exactly as you will one day. They are able to enter the physical plane we inhabit by, to them, the simple action of lowering their vibrations.

One advanced soul I contacted once told me that this action is not a particularly nice one for them. The dense vibrations that form our physical world, create in them a feeling something similar to that which we would experience if we were walking through thick mud. Possibly this is why at every chance, they use the mind and body of a sensitive to bring healing, advice and help to a patient.

Marooned as we are in a physical body, with all the limitations and restrictions that this places on us, it is so easy to fall into the trap of viewing those guardians of healing with nothing less than awe. For as we develop the extra senses that enable us to link in to the higher planes of spiritual life, so we become ever more aware of their powerful intellects, supreme wisdom and the elevated character of their soul enlightenment. To us, with our limitation of knowledge, due to the confines of this human condition, they can at times seem far superior to ourselves with our petty human failings.

In a mental conversation with one of these evolved souls, I asked him, "Why do I feel so inadequate when faced with such brilliant intellects as you obviously possess?"

He smiled kindly at my remarks and answered with the following: "Modesty and humility are fine human qualities and are to be praised where found. Of course, the natural laws, within which all healing operates, demand that you treat God's power with great respect for it must never be misused. That is the reason why every single advancement of your spiritual gift has to be earned by your total dedication to your work. It has not – and never can be – made available just by merely asking, for you must have realised by now the truth in that nothing of any

71

worth is ever gained without personal effort.

"We, like yourself, are merely workers for the improvement and greater fulfilment of the human condition. We neither ask for, nor would accept, any fawning or servility from souls who are living their life's experience. Because of the severe limitations placed on a soul when it enters a body for the gaining of this soul experience, many could be far more evolved than we are, yet are totally unaware of the fact, that is until they leave their bodies once again and return to their rightful position in God's house.

"A person's soul development, whilst he is still in a body, is always reflected in the courage and dedication he shows in his allotted field of endeavour."

Soul advancement is a sliding scale that can work both ways, either spiritual advancement or spiritual downgrading. Some souls have such a bad showing in life, that they may have to revert back to the animal kingdom for a new slant on life's experiences, such is in the belief of the Hindu religion. Possibly this is one of the reasons why many of our pets show such an affinity with humans. It could be they have lived through this human condition and still retain their previous soul wisdom, but exactly like man, not their prebirth knowledge.

Many who are at present living in a body carry great soul wisdom and have an elevated spirituality far removed in stature from the role they have elected to play in this particular life. This wisdom is below a conscious level, whilst their intelligence, however great or small, is a direct result of the genetic pattern laid down by their parents.

The opposite end of the scale from humility is the one that many young souls occupy: they have been born with the potential of a talent in a certain field. This is most noticeable in a purely physical activity such as sport or entertainment. The action of receiving pure adoration from admirers is something they just cannot handle. As a result, many tend to become egotistical and precocious, and have a tendency to look upon themselves as something very special and therefore very important in the scheme of things. The natural consequences of their selfish approach to life is that they never reach their full potential of gaining great soul experiences. Living in a body for them has served no useful purpose in their soul's advancement.

In most respects, I am as normal as you, the reader. I eat, sleep and grow tired and weary. Like you, I can see through the empty promises of politicians, enjoy my holidays in the sunshine and become bored with much of the sheer drivel that passes for entertainment on television. I would say at that point that any similarities between us come to a full stop for I carry a completely different set of values and beliefs to those that society recognises as normal.

I think every sensitive carries with them a secret inner feeling that if the going gets too rough in life, they can always put an end to themselves and return to the security and peace of the spirit world.

The world calls it committing suicide: it is a futile thing to do, for we would be immediately dispatched into another body with similar experiences awaiting us, so to finish our elected life's experiences. That is the natural law.

I have every sympathy with people who become so frustrated, depressed and unhappy over the sheer hostility of this world that they wish to terminate their lives for I, too, have trodden that same path.

It is many years ago now, after I had been full-time healing only a few years.

72

At the time, I was beset by personal problems, worries and depressions over finance that seemed to be insurmountable and unalterable. Additionally I felt so alone in the work of healing. This is the general pattern that happens to all healers once they have progressed past a certain point in their development of the gift. For the path you tread becomes more and more a lonely one, because the gift is so exclusive, your acquaintances cannot possibly understand the pressures you are suffering.

In my case, friends who up to that point at least made life bearable for me, deserted me to walk their own pathway.

I felt completely lost in the world. Whilst I have never, ever, doubted that my healing was doing God's work, when the world has a go at you, a person could do with a little practical help from Him. This did not appear to be forthcoming. I felt I had not the strength left in me that I believed would be required in any long future with healing. How wrong I was.

One day in particular, I was at a very low ebb, depressed and unhappy. Everything appeared hopeless and of no worth. I came to a definite decision . . . I would return home to the higher side of life. I was quite calm and in a way relieved I had made my mind up in so definite a fashion.

The decision made, I drove from Lytham to Fleetwood and caught a ferry to the Isle of Man, with the full intention of leaping overboard when the ship was half way on its journey.

The moment for my demise came. There was no fear in me, I was both outwardly still and inwardly calm. Eternity for me was only moments away. I prepared to climb the rail of the ship but found I could not move a single muscle. My feet were rooted to the deck as I felt a very solid hand pressing down on my shoulder.

I then heard a voice in my mind say: "Don't be silly, my son. The best years of your life are yet to come." It was right – for within moments my depressions lifted giving way to a feeling of aggression and annoyance at myself, having let circumstances drive me to the perimeter of life.

I returned to my healing work freshly armed and with a greater understanding of how the forces of chaos can wreck havoc if you allow yourself to give way to them. So there was yet another of life's lessons in this experience for me.

Life has thrown many such practical, hard lessons at me over the many years I have been healing. Having learnt them and allowed myself to be remoulded into a wiser person, you will realise just why I look forward with eagerness to my body dying. Oh, I enjoy my life here and love the work I have been privileged to perform, for it is an endless source of personal satisfaction, but with my developed perceptions, I know partly what awaits me when my body wears out and stops working. To be truthful, I can hardly wait.

Rest assured that after your body dies, there is no Judgement Day with front seat reservations for the elite, no instant purification and certainly no sprouting of heavenly wings. Life on earth and life hereafter are regulated by the same natural laws that operate the rest of the universe. There is not one single person who can dodge, evade or swerve round these cosmic laws and elude them by paying a paltry fine as a penalty, whether you be John Doe or the Pope!

The natural law I most favour is that 'like attracts like.' It applies to this world as well as the next one. By virtue of this law, I am told by my spiritual friends that there is no single heaven, but an infinite number of heavens available, where souls of like minds intermingle and co-habit.

THE WORLD OF LIGHT

The first time I stepped mentally into these worlds of the spirit was many years ago now. At that time, I was desperately trying to make sense out of my confusion. This particular experience would prove to have a lasting effect and helped greatly in giving me the mental strength to carry on the work of healing. Until this particular time I was prepared to accept that there may possibly be other extensions to life beyond this physical world, but being by nature a rather nosy individual, I wanted to know for certain.

At that time I would spend several hours each day in meditation. On the night in question, I must say that I was not in a very relaxed state of mind. I was struggling mentally to gain contact with intangibles, and having little success. Finally, in sheer exasperation, and to no one in particular, I said, "If there is a life after this one, please let me see it."

Immediately – and there was no going to sleep or sinking into a torpid trance state – I was there. There are no words descriptive enough to fully describe the scene in which I found myself. What amazed me most were the colours. The sky was blue, bluer even than the Mediterranean skies in summer. The grass was an Irish green, only more so. It was as though all my life, until that moment, I had been viewing colours with filters over my eyes. The air I breathed was like sparkling balm to my senses. I felt buoyant and filled with vitality and life. I remember striding through the lush grass that bore just a hint of dew. I was filled with the reckless abandonment of youth. I remember vividly the feeling, it was like nothing I had ever encountered before. To me, it felt like being surrounded by pure love. It gave me such a wonderful feeling of belonging for this sensation and feeling permeated the whole place. Flowers rich in perfume added the final touch to this scene of perfection.

To one side was a thickly wooded valley, from which rose the sounds of many children at play. As I strolled along I felt so happy. Finally, I came across two men who were deep in conversation. They glanced up at me and smiled a welcome but looked puzzled, then one of them said to me, "You should not be here."

That very second, somebody blew on my cheek – and immediately I was back in this life. My cheek still felt cold from whoever had blown on it. The experiencing of such events, gradually gave me such a strong faith in the powers of love, that the materialistic attitudes of many people, met later in my life in connection with my work of healing, left me untouched.

PROOF FOR A MOTHER

Perhaps the best illustration of how spiritual awareness can mend a broken heart was the experience of a lady who attended for healing many years ago. At the time, she was in a shocked and distressed state, having just lost her eighteen year old daughter and her husband within a few days of each other. The great peace that comes with healing relaxed her so much that she asked me if she could sit down for a moment in one of the armchairs.

Within the space of a few seconds she was sound asleep. At that time there was a large vase of red roses on a table. As I watched, one of them began to tremble and levitate out of the bowl. I felt impressed to take hold of it and place it on the lap of the sleeping lady.

After about twenty minutes, she opened her eyes and with a happy smile said: "Oh that was wonderful! I saw my daughter. She looked so happy. Do you know, she was holding out a red rose to me."

"Like the one on your knee?" I asked. Glancing down, she noticed for the first time the rose that I had placed there. With a gasp of pure delight she said: "Yes. The one she was holding was exactly like this." Evidently it had been the practice of the daughter to bring her mother a red rose every week, purely as a sign of the deep love she felt for her. The lady went away content and happy, knowing that eventually she would be reunited with her daughter. I felt privileged to have shared in such an experience.

THE PASSING OF A CHILD

Another moving experience happened to me when I had just started out on my healing mission. I was treating a little girl for advanced leukaemia. A cure was not even feasible, one reason being that healing had only been asked for in the last few days of her life expectancy, but the most important reason was that it was the child's time to return to spirit, for her task in a body was finished.

On the morning of her passing, I had called at the hospital to see her. She was in a small private ward with her parents, one each side of her bed, deep in prayer. The child had been in a coma for all of that day. I tiptoed into the room and stood at the foot of the bed, looking at her. Within a few moments she opened her eyes, gave a look of recognition with a little wan smile, then closed her eyes for the last time. Within a few moments she passed away.

During those last tragic moments, part of my mind had become aware of the spirit presence of a rather fat, jolly faced nun, waiting patiently on one side of the room. She was dressed in a grey habit. It was obvious, she had come for the spirit of this little girl. As my inner vision became clearer, I also noticed that about a dozen other children had come with the nun and were playing around the child's bed. They all looked happy, not a bit dejected or sad over the little girl's soul passing from her body.

The nun walked over to the little girl's spirit form and, grasping her hand, led her out of the room followed by a long crocodile of children who gradually faded from my inner sight through the mists that divide the two worlds.

What made this whole affair so natural to me was the fact that three of the children had straggled behind, as youngsters will, and were still playing on and around the bed. Within a moment or two the nun returned, still holding the little girl's hand and shooed the three stragglers off, in front of her this time.

The completely natural way that the nun came for the child was a new revelation, and certainly taught me that the world's way of looking at death was a completely wrong one, and nobody ever dies alone.

I couldn't even start to explain to the grief-stricken parents what I had seen for they simply would not have understood, but the experience was reassuring for myself.

Much later, when unhampered by emotion, I was able to accept the fact that, in her case, it was the child's time to go in accordance with some cosmic plan. It would appear she had only come for a short time into a body, most possibly to finish off some life's experience or perhaps to give the parent's soul maturity by having to go through the pain of bereavement.

Have you ever seen a soul who has left their body? Your eyes see only in the sense that they convey a message to your brain, so it is this that actually interprets vision. You may contemplate the fact that if these other dimensions of life are so close to this one, spirit forms who are unevolved, carry the same garb and look exactly as they did when they lived in a body, albeit they have no physical substance.

As everything in the afterlife is the expression and outcome of thought, and as such, occupies no time and space, how can anyone say with certainty they have never seen a spirit form, not just once but, thousands of times?

Of course, an evolved soul is instantly recognisable by the strong halo of light that surrounds them, but they are in a minority. All other souls look like perfectly normal people except, they don't cast any shadows.

I MEET A BUDDHIST'S SPIRITUAL HELPER

Many years ago, I visited the home of a business man in Leeds. He invited me into his study, told me to make myself comfortable, and that he would be with me in a few moments.

I seated myself in a comfortable armchair and settled down to wait. Glancing idly around the room, I saw a man standing to one side at the rear. His head was shaven. He was wearing a luminous saffron yellow robe, with one shoulder uncovered. His feet were bare, his eyes closed. I noticed that in one hand he held a wooden begging bowl.

I must say that I felt rather self-conscious with just the two of us there and was beginning to think that perhaps he was a very life-like statue. Trying to open up a conversation I gave a little nervous cough. At this, the man opened his eyes and gave me a big smile. With a nod of my head in the direction of the garden just visible through the window, I said, "The flowers do well in this weather, don't they?" His eyes showed their agreement, but he still didn't speak a single word.

I was a little embarrassed at this thinking, "What a strange man." I glanced round the room and then turning back to continue our one-sided conversation, I could not see him anywhere. Puzzled and alarmed, I shot to my feet for I couldn't understand where he had gone. Just at that moment, the business man returned to the room. I thought, "This man is going to think I am out of my tiny little mind, but I have to have an answer as to who the man in the robe is," so told him of my strange encounter.

He replied to my question in a most matter-of-fact voice, saying, "That would be Chang, my spiritual adviser. You see, I am a practising Buddhist. He doesn't usually show himself to strangers as it does tend to make them nervous. I am pleased. Now shall we get down to business?"

THE HEALING INTELLIGENCE

I call the source that actually dispenses the healing energy, 'the healing intelligence.' My perceptions tell me that it is not just one individual soul attending to a patient's needs and reinstating good health, but rather a gathering of spiritual beings. Evolved souls they undoubtedly are for they bring with them a wealth of caring energies. I would define them as 'souls of light'. There is nothing frightening or the least bit eerie about their presence, but rather a peaceful condition of contentment that settles over you as you receive their ministrations.

Lots of patients who are devoid of 'seeing' ability comment in this feeling of peace and goodness that settles over them as they receive healing, but in most cases that is all they are aware of apart of course from the removal of pain and illness.

Healing carries great and significant implications, for by its very action, it proves the existence of a caring, extra-terrestial intelligence, inspired by a loving creator.

It also proves beyond any shadow of a doubt that a full, wonderful, and exciting existence awaits every one of us after our physical bodies die, and that beyond any shadow of a doubt, each one of us is immortal, even if so few recognise this fact, be it that kid with the runny nose, the duchess with the superior manner, peeking down at the world through her 'lorgnettes', the coalman, the butcher, the baker: all are immortal. Sorry, my lady, but there is no class or society in this new life you are heading for. Everybody is the same, and any status has to be earned.

Do you advocate all developing healers to become psychic?

No, I do not. Not because it is a false path but due to the fact that every person is psychic to some degree, though it is always a good thing to remember that any system of thought expression, however much truth it contains, draws more than its fair share of cranks and spiritually ignorant souls. Some enter the ranks of avowed believers for no other reason than to gain the searched out for reputation of being 'way out'. It's a harmless enough failing as long as you do not take too much notice of what these people tell you.

In my avid searchings, I have heard the most unmitigated tripe, sometimes so wrong as to amount to pure fraud and what I consider pure blasphemy, passed off as coming from the next world. I have also found the most exquisitely evolved philosophy, containing the essence of truth, love and purity.

Profound or ignorant, the contents of any communication from beyond life invariably hinge on the development and general spirituality of the sensitive who is at that moment being used as a channel of communication by the forces of spirit.

Intimate knowledge of the next world is not an essential quality for a person to be able to develop the gift of healing. I must emphasise the point that if you have a calling to heal, it is not only important but essential that you keep the whole tone of your approach to healing on a high moral level. Your attitude is the only key to gaining access to those highly evolved entities that control healing. If you have deep religious feelings, whatever religion you are drawn to or involved in, cling to them desperately, for they will prove to be a rigid bulwark against the scoffers of this world.

Do not become sour as many people do who try to take up healing and lose their ideals because they don't manage to gain instant success. It's a rough old world out there at times, but the experience of overcoming your troubles should enrich you as a person. Do all things from the heart, and I can promise you that your life will be enriched. You will be endowed with wisdom, protection, and right guidance.

If you enter healing for a bit of a giggle, and you are looking for personal power and acclaim from others, you will never achieve anything.

If you are inane enough to open your mind to spirit energies without any higher qualities in your nature, then you're a fool treading on unsafe ground. Your idiotic approach will attract every Tom, Dick and Harry of a low and dubious spiritual elevation that co-habit the lower planes of the spirit world. You could best liken it to holding a census outside your local supermarket; it would include liars, the boastful, the truthful, the reticent, the ignorant and the wise.

There is a completely false premise abroad that there's an immediate purification by the very act of stepping out of the body a person has lived in for a lifetime. This point of view is regularly propagated by the enthusiastic preachers of many religions. Not only is it wrong, but it's a downright lie.

A person who is spiritually aware has an easier task in developing his potential for healing to its maximum than a person well versed in psychic matters. Spirituality is a quality of soul evolvement rather than a system of thought control. Therefore, it is impossible to teach to others.

It is in reality a true reflection of the soul level of that person. One who has this in full measure will do the right thing in life automatically simply because it is the correct thing to do. The higher mind of that person recognises and responds to the needs of the moment in the right way. It is also something impossible to describe in words.

IS THE DATE OF A PERSON'S DEATH PREORDAINED?

Just a few last words on the final sleep of the body. It is in my opinion that everyone has a final date of life expectancy, though I believe that this can be shortened by accident. We tend to break our lives down into years, yet once outside this life there is no such thing as time. Viewing it in that way, one can see how those in spirit look upon the shortening of a life in the body as of no great importance, especially if that soul has fulfilled its life's mission.

Possibly this could well explain why we see people who are on death's doorstep being brought back to life through the intercession of healing. Their life's mission was incomplete. If, on the other hand that final date is approaching and our life is drawing to a close, then under no circumstances would a cure result from a healer's treatment, though the passing on would be made easier for them. I could well foresee a situation in which a terminal illness was cured and then, as this person's living time was expiring, he could well go out and be knocked down by a bus.

EXPLAIN ABOUT THE PASSING OF A CHILD

In the case of a child passing away, one can only express the opinion that this is a planned act. When I meet children with an adult quality it denotes an old soul. Possibly they are suffering from a terminal illness. I am often advised from my healing source that they will not be in a body for much longer and as such have merely come to finish a job in their soul's progression. This is of little consolation to the parents, who have no knowledge of their child's life plan. For those sad, unhappy, parents, I hope these writings provide some sort of explanation and consolation.

CAUTION

I am not one of nature's fools. My reputation of being an honest man was placed soundly on my shoulders in Israel. My reasoning processes examine and evaluate things from every angle and demand double confirmation of everything concerned with my work before I will accept anything as factual. I beg you to be like me, and be cautious over things you cannot prove. I have a gift of discernment that tells me mentally if a statement is not all true. It is odds against that you haven't, so be even more cautious. Place a mental question mark against what you have been told second-hand, saying, "Possible, but not proven." Then make every effort to prove it to your satisfaction one way or the other.

In my searchings regarding my work, I have heard so many half truths spoken that have been accepted without question by listeners. A fabrication of pretty words may sound lovely to the ear, but in many cases that is all they are, pretty words. Rarely are they original for verbal plagiarism is not uncommon.

If by the time you reach the end of these writings, you imagine you are in contact with somebody who has the answer to all life's mysteries, then you will be wrong. But I do know somebody who does, and I suppose that's the next best thing.

The penny should have dropped by now regarding the afterlife and its connection with healing for its so imperative that you fully grasp this point.

The healing I practice, would be impossible without a complete integration with the next world. That is the world of spirit. It is one that every person alive on this planet will one day return to. It is impossible to accept one without the other, though I can tell you from experience that some people squirm uncomfortably over such acceptance. Spiritual snobbery is quite rife: "I am better than him" or "He is a lot worse than me for I go to church and I am religious and to prove it I even arrange the altar flowers". You must have met people like this.

The earth shattering truism regarding the continuity of all life after a body dies is so powerful in its implications that if it were accepted by all mankind, Mother Earth could be transformed overnight into a paradise. There would be no more wars or conflicts. Earth would prove to be a happy place where man could live in complete harmony with nature and his fellow beings.

This will not happen though, because of the difference in soul levels of people going through the system, for there are always a lot of first-time-in-a-body souls around. This is reflected in the traumas imposed by society on all sensitive old souls by this violent and ignorant section of humanity who have no level of soul evolvement to draw upon in order to control their behaviour patterns.

One day, in some life yet to be given them, they will realise that every cruel act, every offence against another person – even the act of mental cruelty – are divine offences. Retribution will be demanded of them for these acts, not in the way we normally think of punishment, but in the lowering of their spiritual status. A fitting judgement would be for the culprit to come back as a victim. Kick your dog, beat your wife or horse – I wouldn't if I were you, for next time in a body could well see you as a dog, horse, or beaten wife, for that's how divine justice works. Isn't it great?

You may find my views rather unusual for few people in this world think the same way as myself, especially so if your life has been narrow and completely orientated towards safety and security, and thereby limited in both scope and expression. The extra-sensory perceptions I have been blessed with are the only things that have made life liveable for me, especially when I have gone through hard times – and fate has thrown plenty of those at me!

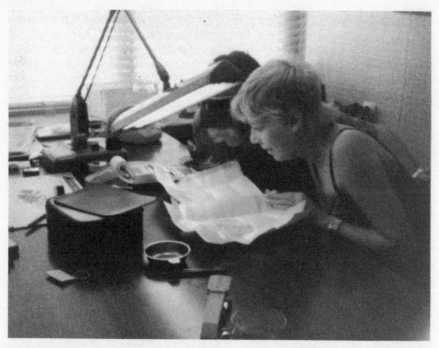

'My lovely Maggie', staring facinated at two million pounds worth of diamonds at The Diamond Centre, Tel Aviv, Israel.

Three years ago, my much-loved Maggie left her body, clutched in my arms, in her sleep, a thing I had been impressed to promise her would happen. But in my child-like innocence, I was hoping with all my heart that it would be at least another twenty years in the future. Only rarely am I told of a patient's approaching passing away, possibly because it would prove a heavy burden for me to carry. Maggie's last words to me were: "Goodnight and God bless. I do love you so much. Thank you for loving me."

Maggie wasn't ill previously, but it would appear that her task on earth was finished and so her heart just stopped and she went back to dad. I was heartbroken, for besides being very close to each other like soul mates, she was my right arm in the clinic. I couldn't understand why she had not been given special dispensation on account of the important work we did.

We had worked together so closely as a team. I healed, and Maggie talked. Since her passing, hundreds of ex-patients have expressed their gratitude for her inspired words of comfort that enabled them to take a fresh approach to life and living. For her part, she could never remember what she had told patients or what they had confided in her. She would say with a smile, "If only I could remember everything the patients told me, I could write a spicier book than Joan Collins!"

Often I would say of her, speaking in fun, that in the morning she opened her mouth and started talking, then she opened her eyes. In reply she would answer: "You don't have to listen. Just as long as you are there." Wasn't that lovely?

Our relationship was a perfect one, for we were so happy together. Our rapport was so strong that many times we did not need words, but could think of each other and the other one would pick up the thoughts.

I was completely devastated at Maggie's passing, and felt that the powers that control all life had not taken full notice of our position. I hate to admit it, but I sulked and was petulant with my spiritual helpers at what I took to be divine injustice. I remember saying to them, "Why couldn't you have engineered a long extension of life for her, considering the good works she was doing and had done previously in past years?"

I received my reply at once: "My son, she had received a long extension of life. She is happy. The grief and hurt feeling is for yourself. Learn from your grief."

On reflection, I had to accept this explanation for several years ago before we met, Maggie had once been certified as being clinically dead. This was following a serious operation that went horribly wrong. She once told me, "Don, I will never be frightened of dying ever again for it was the nicest experience I can ever remember."

She went on to say: "I recall it so clearly as though it were yesterday. I was drifting down this long, pink tunnel, surrounded by a most wonderful feeling of love and caring. Ahead was an intense white light that I wanted so much to reach. Then a voice said so gently, 'I am sorry, my darling, but you have to return to that world for a while.' The next instant, I awoke in the hospital bed surrounded by doctors and nurses, who told me later I had been clinically dead, and that my heart had stopped beating for several moments."

Confirmation that this near-death experience was not an unusual happening came from *The People* newspaper which printed letters from four readers on this subject of out-of-the-body experiences.

Dated 12th May, 1991 they read: "I began haemorrhaging after the birth of my daughter. Then suddenly I was looking down at myself and heard the doctor say he couldn't find a pulse.

Next I was travelling down a tunnel towards towards a bright light. A gentle voice told me I had to go back. Then a dear old friend, George, also told me to go back. Three weeks later my husband told me that George had died on the day my daughter was born."

"Shortly after my wife was told that she couldn't have any more children. I was declared dead after a pit accident.

I was revived, and while in a coma had a vision of walking along the sun's rays and seeing a hand with a long white sleeve, reaching down. I almost touched the hand when I felt myself pulled back. A voice said, 'You are going to be all right and so is your son.' A few months later we learned my wife was pregnant with our son."

"While unconscious in surgery, I found myself floating above my body. The ward clock showed three. Next day I was told that I had 'died' during the op at three precisely."

"When my late husband, an atheist, was delirious, he began reciting beautiful poetry in a Quaker tongue.

When he finally came round, he said he'd been going up a long tunnel towards a brilliant white light, but that something had drawn him back."

"I remember being drawn towards a bright light and then being surrounded by a warm golden glow. Then a voice said gently that I'd come too soon. I'm not religious, but now have no fear of death."

Bereavement is never a happy time, although in theory I suppose it should be. My Maggie had charisma, feminity and what I can only term as style. Long ago she had made me promise to send her out in style if she ever died before me. It was a difficult task, but I kept my promise for she was a great one regarding her appearance.

Our ability to link into each other is still there, although she has lost her body, as well it should be, for you certainly do not stop loving someone just because they have stepped out of their body.

Heartbroken, I dressed for her funeral and checked in the mirror to see that I looked smart enough. It was at that moment I heard her voice in her usual loving bossy manner, saying, "Mr Greenbank. Go and change that suit this minute." I looked down at the suit. It seemed all right. Then I put my reading glasses on, and noticed at once that there was a grease stain down the front from when I had been feeding the dogs, so I returned to the bedroom and changed it.

At the funeral, I was comforted by feeling Maggie's presence sitting next to me. I was filled with a tremendous feeling of spiritual power that came running into me. It gave me an inner elation and a terrific upliftment. This was so strong that I called down the preacher who was conducting the service, and stood in his pulpit.

Pointing at her simple coffin I said: "My Maggie is not in there. That's just her overcoat." For I could see her quite plainly, sitting with a broad smile on her face, watching the service from the third row, next to one of her friends, who verified this to me later, for she, too, felt Maggie's presence.

I went on to add: "Of all the things I could say regarding my lovely lady, nothing could sum up our mutual love for each other as that poem by Robbie Burns, 'My love is like a red, red, rose'."

I then proceeded to recite the poem. My voice became stronger and thundered out as the power from spirit filled me and took over control. The atmosphere in the chapel changed from the usual sadness and dark depressions of funerals in general to one of joyous upliftment.

It was really a time for celebration: a person's task in life was finished. They could forget their cares, fears, and all the sad events that form part of life, for Maggie's previous marriage had not been a kind or a happy one.

Every person in the packed chapel was affected by the spiritually charged emotion and sheer love that filled the place. So strong was the emotion generated that after the service was over, the funeral director came over and said to me: "I have attended tens of thousands of funerals but this is the first time I have ever had tears running down my cheeks. You were both very lucky to have shared such a love."

Maggie spoke to me in my inner mind, she told me to go back to our home and have a party to celebrate her leaving her body. So we went back to the house and broke out four special bottles of "bubbly" she had been saving for a special occasion. Everyone toasted my lovely lady. This pleased her for she stood right next to me throughout the proceedings, giving me her support and comfort.

After I overcame my initial shock at the loss of her physical presence, which took some time because at that period I could see little reason for living out my life, I then realised I was placed on this earth to help others in similar situations, and I was being no less than downright selfish in my attitude.

My lovely lady has returned to me every single night since her passing, just before I retire to bed. I always know when she is present because the dogs walk over and sit by her chair in the lounge. I then prickle from head to foot and can see her misty outline in her chair, and we are able to converse by thought. Our tuning in to each other must be a highly delicate and sensitive affair for if anyone else is present, I cannot reach her particular vibration. I do also often have brief flashes of her during the day and quite often smell her particular perfume, which is a further reassurance.

One event of seeing her made me laugh at the time. It happened when I was treating a patient. I was deeply engrossed in the healing taking place. I had some of our special music playing softly in the background when I became aware of the spirit form of Maggie dancing around the room in perfect time with the music. She often did this when she was in her body.

Tuning in to her, I saw her draw up the side of the lovely yellow dress she was wearing. With a smile and a twinkle in her eye she said, "Do you think I have nice legs, Mr Greenbank?" But what made me burst out laughing was that Maggie was wearing a matching pair of yellow briefs under her dress. She must be one of the few souls in the afterlife to wear undies! Although they were of no substance.

Peter Fosbrook's wife Nina, came several times for the healing of a long standing condition that responded favourably. This night in particular, arriving home after attending for healing, she and her husband went up to bed. The bedroom door was ajar and Peter who was sitting up in bed, saw this smartly dressed blonde haired lady passing the bedroom doorway. She waved to him and gave him a big smile, then vanished. He leapt out of bed, but could not see anyone in the house.

The next time he brought his wife for healing, instead of waiting outside in the car park as he usually did, he came into the healing room with his wife, and told me his strange story. I showed him some photographs of Maggie . . . and he instantly identified her as the lady he saw in his home. So yet further evidence was given me that my lovely lady is still working with me, and for, healing.

In those days of dark depression just after I lost her, somebody gave me a short poem, which had no named author, to help cheer me up. I placed it on a coffee table meaning to read it later. Suddenly it levitated about one foot in the air, swirled around in front of my eyes then settled down where I had placed it originally. I then read it. It states:

"At the end of the tunnel there's always a light,
There's always the dawning after the night,
Always the solace after the pain,
Always the sunshine after the rain,
Look up at the rainbow, arched in the sky,
A symbol of promise when things go awry."

Shortly after Maggie's body died, an ex-patient dropped in to see me. She had known Maggie well, but didn't know of her passing. "Is Maggie having a five minute break?" She asked. "I have just seen her sitting on the seat beside the fish pond in the garden. She gave me a wave of her hand and a big smile when she saw me."

Like most other people – and even with all my awarenesses of spirit – I too like to be reassured that life goes on after the death of the body.

When Gordon Higginson, a well-known medium was visiting Bradford, I went along to hear him speak. He had neared the end of the service and there was no word from Maggie. Suddenly she spoke in my mind, saying, "Don, this is awful. It's worse than queuing at Morrison's checkout." – this is our local supermarket.

Finally the medium came to me for his last proof of survival of the evening. After giving her full name, which is an unusual one, he then described Maggie accurately, Saying, "She has two things to tell you as proof that she has survived the death of her body. This will make you smile. One is that she is in the heavenly choir, and the other is that she has adopted a little girl and is bringing her up in the spirit world."

This was evidence enough for me. Maggie couldn't sing for toffee, and would say to me, "When I die, I do hope they give me a good singing voice for it's something I have always longed to have". The other was that Maggie had always longed for her own child, but it wasn't meant to be, so it would appear that she has been able to fulfil both her wishes in the afterlife. I am so pleased for her.

Readings by other sensitives come to me very rarely, perhaps a handful of times in my lifetime, so mostly I have to rely on my own intuitive perceptions. The elevated soul who runs the clinic, who I have been aware of all these years, was only seen by Maggie once, and then only for a few seconds. She was absolutely staggered at seeing him as large and as clear as life. Being so startled made her lose his vibration, and she lost contact with her vision of this great soul.

Over the years, I have had literally hundreds of seers in the healing room to observe healings taking place – and not a single one of them has seen this elevated soul, therefore it must be a question of vibrations. The higher the vibration of the spirit, the harder it is to link in to him.

Many years ago when I was investigating healing, trying to make sense out of my confusion, I was in London. Having a few hours to spare, I strolled round the Spiritualist Association of Great Britain headquarters in Belgrave Square. After looking round the bookshop, I sat down in the waiting room for a rest. In meditation I heard a spirit voice say quite abruptly: "Who are you? You are different. We can't do anything for you here." So I immediately stood up and left.

Healing and clairvoyance operate on separate vibrations. Usually the two do not mix. I am given advice via a mental voice, only when it is important to the healing, and at such times only are they complimentary to each other. On other occasions they can prove to be a distraction to the healer. I rely on my other intuitive perceptions for the majority of the time. Possibly this is to keep my mind still, devoid of all non-essential chatter.

If I become mentally aware of a soul attached to a person who has come for healing, it is my practice to direct my mind on to the healing aspect and away from the thoughts of that soul.

One of the exceptions was a lady who attended for healing. She came in to see me, such a sad unhappy and depressed soul, full of aches and pains. I knew instantly these had no physical origin, but were largely the result of stress and tension.

She told her story of woe, of how she had lost her husband a few months before and couldn't seem to come to terms with her loss. All the time she was speaking, I was aware of the spirit form of her husband standing to one side. He looked as real as life to me. Ridding himself of his body had not improved him as yet, for he had been – and still was – a bossy chauvinistic person.

Finally, in exasperation I said to her: "Your husband is here. I will use his exact words to you. They are: 'Oh Betty, you do look a beggar in that dress! Black never did suit you. Now buck up your ideas and start living again.'"

She said in reply: "That's him. My name is Ethel, but he always used to call me Betty. Oh, I am glad!"

After receiving healing, she went on her way rejoicing, with all her pains gone and her depression lifted. That is one time that clairvoyance was helpful for the patient.

As I have told you previously, it is my opinion that every person has a date stamp on their life span, and that this is preordained before birth. Confirmation of this came from a most unexpected quarter in a recent issue of the *Journal of the Royal Society of Medicine*. It revealed that "There is a highly significant association between the length of the lifeline on a person's right palm and their age at death."

Three doctors carried out tests on a hundred bodies at Bristol Royal Infirmary and discovered a, "Strong statistical correlation between the length of the lifetime, on the right hand in particular, and the length of their life." Many of these deaths were due to accidents, which gives oneself even further food for thought.

Florrie Greenbank, my mother, was a lovely soul. You would have liked her. Everybody did. She was kind to the point of what many people would call foolish, for I have known her take off her coat in the street and give it to a person who admired it, yet life had not been kind to her. She had been plagued by poverty and hardship. What a joy it was for me to be able to help her in old age so that she was able to spend the last years of her life in relative luxury!

Mum always had certain awarenesses that helped her to live life. She could 'see', but usually only first thing in the morning. She woke up one day to find a man sitting on her bed, looking down at her, with a pensive smile on his face, completely real and solid looking.

He said to Mum: "I once lived here. It was forty years ago." Mum spluttered for she was completely taken aback at this apparition, then the man just vanished into thin air.

Making enquiries later from people who had lived in the village all their lives, she found that a person answering the man's description *had* lived in that house all those years before.

Mum had so many instances similar to that experience that it created in her a very strong belief in the afterlife. She knew that life continued after the death of the body. If Mum had a failing – if you call it that – it was that she loved having her fortune told. She would travel miles with her friends to hear the latest rising star in the psychic field. She was honest enough to say, "I only want to hear the nice things, even if they don't come true, for I have had enough of the nasty one's happen to me."

She lived in her own little world of eternal optimism. Mum called it 'living in hope' and often said, "If you haven't hope, you have nothing."

News reached her ears of a well-known medium who was on a short visit to Bradford. Grabbing hold of her friend – and both full of excitement – they trotted off post-haste to see this person.

They arrived at the back door of an imposing house and rang the doorbell. The door was answered by a lady dressed in a uniform, as some receptionists did in those days. Consequently, Mum and her friends saw nothing unusual in this.

"We have come for a consultation," Mum said. "Is he available?"

"Yes," replied the lady. "If you will go into the waiting room he will not be too long."

The lady in the uniform returned and said, "Now which of you requires the consultation?"

"Oh, I do," blurted out Mum. The lady then asked my mother, "How long have you been in trouble?"

Mum replied, "Oh, for years!" At that, the lady shot my mother a quizzical look as though she was some kind of comedienne, then said: "Well in that case you had better go into that room and take all your clothes off. Put on the dressing gown that you will find there." Mum said, "But all I want is a consultation!" The lady replied, "But he has to examine you to see how far on you are with the pregnancy."

It was at this point that the penny started to drop with Mum. She said to the lady, with a blush up to her hairline: "I have a feeling there has been some kind of mistake. We have really come to have our fortunes told." "Wrong house!" said the nurse, for that's what she was. "You want next door. This is Saint Monica's Home for Unmarried Mother's." Mum told me later they both dashed out of the house and ran a quarter of the mile all the way down Oak Lane, and she always blushed every time she thought of or spoke about that episode.

A patient who came for healing many years ago told me that he had experienced countless events over the years that had convinced him of the reality of a life after death. Perhaps the most amazing thing that happened to him was an apport which appeared 'inside' his clenched hand while he sat in meditation.

I asked him to show it to me. He produced it from his pocket. It was about half an inch in length, metal and felt very heavy. He then agreed to lend it to me so I could have a friend analyse it.

My friend, who is a scientist, took it away, then returned it after analysis. He had a puzzled look on his face. As I had not told him where it came from, he asked, "Where ever did you find it?" He then told me it had proved impossible to line up exactly "with any metal known to belong to this world." The nearest he could reach was only an approximation, for there were certain features of it that had no known comparison.

A patient, Mrs Robinson of Filey, had a remarkable experience via the telephone. One night three months after her son, who was in his twenties, had been killed in a car accident, the telephone rang. She picked up the receiver, but there was none of the usual buzz on the line. Then Mrs Robinson heard her dead son's voice say quite clearly. "It's me Mum," he said mentioning his name. "This is just to let you know I am all right and that I am very happy." Then the line went dead while she on her part was overcome with joy at this reassurance from the world of spirit.

Another of my patients – this one from Bishop Auckland – rang me up late one night in a very distressed state. Over the years I have helped many of their family and found them all very receptive to healing The previous year he brought a friend of his to me for healing. This person was suffering intense pain from arthritis, yet we were able to rid him of all his aches and pains and make his body mobile once more.

It appeared that this patient had suffered a serious heart attack and died about one month before the following incident.

This night in question the telephone rang. The man's daughter answered. "It's me" said the voice of the friend who had died mentioning his name. The daughter recognised his voice at once.

He continued: "I can't talk long. Just tell my wife that I am happy and content. Remember me to that chap in Yorkshire your dad took me to see, for he did help me so much, and I never had a chance to thank him." With those words his voice gradually faded away until the line was dead, except there was no click of a receiver being replaced.

From all my experiences of the afterlife, I have come to the conclusion that it is similar in action to a two-way mirror, whereby those in spirit can see our every action, if they have a mind to, but we are faced with a complete blankness from which only a very limited amount of knowledge and inner sight can percolate through to this lower frequency in which we live.

As wonderful as the life after the death of our body is, each person has an in-built mental block that makes us cling desperately to this life. We call this self-preservation. It is our strongest human instinct and has been deliberately placed there by our Creator as a brake on the inner person returning to the world of spirit before our task on earth is done.

If it were not there, then at the first trouble in our lives – the loss of a loved one, or at the onset of a crippling ailment – it is highly likely we would simply bring our life to a close with never a second thought or fear.

I have been told by many old people that they were ready to die as their bodies had run down and grown old. Most of their partners and friends had died; they were bored with a life in which they had little interest as modern trends and behaviour patterns had changed out of all recognition. This world no longer held any interest for them.

A matron, who I knew very well, once confided in me that many old people died for no organic reason. Feeling they had nothing to live for any longer, they just turned their faces to the wall and peacefully passed away.

Possibly with everyone who has lived a full, useful life, there is a subconscious inner knowledge that their work on earth is nearly done. The in-built block against dying cuts out and is no longer in operation. So it would appear, that like all animals, human beings can apply a death wish to themselves when the mental block of restraint is removed by age.

To be truthful, my feelings as I touch on these further extensions of the life beyond this one, as I often do during my work of healing, is one of nostalga and homesickness. On account of being totally immersed every day in the practise of healing the sick, worldly values have little appeal for me.

I could best liken it to knowing that one is temporarily marooned in an often very unstable physical body, and realising for certain that this life is just a brief halt on a great journey, which the inner person feels impatient to continue.

The inner core of spirit in me yearns for the awareness that it previously had, when once more the hungers of this physical world, the despairs, fears, pain and ugliness, are finally exposed for the lessons that they are and can then be forgotten. It is my private hope I shall still retain the memory of love experienced, the beauty touched upon, and the delights that I have gained through sharing in nature's many moods.

If I were asked to pick one single event that was the most moving to me from all the out-of-the-body experiences that have come my way. I would probably plump for the following, which incidentally I did not see. It is my opinion that the person who did see it wasn't supposed to either.

A Jewish family brought their daughter to me for healing. Whilst I was treating her, for which she gained an instant cure, the mother, who had lost a son when he was just one year old, sat with her eyes closed, listening to the background music that was softly playing.

Suddenly, she saw with her mind's eye an old man walk out of the corner of the room with his arm around the shoulders of a boy aged about twelve. They walked across the room and stopped in front of the mother, who quite clearly heard the old man say to the boy in a kindly and well modulated voice: "This lady is your mother. This gentleman is your father. Now you will have to come back with me." With that, they both turned round and walked away through the mists that separate the two worlds. As you can well imagine, both parents were thrilled beyond words at this experience.

Let me finish this chapter with a smile. One day in a discussion with an oldish man on the theme of a life after death, I was stressing the point of how welcome it must be after a lifetime of toil and stress to relax fully and find perfect peace. He in turn replied with a snort of derision saying, "Fat lot of peace up there as far as I can see, who wants to be sitting on a wet cloud without a coat on, dressed in just a thin nightie with a lazy wind blowing through you, harping away from eight till eight, you can keep it for me."

Somehow I don't think it's like that though!

FURTHER EXPLANATIONS

If you are a man of the world, or perhaps think you are, with your conversation confined to racing, beer, football and women, all I have said previously in this chapter may well be a bitter pill for you to swallow.

Let me try to explain it to you like this. Remember when you go to sleep and have a true dream, not one that comes from eating a heavy supper, and you dream of doing all manner of exciting things. At the time of dreaming, your environment and all the situations you visualise are at that particular moment just as real to you as any of the situations you encounter in your everyday life. Yet your dream is entirely on a mental level of appreciation.

The difference between a dream and the reality of the spirit world is that a dream is merely an excursion of the imagination, whilst the afterlife is one on a much higher vibration and frequency than that which we are now living. I say it is a fraction of an inch to the left.

Another interesting point is, that time does not exist in a dream state. Nor does it exist in the next world. The realms of spirit life that await us when we finish with this one are many and varied. Each one, I can assure you, will be as real and solid to the senses as this one, but with far less restriction of movement. Just remember that, as I said before, you will be able to go anywhere simply by thinking of the place you want to be: the mind boggles at the thought.

There is no waiting in queues at the airport or a train station, being jostled by other people with the same idea as you. Life on other planets? Go check for yourself, though you may have to alter your vibratory rate. That may seem to be no more than a rocky and desolate landscape on one vibratory level, might prove on another to be a second Shangril-la, teeming with rich life and full of beauty.

Isn't it wonderful that the essential part of you – call it what you will, the ego, the soul, or spirit – is immortal? Life goes on and on, with both meaning and purpose. In fact, you couldn't die if you wanted to! You have no control over this fact, for it is one of nature's inflexible laws.

If you still find it hard to conceive something you cannot see, feel or touch, just try and express the following in words, for they are all part of our human make-up. They are love, kindness, dignity, and that word that has nearly gone out of fashion, honour.

After the body dies, each soul goes to his or her dimension – world or mansion, paradise or heaven – on that particular vibratory level to which their soul has evolved. It's a simple and automatic action.

The old-time religion makers were not far out in their description of the life after this. Can you give me a better description of hell than a place inhabited by the greedy, the selfish, the cruel, or any of the other character traits that are displayed in man's lower base nature, and no better description of heaven than a place occupied by innocent children and loving, unselfish souls?

Acceptance of what I have said requires no particular belief in any religion, for it is one of the true facts of life. Knowledge of this nature is a useful asset in living life, for it can bring comfort for the mourner, and a deep joy in ourselves as old age creeps up on us and our bodies prepare to stop working. We can anticipate the joyful reunions ahead. It should banish all fear of death and the act of dying, and is one of the few explanations that make sense of the tests, trials, and tribulations of this life. If this was not so, I can see no purpose for living, learning, or loving.

The difference between men and women are pretty obvious ones. But what, if any, is the difference between the souls of men and women?

We have a saying up here in the wilds of Yorkshire that 'If you want to know something – ask.' So I did just that. I was told by the evolved soul I contacted that the sex factor belongs only to this particular life, and is purely a glandular and genetic affair. After the death of the body, a soul will often cling to the identity of either male or female, purely from past habit.

When eventually they become bored and wish to have further learning adventures in a body in order to gain further soul maturity, they will often elect to come back with the particular sex for which they have a preference.

This could possibly explain the phenomena of homosexuality and lesbianism, such being souls who arrive in a new body, still clinging by habit to the former sex . . . they have a preference for. So I received my answer. If the latest medical discovery in which scientists say they can give the parents a child with whatever sex they have a preference for is true, and if a body is allocated to a certain soul before birth, then I can foresee even more trouble with gender mix-ups in the future.

The explanation given by my spiritual guardians confirmed to me the feelings I have experienced when giving healing in a state of deep attunement. The physical is often forgotten. The touching of souls reveals no difference between male and female. When one touches on the higher, more evolved entities, the impression that comes to me is not one of either a her or him but of a 'being', such as one may perhaps imagine an angel.

Chapter Five

WARNING, WARNING, WARNING OR NEVER PLAY LEAPFROG WITH A UNICORN

THIS chapter has been written solely for the benefit of adventurous souls who love to dabble in an area of spiritual unrest that lies just outside this life. They do this with never a second thought of the consequences regarding their own spiritual safety, for this is an area of unpeace that is potentially dangerous to people's well being.

For want of a better name we shall call this area 'limbo', for that's exactly what it is. It lies between the outer fringe of life and the elevated state of spirit that most people would term heaven. It is not signposted: its limits are defused and unclear. It is essential, if you are enquiring into the world of spirit, that you should know of its existence, and the potential harm it could have on your mental health.

Over the years of healing, I have had to treat hundreds of good, kind, and very well intentioned people, who purely out of curiosity, dabbled in this darkened area of the occult. The condition they finish up in is a befuddled state of nervous distress. I call the healing action needed for them to become normal 'spiritual cleansing'.

If you do feel the need to go aroaming in the mind, do understand that the only protection you have from those capricious and mischievous elemental entities that inhabit this region, is by having a highly developed spiritual code of conduct that inspires and controls your every action in life.

You cannot put on such an attitude on a Sunday, like many church-goers do, and then take it off for the rest of the week. It has to be a part of you. Never forget that without spiritual protection, you are vulnerable to every ill-intentioned force around.

There have been many potentially dangerous situations I have encountered over my many years of transmitting healing. Without the defensive shield of spiritual protection, evil entities could easily have gained entry into my inner person. The possible outcome for me may have resulted in suffering a nervous breakdown, or worse!

I do not intend to go into these situations for it would serve no useful purpose, but these unnerving experiences have made me wary and left me with many uncomfortable memories. My feelings at the time were of being too close to something that was unclean and distasteful.

One such experience I could well have done without will best answer the oft-asked question as to whether limbo is a state on the lower astral plain, where ignorant and arrogant souls co-habit, or merely an illusion propagated by 'hell fire and brimstone' fundamentalist preachers in a futile but furious attempt to make their flocks toe the line regarding their behaviour in life.

After my first hand experience of the following, I would plump for the former. I cannot give you a straight answer as to just why I had to go through it, beyond the possibility that perhaps it was one of life's tests, to see how I would cope with the situation. Maybe it was to show me how rife in this world is the opposition to goodness.

My story starts with the arrival at my clinic of a stack of letters written by a self-styled professor from Thailand. They contained an open invitation to treat many of his countrymen. He told me he already had a list of five hundred people desperately in need of healing. They were suffering from a wide variety of advanced sick conditions. The 'professor' added that my reputation of achieving wonderful results had reached his ears, and that his people were simply desperate for help. The whole affair felt wrong in a way I could not actually put my finger on. No warning of the potential dangers ahead were given to me by my advisers in spirit. They refused to pass any comment on the matter, saying that the choice to go or not was mine alone.

With some inner trepidation, I eventually agreed to go to Thailand, but still felt very uneasy about the trip. After a very long journey of twenty-seven hours, we eventually arrived in Pattaya. We were not particularly impressed, for the town itself, at least on the surface, seemed little more than the usual Eastern tourist trap of sleazy looking bars filled with girls and boys of the town – sometimes it was a puzzle to know which was which – and also dope pedlars haggling with their clients.

The apartment in the hotel that had been provided for us, was palatial, the owner was both friendly and helpful. He placed the presidential suite, consisting of six rooms, at our disposal, and told us we could stay free of charge for up to six weeks if we so desired, as he considered it a great honour to have us to stay there. Later he told me he hoped my presence would bring a feeling of peace and spirituality to the hotel, which had a long history of strange and frightening occurrences, so much so that some of his staff were fearful of entering certain parts of the hotel and grounds. To try and placate his Gods, he had built, at great expense, a huge spirit house in the hotel grounds, but all to no effect. Months after our visit, we received a letter from him saying that the atmosphere had cleared in the hotel and he had not received any further complaints from his staff.

As soon as I entered the hotel, an awful sense of wrongness swept over me. It settled on my mind like a black cloud and I found it most difficult to attune with the higher realms of spiritual life.

The next morning I met the 'professor' who had invited me to this country. We did not gel. He was the complete opposite of everything I hold dear, being avaricious, money-grabbing and with an eye always on the main chance.

He handed me a large packet of paper money, which he had taken for advance bookings from patients who wished to see me for healing. I could well have done with the cash to help run the various charitable works that form part of a healer's task in life, but wasn't allowed to take it.

I handed the packet back, saying, "For some reason for which I can give you no explanation, I am not allowed to treat your people." He looked at me as though I had taken leave of my senses and dismay filled his face. I immediately had an intuitive thought that he had intended to keep a large proportion of my fees for himself.

All I could tell him was the truth, explaining, "There is no power to heal here." For the very first time in all the years of healing, there was 'no' power with me. It is an impossible task to heal without God's energy.

In a desperate effort to understand the reason why not, I asked to see the patients' medical profiles that he had prepared, and the reason became obvious at once why I was not allowed to give healing.

I am no prude, but the profiles read like something out of a horror comic. Aids, sexually induced tumours, every possible kind of venereal disease, advanced stages of drug addiction, and a host of similar conditions, carried by distorted human beings, such as transvestites, kinky prostitutes and greedy pimps.

The calm voice of my spiritual adviser spoke in my mind, saying, "You wondered why we did not caution you against coming here. You must always have your own freedom of choice. It is good that you should know what unpleasant things the world holds. Well, now you know.

These poor, sad people are the victims of poverty, greed and their own base nature. They have been used – and in many cases abused – by selfish and equally greedy people. The price they have to pay is their physical life itself, for there is always an effect to every cause. In their case, it is the loss of both mental and physical health.

How foolish is man. He is only on earth for a brief spell to gain soul wisdom by learning from the experiences that life throws at him. In his naivety, he imagines he can misuse and abuse his body with impunity and thereby never learns the lesson of self-discipline. It is one of mother nature's truths that you always reap what you have sown – and these poor souls had sown badly. Were we to take away their ailments, assuming it was possible no lesson would have been learnt, for they would immediately repeat all the sad things that had happened to them previously. They will be re-educated on the cause of their folly when their souls leave their bodies and return to the world of spirit."

Later that evening, I was standing on the roof of the hotel looking out over the town. The voice spoke again in my mind, saying: "Look, and take notice of what you see". There was a shift in my vision. Hovering like a funeral pyre over this pathetic town far below, was an evil black cloud, swirling around in all manner of grotesque shapes. The voice then said: "There is your evil, born of man's lower self and perpetuated by indulgence. Now go back to your place of peace in England, and feel secure that you bask in the brightness of the higher love that is of the one God."

Within three days we were back in our own country. The heaviness of spirit did not lift from me until we were over twenty miles away from that lustful centre of chaos. So be warned. These forces of evil *do* exist.

Chapter Six

MUSINGS AND SOME FUNNY THINGS THAT
HAVE HAPPENED

TO carry on healing year after year, being constantly confronted with all the fears and depressions that many sick people carry around with them like a sack of coal on their backs, a healer must develop a keen sense of humour to help keep one's sanity. Healing should always be a happy affair, devoid of all sombre undertones. Here are a few examples of how our work is lightened by the often unconscious humour of patients.

A ruggedly-built person staggered into the healing room with a lovely, 'shiner'. It was obvious he had been in a fight. "Whatever happened to you?" I asked him.

"I forgot the first proverb of the Yorkshireman's Bible," he replied. "Thrice blessed is he who gets his blow in first! And I won't forget that ever again."

A while ago a lady came to see me for healing. At great lengths she recounted her long history of illnesses, which included three stays in a mental home for depression.

In a quiet, confidential voice she told me: "I have tried everything I know to become better. I have listened to hymns on TV, bought a bible and even purchased a bloody cross – and I am still no better!" I demonstrated to her how little a thing was causing her pains by tapping the seat of her discomfort lightly with my hand. Within seconds all he pain had gone. She came to see me once more for further healing and said that for about a week she had been pain-free. Then the lady turned over quickly in bed and the pain began again. She had hit the spot on her spine as hard as she could with a long handled clothes brush, but still the pain persisted. She mused for a moment, then said, "You know, there must be something funny about your hands."

Probably the nicest compliment ever paid me was in the following. The healing had gone wonderfully for an eighty-four year old Jewish lady with whom I had struck up an instant rapport. All her pains were removed and on leaving, with a broad smile, she chuckled me under the chin. Paying me her highest compliment she said, "You know, you would make a lovely Jewish boy!"

A coloured lady came to me for help. She explained her case history in a broad Yorkshire dialect, saying, "I reckon now't to them black doctors at the hospital. You can't understand what they are saying."

Many years ago now an old countryman came for healing with a very painful back. Out of politeness I asked him how it had happened. He explained it was a "wrack of t'eye and twist o't goo" that caused it. I puzzled over this new expression. Finally in exasperation as it was obvious I didn't know what he was

94

talking about, the old chap explained further. He was helping his friend to build a new barn. "Have you seen anyone looking at a plumb bob to see if the wall was straight and in line" he asked. "One eye closed, mouth twisted over and backside on one side. Well, that's 'ow I 'urt me back."

The electric lights went off one night in a power cut and we were having to show patients in by candle light. Some people get themselves into such a state when they come for healing. My assistant showed such a man into the dimly lit healing room, he must have been in overdrive for he dashed across and began opening the drapes at the window, thinking it was another doorway. I was just able to grab him by the seat of his trousers before he disappeared through the open window into the back-yard.

Another man sat on the healing chair as I asked him to tell me his troubles. I patted his back in a friendly way. From out of his collar shot a cloud of talcum powder which covered my face, so I said to him laughingly, "Do you want me to sing 'Mammy'?"

Then there was an old man blessed with the wisdom of Solomon, who once explained to me how to achieve the most out of life. He said, "Live every day as though it were your last, and you know, one day you will be right."

On one occasion, I had just finished healing a person who had a very painful spine. Several discs and vertebrae were affected, with signs of arthritic adhesions on either side of his spine. He was freed from all pain, and said that he felt wonderful. I offered him helpful advice as to the best way to avoid further trouble by telling him not to bend too much until the inflammation had all died down.

He replied with a twinkle in his eye: "I have got to bend, lad. My job's digging ditches and my boss keeps an eye on us all the time. He says 'when your head and your backside are level, then – and only then – are you working'".

One arthritic patient who could hardly walk was treated successfully, or so I thought. I felt the limbs and joints come free one after the another as the adhesions were dispersed. However, her progress out of the clinic was just as hesitant and obviously as painful as her entry had been. I remained puzzled until she called in to see me the following week walking quite normally. The patient then told me, when she was in the car, and only then, did she discover that after I had treated her feet, she had put her shoes back on the wrong way.

A patient came into the healing room laughing all over her face. "What are you laughing at?" I asked her. "People are funny," she said. "There's about ten people waiting to see you in the other room. They are having a lovely discussion on, of all things, coffins." I went in and broke that up.

Spare a thought for the Irish lady with a rich brogue. She was lovely and natural, arriving for healing with a huge cross round her neck that would have lamed her if she had dropped it on her foot. Her laboured limb of pain was crowned by the expletive, "By the holy mother of God, me bloody back is killing me!" Healing was immediate in the face of such urgency.

Another time a woman came, telling me she was very worried as she had a lump in her breast. I couldn't sense a sick condition, but had to admit she had a lump. I treated her, but there was no going down in size of the lump, as is usual. She came back to see me the following week, all smiles. It turned out to be a lump in the padding of her brassiere!

On another occasion a patient came into the healing room and said: "There's a

The first sanctuary – 10 Spring Gardens.

The new sanctuary – Oak Lee Hall.

woman in the other room making a scene. She has not come as a patient, but as a companion to one. She is going round asking all the waiting patients what is wrong with them, upsetting one or two who have serious conditions."

I went into the waiting room, knelt on my haunches in front of her and in a quiet voice told her off, or so I thought, for the next patient came in smiling all over her face, and said: "You have just been in the waiting room and told that woman off for being nosy. Well, when you left the room she said, 'Oh, hasn't he got such lovely eyes.'"

Some people are a joy in themselves with their wisdom. One old man once said to me, "If you want to know what God thinks about money, just look closely at the people who he gave it to."

If I could only put into words the sadness in that man's voice remarking on someone who had been left a large sum of money in a will. With nostalgia in his voice he said, "The only thing my father left me was bronchitis."

I shall never understand people. One lady who came for healing brought a shopping list of about twelve things wrong with her. Her attitude was awful, to say the least. I felt little hope of being able to help her, for her list included arthritis and all her joints were locked. She could hardly walk, had pain all over her body, and was as sour as cream that had gone off. I said to her, "if you are at all improved, give me a ring and I will fix you up with another appointment."

She rang me within a few days and still speaking in a sour tone of voice, told me she was slightly improved, so I gave her another appointment.

When she came for treatment I was amazed to find everything was all right, except for just a little bit of pain remaining in her thumbs. She looked at me, her face set and so serious, she said, "Well, at my age you can't expect miracles, can you?"

Every time one particular patient came for treatment, she was so moved inwardly that tears would stream down her cheeks. Apologetically she would smile and say, "You know, I think my bladder is too near my eyes."

My sense of humour often places me in much trouble. Many years ago, I attended a lecture given by a well-travelled speaker on spiritual subjects.

Just before she started the lecture, she told the audience in a very serious tone of voice.

"I am writing a book about my experiences in South Africa. I have chosen the title, which is, *Sitting on a gold mine.*"

Unfortunately, the poor lady spoke with a pronounced lisp and the words came out wrong. I was the only one to laugh!

The quick wittedness of many Jewish persons was demonstrated in the following. A Jewish man from Manchester brought his wife for healing. We managed to gain a great improvement in her condition and she went home delighted. About three months later her husband rang me up and asked if I would treat her again, as in his words, she was ninety per cent better. He wanted her to have the other ten per cent if that was possible. He then said, "Could I have a word with you in private before you treat my wife as there is something important I wish to discuss with you."

The day came for her appointment. Leaving his wife in the waiting room I invited him into my study. "What is it you want to talk about?" I asked him.

"Well," he said, "ever since my wife has been to see you, everywhere she goes, coffee mornings, Barmitzvahs, holidays, and every Saturday at the synagogue, somehow she always steers the conversation around to you. It's Don Greenbank this, and Don Greenbank that. What is it about you?"

"Oh," I told him, "That's just my charisma." He answered as quick as a flash, "Oh, we Jewish boys don't have those do we?"

An old patient who was renowned as a chatterbox, came for the healing of a minor condition – she had lost her voice. Her husband came with her. Usually quiet natured and reserved, on this occasion he was talkative and full of himself. Taking me on one side, half seriously he said, "This is heaven! There's £5 extra if you can make it permanent!"

Some people read words and somehow manage always to pronounce them wrongly. This person came for healing so I asked what her trouble was. She replied, "I have an intense pain in my vaggi-i-arna." I had to think about that one a moment before the penny dropped.

My rather strong sense of humour can at times be open to misunderstanding, so this is written by way of explanation to a very puzzled lady. She will have been puzzled for many years now, for this occured when she rang up my old sanctuary. At this stage I had better fill in the background and explain that, before taking over these premises, they belonged to an advertising agency that became bankrupt. Due to some misunderstanding at the Post Office, their name was listed under our telephone number.

On the day in question, the telephone rang and was answered by my assistant. An icy cool, efficient woman's voice, speaking in a particularly high handed angry tone, demanded to speak to our Managing Director. Every protest of not having one was waived aside so I was called to the phone. "There is no managing director," I told her. "Oh yes there is, and I *demand* to speak to him at once," was her reply, followed by a stream of abuse. "Well, I can't promise, but I will try my best if you will just join with me." I replied adding, "Our Father who art in Heaven . . ." Very gently, there was a soft click as she placed the telephone back on its stand.

Even the most pathetic and distressing of situations can have its lighter moments. Once I was visiting a patient in a Bradford hospital reserved for the terminally sick. Sitting by the side of a patient's bed giving her healing, I became aware of a background noise of somebody talking and the voice was becoming louder and louder, and more excited. I turned round to see who was speaking and there was one of the sweetest souls you could ever imagine, sitting up in bed reading aloud from a romantic novel. So engrossed was she in the book that she was impervious to everyone and everything. With a pair of reading glasses perched perilously on the tip of her nose, and wearing a bed cap from which wisps of silver grey hair peeped out, she was the picture of everyone's grandma.

Her voice rose higher and higher as her reading entered one of the more passionate episodes in her book. It read, 'he drew her to his heaving busom and she melted in his arms; the whole universe dissolved, as their bodies fused together in a earth-shattering wave of pure passion." With the sweetest of smiles, she laid down her book and, still far from reality, said to no one in particular in a wistful tone of voice: "Wasn't that just wonderful? It never happened to me like that, but, oh, I sure wish it had!"

An old lady stamped into the healing room, stripped herself down to her blue hand-knitted vest, sat on the treatment chair, her face set and hard, not saying a word. I threw my mind into her body and could not detect a thing wrong with her.

I told her this, where upon she leapt to her feet and put her clothes back on. Then said; "Oh, that's good. You see I pay three specialists a large fee each year to keep me fit and healthy. I wanted to check if they were doing their job right." With that, she walked out with never even a smile or thanks.

A patient for whom I had gained a great improvement for her sick condition wrote to me telling how, after healing she drove home and on arriving there, found she couldn't move in the slightest and thought she was paralysed. The patient panicked and desperately sounded the car horn to gain attention from some passers by. She told me she felt such a fool on discovering that she had not undone her seat belt!

A medical doctor, who is also one of my patients, told me of one of his patients who was experiencing pains that had no basis beyond tension. He explained at great length how the mind could influence the body, but the patient was adamant in his belief that the cause was physical. Finally, in exasperation the doctor arranged for him to see a specialist. The next time he saw his patient, he came in full of himself and told the doctor: "You see, I was right. The specialist said the pains were 'psycho-somatic'".

There is a part of the North country that is noted for its beautiful scenery and woodlands. They call it the 'Trough of Bowland'. Visitors flock to this part from far and wide. A patient told me she had just come back from a holiday there. "What do you think of the countryside?" I asked.

"Not much" she replied. "You can't see anything for the trees!"

THE FUNNY ONES OF HEALING

If this is to be a true narrative of the healing effort, then I must in all fairness tell you of the other side of the coin, of the funny ones that healing attracts like a bee to honey. Further comment is also called for regarding the many wrongful actions and attitudes adopted by those who are in the process of developing healing.

It is possible that many of them are first-time-in-a-body people. They snatch at healing as a ready-made situation for them to become – in their own eyes – important, and therefore viewed as individuals who apparently have strange and mysterious powers denied to the rest of humanity.

Their actions, as long as you do not take them seriously, can prove to be quite amusing and entertaining for a person with 'some oil in his wick', or in other words, any reasonably intelligent individual.

Unfortunately, the silly ego-activated actions they perform, do much damage to the movement as a whole, for they cast a certain amount of discredit on everyone connected with the work. They make healers in general appear to be good candidates for immediate entry into a 'funny farm'.

The sad thing is that other impressionable would-be healers, may be so impressed by these weird actions and antics, that they might possibly copy them, thinking perhaps it is the done thing. Monkeys are not the only creatures which like to imitate.

Never forget, there is only *one* simple test to assess if a person is a competent healer or not, and that is the amount of beneficial 'results' he gains for his patients.

It is a fact that every unnatural ceremony designed to pad out the act of healing, whether it be used to impress either the patient or the onlooker, will lessen the results of that particular treatment.

By the very nature of spiritual healing, every healer must be in a partial trance state to be able to link in to the source of healing. This can vary from slight to as high as ninety per cent. The word 'trance' carries such funny, strange connotations that a better way of describing the state we heal in would be 'an altered state of consciousness.' This is a much more sensible and descriptive term if you think about it, for that is exactly the state a healer is in when transmiting healing.

It is always best to bear in mind and imagine what effect any strange actions by the healer will have on a newcomer, who is perhaps attending for the first time. If the demonstrating healer's actions prove unacceptable to a prospective patient, he would take one look and say, "Which is the quickest way out?" I for one, cannot say that I would blame him, for any action that involves play-acting is not in the least bit necessary.

Here are just a few of the silly actions by healers I have encountered over the years of healing, together with my comments as to why.

On one occasion, I was warned by a demonstrating 'healer' to stand well back. With a look of great concern, the sweat of strained effort appeared on his face. His arms flailing like miniature windmills, he was, in his words, flinging off great globes of arthritis from a thoroughly terrified patient. He expressed great concern lest he gave arthritis to any of the onlookers.

The result was no improvement in the patient's condition. Here is a person who has entirely missed the basic fact of healing. This fact is, that in no sense does the healer cure the patient. His frenzy of effort served only to destroy all attunement he may have had previously with the higher forces and under these conditions a cure would be impossible. His basic uncertainty was reflected in the desire to impress onlookers. Calmness, and gentle easing movement of the hands to the affected parts of the patient, are all that is necessary. The beneficial results with ailments such as arthritis should be immediately recognisable.

There is one phase of healing ready-made for the exhibitionist, the one referred to in the yellow press as a 'psychic operation'. The theory is that an internal diseased portion of the body is removed by non-physical means. This does often happen during a normal healing treatment, but both the healer and the patient are usually totally unaware of the fact until after medical tests have confirmed this to have taken place.

To any thinking person, it must be obvious that the means, methods and the general approach to spiritual healing, bears not the slightest resemblance to orthodox medical technique in the treatment of illness. Doctors in general are not noted for their compassion and understanding of spiritual law. This is why I find it rather confusing to hear the number of 'dead' doctors that profess to work through these aspiring healers.

This fact by no means discourages a budding psychic surgeon for I have witnessed such play acting as the lowering of non-existent operating theatre lights, mock sterilisation of the hands, the putting on of invisible gloves, the plucking out of non-existent growths and the sewing up afterwards by, if one can believe one's eyes, at least a sail-maker's needle.

100

Results for the patient were nil, but the audience were *very* impressed. This instance is not only an insult to the human intelligence, but a slur on the higher forces of love. the healer, if we can call him that, is taking an ego trip to try and add to his own status. He would be better off joining RADA and becoming a professional actor. Anyone who substitutes nebulous theories for lack of results, has lost completely the basic reason why they took up healing in the first place. This should be based upon love for their fellow man.

One instance, in which incidentally no improvement was gained, was related to me by a patient who previously went to one of these strange people for treatment. After she had been 'treated' the 'healer' walked away, leaving the patient all alone on a chair in the middle of the room, feeling quite embarrassed. Minutes later, the lady healer came hurrying back with a wry grin on her face. She said to the patient: "Aren't I the silly one? I have left one of your chakras (Yogic name for nerve centres) open." With a flip of her finger she closed an imaginary trap door in the patient's head, saying, "You can go now, I have finished". With a wave of her hand in the manner of royalty, the 'healer' steamed off with the panache of one who has just performed a big miracle.

This person is trying her very best to make the act of healing look mysterious and herself knowledgeable but she has no basic ability and will obviously never develop the gift.

Perhaps the commonest role adopted by developing healers is the one of healing in an apparent trance state. Its main attraction to the developer is that by means of self-hypnosis or self-delusion, he or she is immediately absolved from the responsibility, sanity, or rashness on any advice given. It will be noticed to the keen observer, it is usually the personality and idioms of a well-known deceased person that are adapted. Who would dare to refute their assertions?

Indeed, on my travels it may interest you to hear that I have been introduced to not just one, but *several* Dr Karl Muller's, late of Heidelberg University. They display their democratic leanings and linguistic ability by interposing their heavy German accents with flawless Yorkshire "Luvs".

There is, of course, a very easy test of such people, whatever their professed country of origin. That is to speak to them in their own language. It baffles them completely. I have met professed Germans, who cannot speak a word of German, Frenchmen who also have lost their mother tongue, and Chinese who cannot speak a single word of Mandarin or Cantonese. It makes one wonder if the universal language of the higher spheres is English, but perhaps the simple answer is that these people are faking.

One such developing healer claimed he was the instrument of an ex-emperor of Ethiopia no less, and went on to tell to an enthralled audience how he 'flies' over Bradford regulary, eyeing the populace and their carryings on in the local pubs with the jaundiced eye of royalty. Another person had the good fortune, or so she says, to have Nebuchadnezza tuck her up in bed every night. Do you not think that Freud could have a field day with her?

For afters, how about the lady who insists that she has Cleopatra – complete with asp! – help her to heal?

These are definite cases of one-upmanship and really show the infighting that goes on by some to make themselves appear to be someone of influence. There is no basic ability present, hence no results for the patient. The only gift such people will develop is the one of acting.

Without love, caring, and the higher spiritual forces entering into the act of healing, the results of any treatment will always be limited and of inferior value, and certainly prove to be of no value to the patient's sick condition. I would like to bet that those in the world of spirit, who actually manipulate the healing energy, have some jolly good giggles at such behaviour.

When we examine this aspect with potential healers belonging to the more orthodox churches, a similar picture emerges. The status-seeking found in this situation, I admit, is in most cases for an entirely different reason but the subconscious transference effort on the part of the persons concerned is essentially the same however. In their cases it is often a holy figure that is involved in this mental substitution. It is specifically designed to offset at one stroke any prejudices that the sight of an ordinary mortal, doing God's work by acting the role of a healer, may effect their strict conformist congregations.

This figure can be a personalised god, Jesus or even one of the saints. Special terminology is introduced to demonstrate the difference from laymen who practise healing. They have re-christened it 'divine healing', the implication being that it is two steps further up the ladder of purity. The introduction of churchy-type rituals to make the simple act of healing more acceptable to lay people in the church, once again demonstrates the human element's love of theatre. At one such meeting, I heard a quite well-known preacher belonging to the orthodox church who always insists that Jesus in person attends every treatment of his patients and stands on his right hand side. He apologised for his late arrival by saying that Jesus and himself had been held up because they had been treating a person who was suffering from depression and it had taken longer than expected to cheer her up.

Many years ago, I attended a series of healing meetings organised by a certain very dogmatic fundamentalist sect. Biblical quotations were poured in torrents over the poor sufferers' heads. Immediate salvation was offered to those unhappy people in exchange for their ailments. The sanctimonious smugness of the 'healers' involved was to say the least, sickening.

Ailing people were dragged to their feet and told they were healed but sadly, their exit afterwards was just as painful as their entry. The mental defectives were still as unco-ordinated as they had been before treatment. Crutches were not carried out under the patients' arms afterwards; suffering was still heavily written on their faces. Not a single 'cure' did I see that was not hysterical in origin.

The explanation offered to the congregation later was that the poor response was due entirely to the patient's lack of faith. The harsh truth of the matter is, these people were in no sense healers, for the simple and obvious reason that they had no humility, only an arrogant certainty that *they* were exclusive in the eyes of God. Brother, you have to have a lot of conceit to believe that!

On another occasion when I went to listen to a lecture on divine healing, the spokesman, who claimed many years healing experience, could only quote *one* example over those years that had gained a physical benefit for the patient. I heard words, words and yet more words, glibly poured out. Excuses were offered that it was more important for the patient to receive spiritual wholeness than physical freedom from pain. I wondered how they could tell if a patient was spiritually whole? Love was spoken of by people who had no idea what the term

102

meant beyond a romp in bed: charity was mentioned by people who thought it was a five pound note placed with great and deliberate care in front of an audience on the collection plate.

The general impression displayed off by these so-called exclusive men of God in their self-styled complacency was that if any of the founders of Christianity had returned and come to that particular meeting, they would have been refused entry because their robes were dirty.

You must understand that the intentions of this 'funny' minority are often initially of the best. It is also possible that to begin with, a strictly limited healing force *is* channelled through them to the patient.

I am reminded of a Jewish minister I knew who received a full cure from my gift. Possibly because I make healing appear to be easy, he became enraptured by the idea of becoming a powerful and famous healer himself. "It should be so easy for me because of my studies and theological training," he told me. The minister added that he intended going to Israel in the near future to fulfil an important biblical prophesy. His head became more and more inflated with grandiose ideas. Obviously he thought he was the chosen one.

The next thing I heard was he had fallen and broken his leg. A rabbi's wife I related this to said, "Oh, it says in the Torah that whoever becomes two big for their boots shall have their feet taken from them." Nothing more was heard about his healing or his intention of going to Israel. The last news I had was to the effect that his career had careered downhill with a thump.

Because healing does look easy, many developing healers then make the important and very common mistake of not working towards a perfect attunement with the spiritual source. Quite often they become impatient at their lack of results. Consequently they are side-tracked into a preoccupation with way out theories, possibly as some form of compensation for their non-results.

There is a widely held assumption in some circles that spiritual attunement is an easy item to attain, and thus healing can be done in a casual manner. In fact, what most unsuccessful healers do is listen to their own imagination. They seem to believe it as easy as shouting down a telephone that has a direct hot line to heaven.

"Hello God," they think. "There's a man down here with a badly curved spine. Send some healing energy down and put it straight." Then they sit back with a smug smile of anticipation and become very puzzled when nothing happens.

The truth of the matter is that the healing intelligence which attends to every patient's needs is only available when the mind of the healer is in perfect rapport with the source. Every experienced healer will readily admit to a feeling of being overshadowed by spiritual forces at the moment of healing. With experience, one can enter into and come out of this mental state with no effort. But this process only grows gradually and builds up over the years of practice of the gift. This process is purely a mental one, for most onlookers would be hard put to be able to detect any outward difference in the healer's bearing from his normal one.

The actual mental state of the healer at the moment of healing is one of passiveness rather than concentration, the opposite to what one would normally expect for such an action of healing. It is a case of allowing the healing to happen *through* you rather than trying to force a result. When all the conditions are right, it is easy for the healer to gain a good result for the patient.

All I ask, be you patient, healer or enquirer into healing's wonders, is to be aware of the funny people and their actions, for they can distort and taint what should be one of nature's greatest gifts to mankind.

Perhaps if I told you of the good advice I received from a high source, when I first started my ministry, it will make it even clearer. The rules of conduct I should follow in the future were; that I should keep my awarenesses to myself, as many patients would find it uncomfortable to find just how deeply impressed on this physical world were the realms of spirit. I should therefore make certain that my healing work was acceptable to the patient and treat the gift in a matter of fact way. To show humour – for healing should be a happy affair.

The heart of my work would lie in the area of pain and its removal. Always I should strive for instant success for such was the impatience of people in this modern age that anything less would prove unacceptable to many patients. It was also stressed that patients must always come to me by personal recommendation, and that I should avoid publicity like the plague, as this would only attract the ignorant, neurotic sensation-seekers.

Chapter Seven

ILLNESS AND ITS TREATMENT

CONTRARY to the opinion held by many potential healers, orthodox medicine and healing are not complementary to each other. The reason for this statement is that orthodox medicine is often the culprit in actually creating many sick conditions in patients. Medical science, never at a loss for a good word, names such ailments, iatrogenic, or diseases inspired by treatment. The cause is often completely wrong diagnosis, unnecessary investigatory operations or the administering of certain drugs that carry harmful side-effects. These two disciplines of health recovery have nothing in common beyond the common urge to help suffering.

Orthodox medicine generally thinks of the body as merely a mechanical machine comprised of no more than flesh and blood. Like any other machine, at times it develops faults. A healer should look upon a body as a receptacle for the spirit, and that a person's body ought to be directly under the control of that individual's mind. Until this truism is fully accepted as factual by medicine, this gulf of non-understanding will always remain a barrier against full co-operation. There is often a certain servile, fawning, cap in hand attitude amongst some budding healers as regards the status of a doctor. Some aspiring healers even go as far as trying to ape medicine by wearing white coats. Many have developed a fetish of washing their hands in the manner, and with all the seriousness of, a pre-operation scrub prior to giving healing. How could a divine force carry illness? Over the years of being a channel for healing, I have treated thousands of infectious ailments without ever contracting any illness or disease. In fact, I would be most annoyed if I ever did.

While I find actions like copying doctor's rituals rather amusing, it is obvious that the majority of these aspiring healers look up to known medicine and doctors in general with awe as some sort of demi-gods, who have all knowledge regarding illness and how to cure it.

They are actually belittling their healing calling by such play acting, and displaying a complete lack of faith in, and respect of it. Such persons have not the slightest understanding of the many complicated processes of healing. I can well understand doctors having such a patronising attitude of superior knowledge when we pause to consider the many potential healers I have met. They were sincere enough in their motives, but are not the brightest things on two legs regarding knowledge of healing and its practice.

I am reminded of one developing healer, who when asked to explain the phenomenon of cold power directed through her, replied, "Oh, that is because the entity who works through me was an Eskimo when he lived in a body." Another 'healer' who, possibly to boost his ego, boasted to patients that he had so much power he had to treat two patients at once otherwise it would be too much for them to bear and could well knock them out! Strangely enough, nobody received any benefit from him. I wonder why!

Yet another person who, at one stage in his life, I sensed had a good potential to become a healer, went around telling people that one day he would be a much better healer than Jesus Christ! Yet he never made any effort to develop his gift. He is now entering into the evening of his life wondering why the gift never developed in him. Shall I tell him or will you? In such instances it could possibly be that it is a case of 'many are called, but only a few are chosen'.

Healing, by its very formation, tends to attract to its ranks dreamers and idealists. I could never dispute their obvious sincerity, but would certainly cast grave doubts on the intellect of many of them.

Simplicity of thought is a fine human virtue, but it does limit a person from gaining a full understanding of healing's wonders and methods of practice. This is possibly why I occupy such an isolated position for I do not easily suffer fools. If you have an interest in healing, search out and discover things for yourself. Book knowledge is of little value except to confirm what is possible. Be as honest as you can with patients and this will be respected. Never, ever promise a result: let the result of your efforts speak for themselves. Do not, when talking about the subject, adopt an air of mystery concerning healing in an effort to make yourself appear more knowledgeable and the healing process a more complicated affair than it really is.

Recognise and accept the fact that in many areas regarding the treatment of sickness, spiritual healing when administered by one of the few fully developed healers there are in this world, is far superior to any treatment orthodox medicine has at its disposal. Of course you may deny all that I have said, especially if you are one of those who believe that medicine has all knowledge regarding the treatment and curing of illness, and your faith in medicine is so strong you imagine there is a specific drug to cure every ailment.

If you do think in this way, then it is highly likely that in comparison with a graduate from a medical school, you view a healer with a patronising attitude as one who possibly has a great urge to help sick people – and that is all.

My answer is this. If it were possible, compare the number of ailments treated with success by your local doctor. The figure is only about forty per cent of all diseases are actually treatable. Of these ailments, many are not curable except by surgery, which should really be seen as a sign of failure. What medicine can't cure, it will cut out or off.

A doctor also has at his disposal a vast selection of chemical drugs, and to confirm his diagnoses, the back up of the many complicated machines in hospitals. Compare this with a healer's success rate with similar conditions, all he has are a pair of hands and spiritual attunement. Once done, I have a feeling your faith in medicine would be shattered, and you will realise that medical science is even now still in its infancy.

If you sat as an observer in my clinic for just one day and heard all the adverse, acid comments by patients regarding medicine in general – and remember the majority have been through various forms of medical treatment – you would hear of wrong diagnosis and medical opinions they have been given by doctors, and of the many non-effective treatments tried. See the immediate improvement that healing shows in their ailments, and you would leave my clinic totally convinced of the power of healing.

Listen to a statement made by a well-known and famous consultant. It is a plain admission that medical knowledge on how to treat many of the complicated issues of sickness is still in its infancy. If he, with a lifetime's experience in the treatment of illness, can accept the fact, then why can't you?

His statement said that, **"Not all symptoms are diagnosable, that not all diagnosis are treatable by any form of known medicine. That there is no one treatment for any one particular illness for the reason that patients vary so much in their response to different treatments."**

Another leading consultant said, "Show me a drug that doesn't produce adverse side effects, and you will be showing me a useless one."

According to the *British Medical Journal* four out of ten patients who are given pills develop serious or uncomfortable side effects. Dr Patrick Pietroni, a senior lecturer at St Mary's Medical School in London, claims that one in six people in hospital are admitted because they have been made ill by doctors. He also admits that forty per cent of the information which influences doctors' decisions about prescribing a certain medicine comes directly from drug companies' literature.

Did you know, for instance that there are about two thousand deaths a year in this country alone that can be traced directly to barbiturate drugs. In just one year, nearly eight million prescriptions were issued for these drugs. During this same period, nearly nine million prescriptions were issued for non-barbiturate hypnotic drugs; twenty million for the common tranquillisers, and seven million for anti-depressant drugs. That is surely enough to turn the whole population into mental cabbages.

To prove the case further, if you are still in any doubt, the rear section of this book contains some of the tens of thousands of cases that have been cured through my gift of healing. All of them had previously been through the hands of orthodox medicine without success. The cases I quote were taken completely at random from my visitor's books. I have mainly chosen cases with an element of pain, for its removal is an instant indication that help *has* been given. The permanent character of healing is shown by the fact that many of these testimonials were written years later. The originals – plus nearly a hundred thousand more, can be examined gladly, by any researcher who I consider is biased in favour of spiritual healing.

I must stress that spiritual healing is not for everyone, and neither is it a magic bullet with the in-built power to heal all sick conditions instantly. However, if the patient's ailment lies within the laws of nature and the condition is not genetic in origin, much can be done to help most sick people.

The countless ailments that are allocated for a healer to treat – and in many cases cure – are so varied and complicated that ten medical consultants could not possibly have an intimate knowledge of them all. Nor indeed could the person who calls himself a healer if he was working on his personal knowledge alone. Fortunately, he has the resources of the spiritual kingdom to draw upon for assistance, and they *do* have the knowledge.

This unique source of health has a detailed awareness of every sick condition. Once healing has been applied for, it is usual for a remedial energy to be sent immediately to the patient.

I often hear the statement from enquirers that, "I have been to a healer for treatment and was not the slightest improved afterwards." This could well be the case if you have been to see a person with an undeveloped gift. Without the gift's development, little will happen for the person's benefit, beyond the gaining of inner peace.

So you see the term 'healer' is a general one. We can compare it to the world of sport, say football. Two people call themselves footballers. One plays for the local team on a Saturday afternoon whilst the other is a star player for a first division club. If you are a Saturday afternoon player, how do you get into the first division? Exactly the same applies in healing – by experience gained through application, plus natural talent.

I know full well we are living in an age of instant everything, from coffee, to how to be an atomic scientist in ten easy lessons, but not in reference to access to healings wonder's.

The faculty of being able to tune into the life-enhancing energy of healing is a gift from our Creator. It is specifically designed to reassure the patient's soul and give him an inner contentment by being in tune with the infinite as well as the actual removal of illness. It certainly is not something designed to give the healer an enlarged ego.

It is thought in some quarters, that the majority of a healer's patients are people suffering from nervous disorders, and who must therefore be neurotic in temperament. To set the record straight, here is just a fraction of the many sick conditions that have been treated successfully in my clinic.

Arthritis, rheumatism, fits, nervous ailments, neuritis, conjunctivitis, menieres disease. All heart conditions, which include hole in the heart children, angina, mitrel stenosis, and blocked arteries. Sinusitis, thrombosis, ulcers internal, varicose, and stomach. Varicose veins (rarely do the veins alter in appearance, but it is usual to be able to remove the pain.) Internal cysts and tumours, breathing disorders which include asthma, bronchitis and emphysema. Migraine, colitis and Crohn's Disease. Eye ailments, such as cataracts, glaucoma, tunnel vision, scarred retinas, lazy eye, and ulceration of the eyes. growths, rodent ulcers of the skin, malignancies, pancreatitis. Stones in the kidneys and bladder. Cystitis, hiatus hernia, goitres, Bell's Palsy, phlebitis, poly-neuritis, acidaemia, fistulas, eczema, nephritis and other kidney complaints. Infertility, Padget's Disease, haemorrhoids, spinal curvatures, shingles, and spondylosis. Deformed spines. Reynaud's Disease, tuberculosis, insomnia. Loss of hair and alopecia. Thyroid gland problems, either under or over active. The after-effects of strokes, meningitis, glandular fever, slipped and prolapsed discs. Displaced vertebrae, hardening of the arteries, mastitis, locked joints, pulled tendons and bed wetting. All forms of deafness, including tinnitus, and perforated eardrums. All forms of pregnancy problems. Severe septic infections. Wounds that will not heal by other methods. Anaemia, and other blood disorders. All skin eruptions and conditions and pains that have no known medical explanation.

Some patients carry symptoms of ailments that do not fit into any single medical category. I have known many cases where healing has had to cure several different sick conditions before the patient is at ease and free of pain.

It is often in the field of what I call 'medical question marks' that the healer is able to bring about rapid recoveries, even when the patient has been suffering from those unusual symptoms for years. We find that patients have been carrying a completely false symptom, and in most cases treated for years for a condition they were not suffering from. Is it any wonder they did not recover.

Recoveries occur via healing by virtue of the fact that the guardians of healing know exactly what is wrong with the patient, and often have the means to put right the cause of the distress immediately.

Genetic problems are not curable as we understand the term, by healing or by any other method. Nonetheless often great improvements can be shown in behavioural patterns.

Nature is neither cruel nor unkind, though it may appear so to many who are suffering. Living as we do in an age of surface sentimentality we tend to lose sight of the fact that nature is a realist.

Mankind is a part of nature just the same as any other of the animal kingdom, therefore he is answerable to the inflexible basic laws that regulate all living things. This states that only the fittest shall survive, something we humans find a very difficult fact to accept.

If you offend the laws of nature, there is a penalty to pay. For instance, wild animals will never interbreed for they have an inbuilt code against doing so. Domestic creatures are often deliberately allowed to interbreed and the resulting outcome is often shown by a nervous temperament, unsocial behaviour and common internal organ failures.

I often hear a protest of, "Why did God do this to us?" by the parents of a child wrongly made or born deformed as a result of drugs a mother was issued with during pregnancy. On the other hand there is the interbreeding with close relatives in some certain closed societies. This has the effect of gradually weakening the genetic strain, often to a state where these societies have their own particular common ailments. The malformations of unborn bodies is sometimes the result of radioactive fall-out from nuclear accidents.

Millions of pounds are spent annually on research into keeping our wrongly made children alive, all to little effect I am sad to say. My heart goes out to the parents of children who are deformed, for experience has shown me it is futile trying to change the mould in which a person is cast.

Minor genetic faults are curable in some patients. For example, the heart of a Down's Syndrome child can often be strengthened. We are frequently able to give some children an extension of life and have had cases where we have been able to give a sick child the ability to walk where previously they could not. However, in no case can I remember healing changing the genetic code of a child so they became what we would recognise as normal.

Parents of such children will often harbour such a sense of hidden guilt that they found a new charity to help research into their child's complaint in a frantic but futile attempt to absolve themselves of this guilt. Previous to their child being born wrongly made, they would never have given a second thought to such ailments. This, of course, is good for the parent's maturity of soul. While medical progress in this direction is doomed to failure, some good does transpire of such unfortunate happenings.

It is a case of we humans placing too much emphasis on the body dying. If only more people could just accept the fact that if we are placed in a wrongly made body, when it dies, another will be provided for that soul to have a home in which to live out its life's experience. This is the only logical and feasible explanation I can give and one that also makes sense.

THE FOUR ACTIONS OF HEALING

For clarity, I have broken the healing action down into four parts, but in practise it will be found that most treatments are a combination of all four.

THE MENTAL

In this part, we refer to all sick conditions whose origins lie within the mind. You will find such conditions often refered to as 'psychosomatic ailments', the actual cause being mental, the effects physical. It is worth noting that seldom can the patient himself see the connection between mind and body. Only later, after the disappearance of the sick condition, is the patient able to assimilate and accept this fact.

For instance, most skin problems fall into this category – eczema or psoriasis – as well as loss of hair and also many allergies. It is a useless exercise to treat just the symptoms by ointments and salves. First, the mental state of the patient must be made calm and tranquil, and the inner person at peace with themselves. Only then is it usual for the symptoms to disappear quickly.

Next, we advance to mental illness in which there is an imbalance in the patient's brain, causing either hallucinations, or a conviction that they are being persecuted. Sufferers might behave irrationally, as in the case of the split personality of a schizophrenic sufferer. A small number of such cases can be due to possession by an earth-bound entity still trying to cling to this physical world through the patient's mind. In my opinion, it is preferable in such instances, for the healer to have 'no' physical contact with the individual concerned whatsoever, mainly because some patients with such mental problems tend to resist every verbal advance made to them so strongly that at times a healer can suffer what I can only describe as a psychic backlash. This, I can assure you, is a very wearing and tiring ordeal.

This mental backlash happens in spite of the fact that the healer is not personally involved in the treatment, beyond the simple action of asking for help for the patient from the spiritual source. It is then the sole responsibility of the healer's spirit helpers to detatch the entity from the patient and guide it towards the light of God.

Some come for healing suffering from nothing physical, but are in a state of what I can only term 'unpeace'. They are nervous, often frightened of something intangible, and frequently feel full of body tension with aches and pains. Mentally they feel lost in this world. Often such people feel that life and living holds little purpose for them. To such individuals who are invariably extremely sensitive in nature, healing is like balm to their senses. Within a few moments of treatment, it is usual for them to become serene and peaceful, and in a perfect, relaxed state. I can best liken this to the state mentioned in the Bible, 'The peace that passeth all human understanding', because it is impossible to describe, something you have to experience to know.

110

As a healer, I try to educate people into tuning into this state of grace. Many ex-patients tell me they can achieve this by the act of 'thinking' themselves back into the healing room in my clinic. Some feel the need to attend for healing once a year for a tuning in. They will often refer to this when they ring up for an appointment as 'a ten thousand mile service'.

Frequently when this spiritual peace comes to a person, they will fall into a light sleep state. In this, they are often aware of everything around them, but it is of no interest for they feel detached, often to such an extent that they describe the sensation as 'floating'. They feel in a weightless state, but in a completely altered state of consciousness.

It also creates a nice feeling for the healer as he sees the patient's face become tranquil, the lines of worry drop away and they become at peace with the world. Afterwards, some even ask with a smile, "Do you do bed and breakfast?"

A very few highly sensitive patients will fall into a deep trance state similar to a heavy sleep. In that state they will often be aware of spiritual beings, usually in the shape of lovely coloured blobs of light. It is possible this state is induced by the guardians of healing so that the spirit of the person can be transported into the heavenly kingdom for a soul reviving as, when they eventually awaken, are always refreshed and look on life with a renewed interest.

You may well ask why healing isn't permanent in such cases. The reason is that to recover from an illness, you must first be ill. These people are not ill, they are just 'out of phase', speaking in a spiritual sense.

Other reasons for the reoccurrence of pain is that the basic law of healing says that for a cure to take place, the actual cause must first be removed. If the basic cause of a person becoming tense and fearful is society itself, with its materialistic attitudes that are blatantly thrust at one from every direction, then an individual cannot retreat from life and go and live a monastic existence in a cave somewhere. Life has to be lived, but from experience I know that it is possible to achieve a compromise and keep the world of false values at arm's length, as I do.

The powers that run my life have given me precise instructions on how I must run my healing ministry. There are certain sections of people I am not allowed to treat more than once.

On the first treatment, like every other patient, healing is offered to them. If they are unable or unwilling to take advantage of my gift, then I have specific orders that treatment for them must be terminated. These patients are mainly the pure neurotics, who are insensitive to anyone bar themselves and totally preoccupied with self. They also often suffer from ailments manufactured in their own imagination.

Such is the complexity of the human make up, that only prolonged psychotherapy would stand any chance of changing such a person's personality to a point where they would recognise their own faults and make them fully aware of the fact that others have needs as well as themselves.

Orthodox medicine may have branded other patients as neurotic. Indeed, on the surface they will display similar symptoms. It is at this point any similarity ends, for they often prove to be the sensitives of this world. For myself, giving them peace and tranquillity is a happy and easy affair. Many who have attended for healing say afterwards it is like coming home. Healing for them is an experience that they treasure for the rest of their lives.

This is the reason I have been given orders always to treat a person once. Over the years, I have known the most unlikely people obtain great benefits from healing while others, who at first sight one would have said with certainty would respond easily, do not.

It's a pity we are not issued at birth with a tag from God, telling everyone of our particular level of soul evolvement. It would certainly make the task of a healer so much easier for, sadly, it is a fact that only old souls respond easily to healing.

Although a lifetime seems endless when you are young, the work allocated to a healer in his lifetime seems barely enough. Therefore, a healer's time is precious. He must conserve his time and gift for those God intends it for.

PART TWO

These are cases where the body is attacked by virus infections or rogue cells in which the immune system is unable to overcome the condition. This can happen in any part of the body, causing pain and inflammation, which in turn can affect other organs in close proximity.

The medical way is to treat the condition with chemical drugs, which invariably often carry dangerous side-effects for those used are not selective enough to confine their effects to just the diseased organ. In fact, sometimes some of the side-effects can be worse than the symptoms the patient carried before treatment. There is a saying that a new virus comes into being just one step ahead of the latest medical cure.

The actual part the healer plays in the curing of such conditions is, to an observer, a very simple action. The healer just places his hands on the affected parts and seeks attunement with his spiritual advisers, with a mental request for them to send a remedial energy to the sick condition.

In these cases, what a healer is actually doing is using his energies to form a spiritual upliftment for the patient so that every atom of the sufferer's being is elevated, often to such an extent that he is hardly in this world of matter. It is in this state of energised matter that spirit helpers can work directly on and in the patient.

It can be very interesting from a healer's point of view, for many times I am aware of my spiritual helpers actually walking into the physical body of the patient and treating the affected parts with various energies that have an effect on the molecular structure of the diseased parts. The patient's physical body is held in this state of refinement by the concentration of the healer; the individual is rarely aware of all that is being done for his welfare.

It is usual for the patient, whilst not being able to identify the various healing energies that will come to him during treatment, to feel either a strong heat or intense cold coming from the healer and penetrating deep within his body.

As this apparent heat and cold is not physical in origin, it is definitely part of the healing process, but not, I feel, the actual healing energy. It is certainly an energy field, which I liken to a life force. It has the capacity of being able to penetrate apparent solids, such as a plaster cast or steel corset. By experimenting, we have even found that it easily passes through three inches of lead. Radioactivity of a very powerful order, would be stopped by such a barrier. The patient will only be aware of the pain being soothed away: he will feel relaxed and peaceful.

I have been informed by some clients they have been aware of the heat of the energy of healing for several days after being treated, the heat gradually fading and decreasing as the sick condition passes. Besides the betterment of the affected part, it is obvious by the feeling of well-being and added zest for life the patient has after healing that his or her immune system is also strengthened and fortified.

Chapter Eight

THE AGE FACTOR (PART ONE)

IT is a fact of nature that bodies are only built to last a lifetime. It is another basic law of nature that as they age, so the composite parts and organs begin to wear out and no longer work as effectively as they did when we were young. The heart action tends to become erratic as veins and arteries become clogged with toxins and thereby lose their elasticity. Eyesight tends to fade with age. Hearing becomes less acute. There is also a decalcification of the bones, causing them to become brittle. This is why there is a tendency for bones to break more easily in elderly people.

One doesn't require a towering intellect to realise that it is not within the laws of nature to make someone of advanced years into the condition they were in their teens. Nevertheless, we are often gratified to find amazing differences in elderly patients after healing has been administered.

This response is especially noticeable when they are suffering from ailments that carry a large measure of pain which in turn is causing them to have a complete lack of mobility. Often the improvements shown are so dramatic that life becomes meaningful again, and they are able to spend their declining years in comfort.

We have known cases where before healing limbs were wasted, painful and virtually useless. After treatment, they became mobile and pain-free, with muscles reformed. There's an old saying, 'What you don't use, you lose', or it could also be, 'What you can't use, you still lose'.

Quite often after healing has been administered, hearts will begin to work more effectively and the pulse will beat stronger and steadier and the patient frequently gains more energy. All manner of pains simply disappear, for such is the power of spiritual love.

A nice little story regarding this age factor illustrates the fact that if you can keep your sense of humour and stay young in heart, then you will certainly grow old gracefully.

I invited a ninety year old 'Dolly bird' to come into the healing room. She was dressed in the height of fashion, having a trim figure, with painted finger and toe nails, high heeled sling backed shoes, blue rinsed hair and her face made up to the nines. In all, she stood about five feet tall in her socks. I said to her, "Come with me Mrs So-and-So," mentioning her name. With a twinkle in her eye and her mind obviously as bright as a button – she snapped back at me: "Young man, I am not a Mrs, but a Miss. It was only last week I went down to see my dear friend, the funeral director. I have made full arrangements to have a little notice placed on my tombstone."

"What does the notice say?" I asked. She replied with a broad smile; "Oh, it's short and simple. It goes like this. 'She may have been a Miss, but she didn't miss much'."

PART TWO

PAIN

It is in the area of pain – and the freeing from it – that is an exciting one from this healer's point of view. It is also of great interest to any observer present as the results of the healing effort are instantly recognisable.

The signal of pain is a message to the brain that something is distressed or malfunctioning in the body. In some cases, the pain can be a mental brake to stop us overdoing things, thereby causing further damage.

Our bodies are a mass of sensory nerves whose numbers run into the millions. For instance, every single pore has a nerve running to it. These give both our conscious and subconscious minds a full picture of everything our physical body is experiencing. Without these safety checks, we would be always in danger of damaging our bodies by lifting weights that were beyond our strength or burning ourselves, for we register heat and cold via our nervous system. This, in turn, keeps our blood at a constant temperature, our bodies opening and closing pores in a constant wave of motion, all under the control of our subconscious mind.

I have emphasised this fact to show how complicated is the human body, so complex that even our modern medical doctor with all his equipment cannot identify many causes of pain in a patient. Therefore, he has to resort to the blanket effect of pain-killing drugs in an often futile effort to overcome pain by dulling the transmitted message to the brain.

The curing of pain via a healer is a completely different affair from any of the other illnesses previously described. During treatment my whole body and mind are used by the authors of healing and when healing, it is usual for me to feel closely overshadowed by loving energies. With experience, I can detach a part of my mind and converse with the patient in a normal manner, but the main part of me is in tune with the infinite.

I usually attain an instant diagnosis as to the cause of the pain, and am given the exact remedial action needed to put that condition right. All guess work concerning the reasons for a particular pain are eliminated. With the information and the healing energy provided, it is quite usual to be able to disperse the pain and put right the cause immediately. It is a matter of record that we have treated literally tens of thousands of patients suffering from severe pain just once . . . and they have gained a complete cure. This is even in cases where the patient has in many cases been treated by other methods, spread over a period of years, with little or no benefit.

One important aspect I have discovered regarding the issue of pain is that people have different tolerances. In other words, what might be merely a dull ache to one person, may be agony to another. I have examined some patients and found it hard to accept that they have been able to do manual work, when theoretically, according to my senses, the condition was so severe, most other people would have been in agony and completely unable to do any kind of labour involving effort.

Most pain is caused by trapped nerves from the spine. In many cases the misalignment causing them to be trapped is so minute it would not show on any diagnostic medical machine. Over the years of practise, my hands have been guided to the exact location of tens of thousands of nerves that were the cause of pain or were making parts of the body malfunction.

Even today, after a lifetime spent in healing the sick I still do not have a complete knowledge of the nervous system. If, for instance, I have a patient suffering from certain symptoms I have not encountered before, I say mentally, "Show me." Next I slowly move my hand down the patient's spine. Such is my rapport with the source of healing that my fingers will be attracted to the *exact* place causing the pain.

I am not allowed by the source of healing to give the exact location of the many thousands of nerves that experience has taught me cause internal pains both in the body and the limbs. Quite simply because any experiment by an unskilled healer could easily result in the production of even more pain in a patient – and that would not do the cause of healing any good at all! If you are a potential healer, as your gift matures, so all these sources of pain will be shown to you, but only when you are mentally developed to handle the information in the right way.

To give you an idea of the number of sick conditions that arise from the spine, here are just a few examples. You will not find many of them in any medical book, but their effects and positions have been proved to me by the experience of applying healing.

It is usual for orthodox medicine to treat symptoms. From my experience I know you have to find causes. These may be far removed from the pain being experienced by the patient.

Nerves running from the neck into the head can cause or aggravate the following conditions: pains on the top of the head, in the teeth or hinge of the jaw. In some cases, the patient will experience trouble in making any dentures fit properly and may also note great pain while eating. Certain out-of-place nerves from the neck can affect the eyes, cause pain in the ears, create some forms of deafness. Bells Palsy, and other forms of partial paralysis of the face, wry neck, heavy eyelids, floaters in the eyes, sinusitis, inflammation in the eyes, constriction in the nasal passages, hay fever, loss of voice and a paralysed larynx.

Difficulty can often be experienced in swallowing foods. Other trapped nerves in the neck might cause headaches, disappearance of feeling in the lips, loss of sense of smell and taste. The ears can be affected, causing lack of balance, dizziness, noises in the ears and, of course, deafness. Pain can be caused in the hinge of the jaw so the patient looses the ability to open the mouth properly. I have known some so advanced with this condition that they could only take nourishment in liquid form.

Inflammation can be induced in the trigeminal nerve which may be so intense at times as to nearly send the patient insane. The medical treatment for this condition is normally pain-killing drugs, which are usually non-effective. The only other medical alternative is to perform a sympathectomy operation to sever the nerve. This surgery can result in partial paralysis of the face and dead areas.

The patient might then experience what is known as 'phantom pain', for which there is no known medical remedy.

Trapped nerves in the spine can also cause swelling of the glands under the arms or those in the neck. It can similarly cause the neck tendons to tighten up so it is painful and restrictive in movement. It can result in loss of voice, and a tightness in the chest, causing constriction of breathing, making asthmatic problems worse. The gullet might tighten up to such an extent that the patient can often experience great difficulty in swallowing food.

Trapped spinal nerves can cause patients to have spastic stomachs in which they are constantly sick, feel a stomach unrest or have actual pains therein which may lay the ground for peptic ulcers. Nerves from the same area can cause inflammation of the gall bladder, liver upsets, and pancreatitis.

Other conditions where the cause is from the spine are inflammation of the guiders and tendons that go to each finger, causing pain in the hands, discomfort in the thumbs, deformity of the hands, and tingling in them. A 'Tunnel' operation on the wrists will often be recommended by doctors which invariably proves unsuccessful as the nerves causing this condition come from the spine, *not* the wrists!

Tennis elbow often also originates in the spine, which has the effect of contracting tendons that cause the actual pain and inflammation in the elbows.

Frozen shoulders frequently arise from trapped nerves in the spine. This has the effect of pulling the arm into the shoulder socket, causing an inflammatory condition. Reynaud's Disease is often due to certain nerves that cause muscles to be under permanent tension. This in turn has the effect of compressing arteries, allowing only a limited blood supply to penetrate through to the extremities. This condition can, over a period of time, deteriorate so much that the finger and toe nails become distorted and blackened. It is then possible for a gangrenous condition to arise in the feet or hands.

Some heart conditions can be aggravated by trapped spinal nerves. This has the effect of causing the heart to fibrillate or of compressing chest muscles and can produce similar symptoms to angina. Migraine, where the cause is not an allergy to food, is often due to trapped nerves and can usually be removed from the patient immediately.

When treating all breathing problems and other conditions of the respiratory organs, such as asthma, bronchitis and emphysema, I have always been impressed firstly to make the spine flexible and mobile, thus enabling patients to make full use of their lungs. In all these conditions, I have found that the patient is only using a small proportion of their lung potential.

Nerves from the spine run into the legs, knees, ankles, hips, and feet. Trapped nerves can cause pain in all these extremities. The root cause of a patient developing bunions is a nerve from the back that runs into the big toe. This has the effect of pulling the toe into its joint which in turn causes an inflammatory and painful condition. The joint becomes enlarged because the defence mechanism has sent a calcium carbonate deposit around the joint as a protection, then a bony structure forms, often to a large and uncomfortable size. The medical treatment is to operate on the toe, cut a portion of bone from it to lessen its size, scrape the joint and then stiffen it so the toe is immobile. This can sometimes result in a certain loss of poise as we use the big toe as a balancing aid.

117

It is quite usual for healing to show dramatic improvements in this condition, often diminishing the swelling and gaining mobility to the toe, lowering the pain to a bearable level.

Cramps and pains in the shin-bone can originate in the lower back, as, do certain nerves running into the knees, that quite often give rise to the wrong diagnosis of arthritis or cartilage trouble.

In my opinion, the most important item in the keeping of skeletal balance is the pelvis. Once it tilts, it can act like a row of dominoes falling down, effecting the rest of the vertebrae of the spine, causing painful conditions all over the body. Strangely enough, it is not usually the lifting of heavy weights that causes the pelvis to tilt, but the turning action of the body, when the spine is loaded and under tension. Over the years, we have treated thousands of nurses for this one condition alone, which is usually caused by the simple action of lifting a patient into bed or out of a chair.

A 'slipped disc' is a misnomer. They do not slip, but they can burst, for a disc is just a sac of fluid between the vertebrae. I can assure you that a truly prolapsed disc is a very rare affair. Patients often come for healing and tell me quite blithely that they have been informed by their doctors they have several slipped discs. I can only answer: "Nonsense! If you had just slipped a disc, the odds are that you would have to be carried into this room."

Most cases christened 'slipped discs' by medicine, the actual cause of the pain is that some of the vertebrae have moved slightly. These are literally nipping the disc, thus compressing and trapping nerves, thereby causing inflammation.

The curing of a so-called slipped disc often involves the straightening of the pelvis. I call it 'thinking it' back into position, for that is exactly what I do. No pressure is needed for the bones move back into their rightful position under the influence of the healing energy. How can an energy move bones? Some patients find this very hard to accept, even though the pain has gone and after I have pointed out the dramatic change in their body posture. So I am usually impressed by my advisers lightly to touch one of the patient's vertebra. There is often a loud crack – and the patient is all smiles for then they feel that something positive has happened to them, as indeed it has, but in their case it was several moments previously.

This simple operation as far as healing is concerned, of replacing a twisted pelvis into its correct position is something orthodox medicine has no answer to, as it is rarely noted by doctors. It does not generally show on X-rays mainly because most X-rays are taken when the patient is in a prone or reclining position. In that position, the skeleton of the body partially straightens.

The usual medical explanation – and it is one I have heard several hundred times, is that the patient is told by doctors that they have one leg shorter than the other, as this is the effect a tilted pelvis has on the body. Some consultants will then recommend the patient wears a special shoe with a lift in it to compensate. In actual fact, all this action will do is to make certain that the condition is permanent. The only time one leg is shorter than the other, is by a bad breakage or a pre-birth accident in which the body is malformed.

I have also discovered from the experience of applying healing that there are many conditions labelled by medicine as 'arthritic' that is not caused by arthritis. Rather than the condition being an actual disease, the origin can be often traced to

118

an accident that has trapped spinal nerves, imposing certain pressures on joints and muscles, causing a localised inflammatory condition easily mistaken for arthritis. X-rays of this condition can be misleading for both arthritis and inflammation, in fact according to one of my doctor patients, this shows up as a cloudiness on an X-ray plate. Invariably the prognosis is the one of arthritis. I wonder just how many corrosive drugs have been issued in error due to this fallacy.

Back pain in ladies who are in their middle years is such a common thing that I have made a careful study of it. One frequent cause I have never heard mentioned before can be traced back to when they were pregnant. In nearly all cases where a lady did not 'show' much when she was carrying a child, they later develop back and posture problems. It occurs because she has carried the child against the spine, and deformed it by the internal pressure moving the spine backwards creating an outward curvature of the spine from just below the shoulder blades to the waist. The spine then becomes calcified in a position that is 'out', and the condition becomes permanent. Trouble may not occur until years later. Happily, this condition responds easily to healing. The healing energy softens the adhesions and enables the healer to deploy the spine to its rightful position.

There are certain nerves running from the spine into the muscle that operate the bladder, the action of which gives a person control over the passing of water. If these vital nerves in the spine are affected, then the brain will receive a distorted or 'no signal' message from the body, which can be a great embarrassment, especially when the patients are in their teens or contemplating marriage.

We have treated hundreds of such instances of poor bladder control which often results in bed wetting – with great success, and found that rather than the problem being psychological, as is often implied by doctors, these cases are really mechanical. If the various nerves that are causing the condition are reseated, then immediately full bladder control is gained. Sometimes the problem will just be during the hours of sleep at night. The reason for this is that the spinal position in repose is vastly different to the one when a person is standing upright.

Certain nerves from the base of the spine run into the colon and can cause a spastic colon or diverticulitis. Eventually the condition can deteriorate into Crohn's Disease, perforation and ulceration of the intestine. The root cause in my experience is that certain nerves from the base of the spine are affected. Their action in this state is to place the colon under constant pressure, compressing it into a tight mass, thereby causing inflammation and, over a period of time, ulceration. Medicine usually treats this condition by prescribing the patient a diet of roughage. Rarely is this action successful. Quite often the patient's life increasingly revolves around bowel movements, sometimes to such a degree that many grow frightened of leaving their homes for fear of being 'caught short'.

We have had many cures of this condition, even when patients have had the ultimate medical answer, an operation to shorten the bowel, by cutting out the perforated section. This, incidentally, is not always effective.

Pains in the abdomen, painful menstruation, and even some cases of infertility caused by blocked fallopian tubes, can often be traced to peripheral spinal nerves. A tilted womb; pain in the testes and enlarged prostrate gland symptoms; a bearing down feeling in a lady, that will often be misdiagnosed as a prolapse of the womb; heavy flooding during periods; cystitis and other urinary problems; in

119

all these conditions trapped spinal nerves often play a big part. It is usual to gain an immediate relief for a patient once pressure is relieved from the offending nerves.

Haemorrhoids can often be caused by stress and are therefore classed as being of a nervous origin. One interesting point regarding this condition is that the healing energy which comes for this ailment, is always icy cold. When treating 'piles' I am always impressed first to check that the coccyx is not out of position. If it is only slightly out of alignment it can induce pain in the seat and in extreme cases, as in an accident, it can cause partial paralysis in the legs. Haemorrhoids generally usually respond well to healing and it is usual for any bleeding to stop immediately.

SKIN CONDITIONS

Eczema and psoriasis can be both unsightly and irritating. Experience has shown me it is a waste of time simply treating the symptoms. I am always impressed to treat the kidneys, possibly because they are the filters of the blood, and both ailments are basically blood conditions. It is usual for the itching to disappear within a few moments of being treated, but the unsightly eruption can take several weeks to clear entirely.

OTHER CONDITIONS

There are certain nerves that run directly from the spine into the stomach. If these are misplaced, they may cause constant flatulence in the patient, and bring about an excess acidity of the stomach that can over a period of time encourage ulcers.

Other nerves from the spine run into the knees, groin and ankles. These conditions can be misdiagnosed as a torn cartilage, torn tendons, (eyewash), or arthritis in the legs (Bunkum) which are often operated on to little avail.

Varicose veins are usually blamed for certain leg pains and support stockings issued as a medical aid. Quite often the pain can be from sources in the lower spine. If certain nerves contract the tendons that go to the knees, this can often cause intense discomfort.

Many internal sick conditions can be aggravated or actually caused by certain spinal nerves. We have known many cases where orthodox medicine was in a quandry as to the reason for certain pains a patient was suffering from. I have known surgeons go as far as to perform exploratory operations in a fruitless attempt to find the root cause of the pain. Invariably they have been unable to come to any definite conclusion. The patient has been told they must learn to live with the condition, or doctors try to place the blame on the sufferer by saying that as they were unable to find the cause of the pain, it must be imaginary, then arrange for the patient to see a psychiatrist.

Not all conditions cured by healing are able to be confirmed by medicine. For instance, only another biopsy could confirm if the cellular structure of a malignancy has been changed to a non-malignant growth. Often medicine will not go to the trouble of re-checking a patient after they have received healing for an illness of this nature is incurable in doctors' minds, therefore the patient lives on in fear. I could quote many instances of this where changes have taken place that are non-pathological. One in particular was a lady completely blind in one eye who came for healing. The condition was so severe she could not distinguish between light and dark.

After receiving healing, her eyesight became so acute in the once blind eye that she could thread a needle! She had been awaiting an operation for which little hope of any success was offered. On returning to see the medical consultant at the hospital, after examining her eye he pronounced there was no difference in it saying she was still totally blind. The patient pulled a needle and thread out of her handbag, proceeded to thread it with the use of her blind eye, then read the eye test chart from top to bottom with no hesitation.

The consultant in turn, was amazed, and could give no rational explanation as to how she was able to see. No operation was performed and the lady has kept her sight. Such is the power of healing.

What I have written in this chapter, is only a small part of the areas of sickness covered by a developed healer, but you will have gained a small idea of how involved and complex the work of healing can be as well as the mass of knowledge regarding sickness that is available to the healer from the spiritual source.

It must be obvious to you by now, that spiritual healing is an exact science. Not from the earthly healers angle, for we only have a limited knowledge, but from the spiritual source that dispenses the energy. More so, than our physical science, on which this modern world is based. Much is possible and what can be done will be done, by healing.

The thought just struck me, that considering all the ailments that could effect the human body, it is a compliment to our designer that so many people manage to reach old age.

Chapter Nine

JOIN ME IN A DAY'S HEALING

I am often asked by puzzled ex-patients: "We have read your books and received health from you. When you are treating us you make it all seem so easy and simple, but exactly how does your mind operate so you are able to produce these wonderful benefits for sick people?"

In this chapter, rather than just exercising the intellect by reading my opinions about healing, *you* are going to share in a day's healing and view the healing scene through my eyes and with my senses.

As far as I am able, working within the frustrating confines of words, I shall attempt to paint a full picture of the many emotions, senses, and awarenesses that come to a healer as he acts as a receiver and transmitter of the healing energies. Obviously this is bound to be a limited picture as it is impossible to put many of the healer's senses into words.

There is a normal, average day's healing ahead of us. Here we sit, the two of us, twiddling our thumbs, eagerly awaiting a flood of medical 'incurables' who will soon be arriving for help. Is it any wonder there is always a little apprehension before the day's healing starts?

I have no banks of sophisticated disease-tracing equipment at my disposal; no monitoring devices; no short wave equipment for dispersing inflammation; no patient's past medical records or notes and the opinions of other medical consultants . . . just a pair of hands, plus an energy of life that floods my whole being and a sensitivity so finely pitched that at times it can be downright painful.

As of this moment, you are now linked mentally to me. We will see how you handle the clear thought from a patient who believes you are possibly a crackpot. What is more, when you receive a thought like that, you can't answer it verbally: you just have to keep a smile on your face and hope that the powers which work through you will prove the patient wrong.

To make the work of healing acceptable to patients, I have to present healing in a matter of fact way. Not one client in a thousand has any idea of the great mental effort required by the spiritual source and myself to take away their illness.

So finely tuned is this mental rapport that it can be inhibited and very occasionally sent flying right out of the window by the attitude of the patient. Many people take pride in saying, "I have an open mind." The reality is that very few do, for whether they are aware of it or not, most people are greatly influenced by the opinions projected by the media, which is essentially biased towards a materialistic outlook.

So when a patient arrives for healing with a suspicious attitude towards you and your work, quite often this creates an atmosphere in which you are left confused and completely out of phase with healing's source. This is not only ego-destroying but effectively places a brake on any healing happening at that moment.

Unlike most healers, the majority of my patients are quite ordinary people who come from every walk of life. Most arrive with no pre-knowledge of healing. All of them will have come from personal recommendation given by someone who has been helped greatly in the past by myself, but my work, the 'how' bit, will be a complete mystery to them. The majority of patients are easy for me to treat, with no spiritual hang ups. It is just the odd one or two a day that makes my job difficult to the point of being upset inwardly by the bad vibrations they carry.

The effect 'funny' patients have on me is so great that I would gladly pay them not to come and see me for help. On the plus side, with those receptive to healing, applying it is a complete joy to me. What can we expect from all these people who are at this very moment putting on their hats and coats to come and see us?

Well for a start, very few have any idea as to the true nature and actual cause of their ailments. Any previous hospital treatment will have been devoted to treating the symptoms. Our task is to find the true cause of the illness and correct it and it is then usual for any symptoms to disappear at once.

There will be added obstacles for healing to overcome in these patients in the fact that a number will be hooked on some form of chemical drug, either of the pain-killing variety, steroids or antibiotics. These drugs will be having a stimulating or subduing effect on various parts of the body, therefore there are bound to be some serious side effects. The patient may be just as addicted to these drugs as they would be if they were taking hard substances such as heroin or morphia. They will be totally unaware of this fact until they try to cease taking them.

Many patients coming to see us will be having treatment for conditions they are not even suffering from as wrong diagnosis is not a rare occurrence.

Those visiting us will cover a whole spectrum of varying mental attitudes. Each will have a different effect on us. These attitudes – not healing – are what makes a healer exhausted after a day's work. If all patient's came for help with the right approach, giving healing energy and gaining consistent fantastic results would be easy to the point of bliss for myself.

At the other end of the scale, one's feelings can vary between annoyance and amusement as I can sense the patients trying their level best to place healing in a slot that is acceptable to them. They will try every other category but the correct one of applied divine energy. Some squirm over the 'mind-over-matter' bit, though not one person in ten thousand understands the true meaning of the term. The patient's own body tension, especially if the condition is of years standing, can impose a 'locked up' effect so much so that on rare occasions the mental healing of the condition cannot instantly overcome them entirely. In such cases I run over the points of pain with the energy coming through my hands.

The baffling thing to everyone is, "How can bones move back into their rightful position and the pain be removed when I am sitting at least ten feet away?"

It has even been suggested by some cynical patients that I have hypnotised them so they no longer feel pain. In those cases, only a period of time without pain carries to them full conviction that they are indeed fully healed. One can understand that this cynical mental yo-yo action is motivated by suspicion, but it is still irksome.

The actual truth of the matter would certainly be much harder for them to accept if I told them I gain these wonderful regular results by sending a specific request through my mind direct to the next world, telling spiritual helpers who administer the healing exactly which bones to move to gain help for the patient. Even though this is true, it would sound barmy.

Before we start the day's healing, let me state that the awareness – or much of it – is like all abstract things, very difficult to express in words. It is a combination of instinct, of 'seeing' inwardly, 'sensing' and a 'knowing' so strong I would stake my life on it being correct. That 'knowing' extends to if whether a full healing is likely at a particular time, or whether as much help has been given as is possible, and it would be futile to continue further. I also 'know' when to persevere with a treatment as a good result is imminent. There must be a total immersion by the healer, in the healing taking place, for him to give direction to the channelled energy. If the healer is casual in his approach, only a limited result will be forthcoming.

One's personality when giving healing is split. Although to an outsider I may look normal, act normally and can even converse with the patient in a seemingly normal way, the inner person feels apart and withdrawn.

Such is my spiritual attunement that I am often inspired to ask pertinent questions regarding the clients' ailments, which are often completely outside my normal knowledge.

I can only say that when I am transferring healing energy I am in a state of grace, with added confidence and a greater range of senses than one would normally register. I call this an altered state of consciousness. So highly charged is this mental state that often the tick on someone's watch sounds overloud to me.

My memory, which is usually akin to an absent minded professor undergoes dramatic changes when healing. If a patient comes to see me, even though it may be years since I last saw them, as I touch them there is usually a complete recall of his or her background, ailments and personal troubles. Yet when that person leaves, all knowledge of them goes with them. Quite often after a full day's healing, I have great difficulty in remembering who has been to see me for treatment on that day.

The responsibility of a professional healer is great for although at times one may joke and pull people's legs in order to lighten their tensions, there always remains the awareness that for many, my work is their last hope.

It is nearly time to start our day's work. Firstly, a few moments of meditation to gain that essential 'oneness' with the higher forces of love. The ingress of peace and the feeling of being overshadowed by caring energies tell me that all is ready. I ask my receptionist to bring in the first patient. A lady is brought into the healing room, her face shows both her trepidation and pain. I welcome her warmly to put her at ease and motion her to sit on the treatment chair. This is an easy one as I 'see' the cause of her trouble is in her back, causing pain in the neck, arm, elbow, knee and ankle. As is my policy, I ask for a description of the symptoms. They agree exactly with what I have sensed. This I always do because the balance between 'reading' fears and 'reading' actual symptoms is a very delicate one. It is easy to misinterpret a patient's signals, even with great experience. That advice was given me by Harry Edwards.

The patient gives me a brief history of her illness, not necessary for me, but perhaps helpful for her. It started with a severe fall on a bus which lurched forward before she had a chance to sit down. That was about two years ago, she tells me, then goes on to describe in detail the hospital treatment, consisting of heat treatment, which was a complete waste of time. Traction was also non-effective. Finally, as a last resort, a plaster cast was fitted. We hear of the drugs tried to no effect and the different specialist's opinions. I stand the patient on her feet, and show her just exactly what is wrong. The pelvis is tilted on one side. Six vertebrae are imposing pressure on certain discs, thereby causing pain in the legs and hands. I also show her just how limited the movement is to one side in her neck.

I tell her to sit down, relax and close her eyes while I try to 'think' everything right. She looks at me as though I have gone mad, but decides to humour me. I sit myself in a chair facing her and seek healing. Mentally I pass on the exact condition to my spiritual helpers by going over each part that needs to be relocated in her body. In my mind's eye, I can vaguely 'see' both her physical and spirit bodies. In the meanwhile, the patient has not closed her eyes or relaxed in any way, but is staring at me suspiciously. However, this makes no difference.

I open my eyes and give her a smile, telling her, "Stand up and see if you have any pain now." She stands up with a puzzled look and admits she has hardly any pain. I show her the changed attitude of her body, of how her pelvis is now level. Her neck has full mobility, she can reach her toes without pain. All this is without touching her.

There are still one or two places in her body I sense are sore and slightly painful, these will need further healing. My hands find the source of the trouble and mentally I seek a dispersing of the inflammation and sediment around the offending parts. It feels 'right'. There is pulsing from my fingertips which often manifests when parts of the body have to be moved into their rightful position. A hardly audible 'click' sounds as the vertebrae move back into their position. All soreness goes at once.

This part of healing she can understand, but not the 'thinking'. A smile, a handshake and the healing is done. She leaves the room walking with confidence. Possibly she will later muse over what has been done for her, and by whom. Perhaps she won't.

That is how I heal now, while the following is an example of how I once worked, delving deep into a patient's mind to find the actual cause of an illness. I have found that being able to 'read' a patient as in the following is a tiring and exhausting experience for the healer. It has been revealed to me that this is the task of the healing intelligence that directs the healing energy, and is not my responsibility.

As pressure from the large number of patients wanting healing from me has grown, so I have cut out all the 'frills' from my work, both for the sake of simplicity and for the speed of healing.

The next patient comes into the room. She is middle-aged with swollen legs

125

and hands. "I have got osteo-arthritis," she tells me with no little pride. I cringe inwardly and feel sorry for the lady, for her attitude states quite plainly that the illness plays an important part in her life. She shows me with great relish the various pills, which include steroids and other potions which could explain the swollen legs.

It is on the tip of my tongue to ask why she has taken them for the past ten years if they were not curing her ailment, but I suppress the idea as I know too well the answer – "Well, think how bad I would be if I had not taken them." Looking at her swollen hands and legs, I wonder.

Sensing from her the general feeling of antipathy, negativity and overall flatness of spirit, I have doubts about her responding to any therapy, including healing. There is an undercurrent of fear and general unhappiness as I touch on her mental state. A picture builds up in my mind of all the factors involved in the cause of her illness. It is by no means a simple one of a purely physical condition, but what I call 'a poverty of living', all her life being modelled around the word 'respectable'. I can sense that the only happy period in life was when her children were small. They have now grown up and left her so there is little else in life but the mundane daily chore of living, with an uncaring, unsympathetic husband completing the picture. It is no wonder that the illness is so important to her.

I keep this information to myself as it would be of no help to her recovery if I repeated my impressions. For her to be healthy, she has to be made happier and her inner person needs to be stimulated into having other interests rather than the one of her illness. It is my hope that she will gain an inner awareness of the caring forces of healing. The case is now entirely in the hands of the healing intelligence, who will impress constructive thoughts into her mind.

Firstly, the physical condition must be dealt with to show her it *is* possible for the illness to go. I treat every joint in turn and can sense the adhesions being dispersed and mobility return to the limbs. Most of her pain has now gone and I can sense a spark of response in her. Her quavering tone of voice gives way to an interested, "Oh, I haven't moved that in years." I seek peace for an unpeaceful mind and happiness for an unhappy condition. It is out of my hands now and into hers for I know I have tried my best. So has the source of healing.

Like every other patient, a choice has been given. She can reach out and grasp the help and warmth of healing or alternatively let slip all her gained benefits and return to her previously unhappy, painful self. Often ailments such as hers – especially when they have reached the chronic state – require a period of time to cure. If such a person gains extra relief and the pain diminishes every visit for healing, then I am content. She departs, incidentally walking considerably better than when first entering the room.

Our next patient carries before her a wave of confusion. She tells me she is suffering from 'nerves' but I cannot sense this. She says she is hypersensitive and that everyone goes out of their way to hurt her. My senses say, "selfish, neurotic and completely self-engrossed."

Mental impressions flow into my mind regarding her make up. Her remarks are as cutting as a cold chisel. She is what I call a 'one way sensitive'. It is painfully obvious that some time in the past she has been hurt emotionally and the experience has soured her to a point where she is critical of every thing and every one. Clearly there is a total lack of affection in her life which is entirely due to her own attitude of just wanting to take affection and never give it.

A complete lethargy drapes itself around me and I wish the clinic was finished for the day. Then it dawns on me that this is merely a mental effect from the patient, I have made the mistake of placing myself too much in sympathy with her. Healing in cases such as this should be given at arm's length figuratively speaking.

Draw too close to such a person and you as a healer will be filled with all the debris that a resentful mind carries around with it. Healing-wise, the emphasis for such a person is on the elevation of the mind to a state of harmony and peace. The 'asking' is for these qualities to be given to the patient permanently. It shows a certain reaching out in her on some level that she has even 'wanted' to come to me for healing or does she merely seek attention? Only time will tell its own story as to how she will respond.

Let me state at once that in no sense does a healer judge a person: what he gains through his instincts and senses is an assessment of the many factors involved in making someone complete and healthy.

Our next patient bustles in complete with a large package of X-ray plates. He tells me quite proudly of how many thousands of pounds he has spent of non-effective treatments, and of the various medical specialists visited in the last ten years all giving him different diagnosis as to what was wrong with him. These medical opinions ranged from arthritis of the spine, trapped nerves, fibrositis, sciatica and the latest one, an abnormal condition of the spine probably caused by a difficult birth.

Many non-effective treatments had been given him over the years, including one in Israel known as cupping, in which hot flasks are placed on the spine, presumably to help draw out the inflammation.

My treatment begins by sitting in my chair and 'thinking' the-out-of-place bones trapping nerves, back into their rightful position. This was certainly not what he had expected. His attitude annoys me, though I should be above becoming irritable, the apex of healing development is shown to people . . . and they cannot accept or respect it. It is an exclusive gift. I know of no other healer with this special ability of directing the unusual energy which has the quality of being able to move bones back into position and re-position trapped nerves immediately.

This is not by myself I hasten to add, since all I do is put in a request for help for the patient. I demonstrate how his body is now free from pain and fully mobile once again. He scratches his head in bewilderment, gives, me a suspicious look and says, "I don't understand."

I reply: "Of course you don't. What I have just demonstrated is something entirely outside your previous experience. Test what has been done for you in any way you can think of. Then be grateful to Him," I tell him, pointing a finger upwards.

He then does everything that previously gave him pain, which included laying down on the floor and rolling over, which puzzled me until he explained he could never do this in bed. He warms to me as the penny begins to drop within him that he is now cured. This client leaves the clinic a happy man, and certainly a very puzzled one.

Treating a four legged friend, thirteen years old, previously it nearly died with a heart attack and could hardly see with cateracts. The eyes have now lost their blueness and she can run and romp around like a young puppy.

My next patient waddles in. She is ten years old, with a dry nose and a bushy tail. We strike up an instant friendship. There is a wince from her as I run my hand down her spine and sense varying degrees of reaction from her rear end which confirms in me the 'feeling' that this is a case of partial kidney failure, resulting in water retention and high blood pressure. There is a surge of healing power; the dog starts panting and settles down with a contented grunt. By now, her eyes are fluttering, which is a sure sign that healing is being received. Within a moment or two I feel impressed to withdraw as I know intuitively that full benefit has been gained for the moment.

I am told mentally that she will need another two treatments, spread over a period of time, then should be perfectly well again. There is a spring in her step and a sparkle in her eyes as she departs with a last wag of her bushy tail through the doorway.

With animals, the first signs of returning health occur when the coat becomes glossy, the nose wet and the eyes bright and sparkling.

A gurgling, bubbling baby is brought into the healing room. The parents tell me that one foot is deformed in that it is pointing to the side. They have been told by hospital doctors that this condition is the opposite of a club foot, and that a bone is missing from the child's ankle. Doctors say that when the child is developed enough to walk, a special boot will have to be worn. My senses guide me to the child's hip which I sense has been partly dislocated at birth. I can feel the healing energy at work under my hands. Excitement mounts in me as my awareness tells me that the hip is going to give under the healing. Taking hold of the child's foot in one hand and placing my other on the hip, I feel impressed very gently to turn the foot. It comes round as if it were on an oiled bearing and the baby gives a happy chuckle. Both feet look exactly the same now, with full movement. The healing is complete. There are tears in the mother's eyes and a lump in my throat as they depart. In those few quiet moments, one wonders just how much mental anguish this child and its parents have been saved.

A man in his mid-twenties walks in next: he tells me that for three years he has been in constant pain with a stomach ulcer. Medications have not made any impression on his condition. I hear the inner voice speak in my mind saying, "The cause of his pain is from his spine: it is one of the peripheral nerves." I run my hands over his stomach, which is hard and distended causing the patient to wince as my fingers probe deep, sensing and feeling. There is a strong reaction from my other hand, the one touching his spine.

A flash of insight shows me the nerve causing all his trouble which is indeed one of the peripheral nerves. Now, as I sense the adhesions are dispersed, comes the moment when we will know if my intuitive thoughts are right or not. I gently bend him backwards over my hand. Within a moment all the pain has gone from his stomach. A few more seconds healing in the stomach area with the energy pulsing into him and within a short time there is a complete relaxation of his muscles and the treatment is finished. He can now dig his fingers into his stomach with no pain. The patient may possibly have to come once more for help, but I know that already the condition is considerably improved.

The next few patients are suffering from arthritis in varying states of advancement. There is nothing extraordinary to relate beyond the considerable lessening of pain and more mobility given to the limbs.

We treat many more patients during our session together, some with eye troubles, others with hearing difficulties. One person with very severe varicose veins has developed phlebitis; this was a quick healing, with all pain being removed immediately.

The penultimate patient of our day arrives, carrying with her a huge medical question mark. Every medical expert – and she had seen five – gave her a different opinion, offering a totally different kind of treatment, with no improvement in her condition. The patient was suffering from these symptoms: pain in the back, head, shoulders, hands, thighs, knees and ankles and she was in a pitiful condition. I run my hands over the areas of pain and feel strongly that for the moment I should ignore them as they are only referred effects. My instincts draw me back to the spine where I discover there is a slight lateral curvature.

I gain a strong impression that this was caused by a bad fall in her early life which the patient confirms. I give a few moments of applied healing with a specific directive to disperse the many arthritic deposits I can sense have formed around the spine. I then 'know' that the moment is right to return the spine to its rightful position. Gently and painlessly, the spine moves and straightens exactly like a rusty gate. There are many loud creaks and clicks as it does so.

That was the true cause of all her trouble, now to deal with the effects. Only a moment or two is required for all her pain to disperse, and full mobility and freedom return to her limbs. It is amusing to watch her reactions: amazement and astonishment give way to thankfulness as we invite her to walk around the room. At first her steps are hesitant, but with every new step she gains fresh confidence. To her, this bears the stamp of a miracle, but to the healer who has seen such things happen many times before it is a careful application of divine energy.

This entails the prompting of the healer's mind and body by an intelligence who has a full knowledge of the patient's ailment and the ability to direct the healer's hands to instigate a cure.

The last patient brings us both a smile. She limped in with obvious pain, and said, "You have to make me right in two weeks time."

"Why?" I asked her. She replied: "I am going around the world on a three-months cruise. What is more, I have gone every year for the last ten years." This puzzled me because she was very poorly dressed.

"Oh" she said, obviously sensing my thoughts. "I keep my best clothes for on board ship. Up until ten years ago I was as poor as a church mouse then a distant relative died and left me a row of houses. The rents pay for the cruise."

"What do you think of the world!" I asked her. She thought for a long time then said, "Eh, Tahiti, is a mucky hole!" I then replaced the trapped nerve in her back that was generating the pain in her leg to which improvement was instant. She breezed out with no sign of a limp.

So my friend, today you have been a healer. Try as I may, I have perhaps been able to put into words only a tenth of the actual interplay of 'seeing', 'sensing' and 'knowing', and sheer instinct a healer uses. You should have grasped the idea as to how the 'how' part works. We have seen about twenty patients. Only one or two have not responded. Come with me, and let us have a cup of tea. We have earned it.

Chapter Ten

HOW DOES RELIGION INTERACT WITH HEALING?

ORTHODOX religion has failed miserably in offering to the common man an answer to his apparently simple question, "Tell me about God and how best He wants me to live this life He has given me, and teach me how I can be a happier person in the process."

Mealy mouthed clichés given as an answer by many clergy carry no impact, meaning or general understanding.

To guide you safely through life, all you need to do is follow the inbuilt instruction chart implanted in your mind at birth. This is our conscience. Follow it to the letter, and try your very best whatever circumstances of life you find yourself in.

I grow weary of being asked the questions, "What religion do you subscribe to?" or "Are you a religious person?" by people enquiring about my healing work.

Why these questions are asked in the first place baffles me, beyond the fact that people in general like to use name tags for everything and everyone. This immediately places you into a certain slot in their minds.

My reply to them – and you, is this: healing is one of nature's gifts, specially designed for mankind's benefit. **The source from which all healing stems is so spiritually evolved that it transcends every religion and clashes violently with none.**

It has never been my intention to tear down accepted beliefs, even when I know for certain that they are diametrically wrong. All I do ask of people is for them to enlarge the theme of their beliefs so they may integrate them into the reality of living.

I write this chapter only because I have been asked to by puzzled ex-patients. If you are expecting flowery language and pious, plaintive squeaks, full of 'thees' and 'thous,' sorry, but that is not my style.

I would admit that my viewpoint of religion is a confined one for I have found my footpath to the higher forces of love through the framework of healing. Obviously there are an infinite number of ways both to receive and appreciate a state of oneness with the forces that regulate all life. The word we use is 'spirituality'.

Of one thing I am certain: religion was never intended to be a separate part of people's lives, confined as it often is, to a one-hour-a-week visit to a place of worship.

My natural sympathy is with the underdog, the lost soul, the poor and the oppressed and all those in need. I have always viewed with deep distain society founded on the possession of objects rather than the love and caring for people.

The instigators of the world's religions were all humble men, devoid of personal ego, whose lives revolved around bringing to the common person a measure of reassurance regarding the temporary nature of life in this world and the immortality of his soul after his body dies.

Life in mankind's early days may have been primitive by todays standards, having no hot and cold running water but exactly the same as today, the world was flooded by the greedy, the selfish and the power hungry.

The whole of our present-day culture is essentially biased towards a materialistic outlook. This fact alone makes living a genuine religious life difficult to say the least.

Shall we examine the mess that mankind has made of this world and how his un-Godly behaviour has come to be recognised as the normal? Perhaps this is one of life's tests, to see how you cope with the situation.

There is a tendency for history to smooth over the less noteworthy conduct of those who formed our early society and class system for in those days, as now, anything went, bar cheating at Ludo.

The majority of the well-heeled section of our society originally made its wealth by disregarding every good principle it has been taught by the church. This was done in the name of progress, but the real reason was sheer greed. Great wealth was formed for the few at the expense of the sweat and toil of others. This often had to be paid for in the shortened lives of the workers in and after the industrial revolution.

Previous to that, the wheeler-dealer of those early ages had other ways to keep the wolf from the door, such as sheep stealing, cattle rustling, smuggling and that nice little earner, slave traffiking.

As we pushed the frontiers of our empire ever outwards, fresh lands were conquered and plundered in the name of progress. Our government at one time even instigated and condoned the issuing of opium to the Chinese to gain entry into that country for free trade. This was the instigator of the infamous Boxer Rebellion in China. It is no wonder that the Eastern people still have an ingrained suspicion of Westerners.

So you see there is nothing new in unhealthy wealth, and those far off days of corruption and plunder formed the basis for today's prosperous society. This system is so deep and advanced in our society that it is impossible to change, and under whose standards we all must live. We call it civilisation. Its methods of trade revolve around a consumer society, one that is well on its way to destroying much of our natural world. Many people argue the advantages of communal ownership, but in practise a classless society simply doesn't work either.

Poor Mr Average Person, whether you realise it or not, is trapped in a closed social class system. The key to your position in it is clearly and automatically defined by the number of noughts in black on your bank statements.

Most Western religions have changed from their founder's original conception to the one of being money-orientated. Many such churches now have full coffers and own vast tracts of land. Some of these lands contains the swankiest bordellos in the country, and only pay lip service to the piety and love contained within

132

their religion's original founder's concepts. **Whether they know it or not, they are now capitalistic churches, with capitalistic values, catering exclusively to capitalist's congregations.**

Therefore I no longer find it curious or a complete puzzle as I did once that the only 'knockers' against my work of healing have come from the clergy of such churches. All other faiths have received my gift with great gratitude as to its origin.

I am not about to bore you with details for I consider these encounters with such closed minded clergy, petty and only a minor irritation. Being a loner in my work, completely without the protection that comes from belonging to a particular sect or society, has many times, left me smarting with annoyance. Whilst not wishing to generalise, I can only comment on that small minority of churchmen who have made regular and vicious attacks on me over the past years – even from one who now lives in a bishop's palace! Isn't it a strange contradiction of the teachings of Jesus that bishops should actually live in palaces?

From their comments it was painfully obvious they had not the slightest idea what my lovely work of healing involved or the source from which it is generated. Can you explain why there is such a vast discrepancy between their words and their deeds with those people of the cloth?

Cultures that are often looked upon as being primitive and backward have the basic facts about religion very much in perspective. Did you know, for instance, that the North American Indian nation had no word for religion in their language and that they shared everything as an accepted matter of course?

They were taught from infancy that their daily lives should be composed of prayerful acts and a close intergration with nature, coupled to a loving concern for their neighbours and none of these things could ever be separated and many people have the audacity to call them heathens!

So it must be accepted that being kind, caring and loving makes a person religious; no prayer meetings, no singing, no rites, no dogma, no studying of religious books and certainly no judging of another. Note the simplicity of requirements. These self-same virtues form the basis for every one of the various schools of philosophy that we collectively term religion.

One aspect of life that has often puzzled me, being such a simple soul, was why this need for so many religions? If they all teach the same truth, why wouldn't just one do for everybody?

My answer came from an Indian guru, Sri Ram-Krishna. He was explaining to his followers why there was the need for so many different religions. Roughly translated, he said simply that there are many ways of serving fish – it can be boiled, fried, baked, sliced, boned, or mashed for a child. It is neverless all fish. Each person receives the same basic goodness and nutrition from it but because people's palates and tastes differ, it has to be served in different ways to become acceptable to each individual.

That answered one of the question marks in my mind for I fully accept that if you sense the inner peace contained within some Buddhist monks, see the tranquillity shining on the face of a true Eastern mystic or hear of some Christian's attitude of loving charity, then you realise that all these people are sharing similar experiences. Natural laws are being expressed by actions. The rewards of these actions are shown by the peace and contentment in their lives.

Religion fulfils a deep basic need of man to help him gain a feeling of nearness and security with our Creator. This inspires the quality we understand as faith. I believe that to achieve this state of oneness is simplicity itself, and that what most people mean by the word religion is really theology.

My belief is this: that every time you are caring and loving, in whatever circumstances of life you find yourself, you are being religious. At that moment, there is a link between you and your creator.

We live in a world of matter and show. Some people collect religious books for no other reason than to show the world how 'holy' they are. Ornate trappings are placed in mighty palaces of worship that are specifically designed to impress God. All they do is impress man. These displays of weath are tainted by the same primitive belief that was coupled to the worshipping of grotesque idols and the eating of your enemies flesh with relish – this is still done in some remote parts of the world – the idea being that they may inherit their enemies bravery. Even the act of Holy Communion practised in the Church of England – and considered by many to be the height of spirituality and a token of the person's faith – carries with it a primitive cannibalistic undertone, the wine being Jesus's blood, the bread his body.

The trappings of earthly wealth and pompous behaviour performed by that sect's devotees can never carry any impact with a God who considers every human being an equal. Rest assured, that He is not bothered, or even slightly impressed, whether you have two cars in your garage or if you ride an elephant to work.

When idly musing, I have often wondered if on a Sunday morning God says to himself: "Oh, bother, it's 'gimme day' again. They will be all at it saying, 'Oh God, give me this, and give me that.'"

It has often been asked of me, "Do I have to be religious to receive healing?" The answer is a firm, "No!" I have pondered long and hard searching for some common denominator as to why some people respond more easily than others to healing for it is fact that they do.

The only rational conclusion I can come to is that those who do respond readily are old souls who have been in a body possibly many times. Invariably they are 'natural' in their approach to life and do not carry any false fronts seeming to remain unaffected by other people's earthly success. It has nothing to do with belief, or lack of it.

So exclusive is the true nature of spiritual healing that it should never, ever be delegated and downgraded to the role of being just another fringe medicine therapy, which has severe limits on its ability to cure sickness, as is thought in some quarters.

As a healer, I consider I have been given a definite mandate from the Almighty in the form of this gift of the spirit to channel and offer His exclusive energy to humanity.

In view of this fact, we treat patients with no particular religion and people from all religions, no matter how far out they appear to be in their beliefs. Nevertheless, I never cease to be amazed at the strange antics and arrogance displayed by some avowed believers.

Some time ago now, a party of Arabs from one of the embassies in London arrived at my clinic to see me. It consisted of two ladies in startling black and gold masks, together with a half dozen gun-waving bodyguards. They were shown into the waiting room by one of my staff, and asked to wait a few moments as I was busy treating another patient.

Suddenly, the door of the healing room crashed open. One of my cleaning ladies dashed in with an alarmed look on her face and said; "Please come at once! The toilet and the washroom are awash with spilled water. Without a by your leave, they have gone into your private rooms." Firstly I went into the washroom where from the state of things, rather than having a wash – it looked as though they had been having a ritual bath – for they had used all our hand towels and left in one corner a huge pile of silver washing bowls.

Puzzled, I then went to my private lounge and noticed, like four little sentries, two pairs of ladies shoes left neatly outside. Peeping round the door frame into the room, I saw that they were busily occupied, praying their little hearts out. They had a big compass with them to identify the direction of Mecca. I now know that Mecca lies halfway between the drink's cabinet and the fire place!

It turned out that they had come all the way from London not for healing, but to confirm or deny one of the women's fears that her husband was being unfaithful to her!

It needed the wisdom of Solomon to answer her. From my perceptions, I was instantly aware that her husband was indeed unfaithful to her, but my task in life is to heal, not predict someone's future or comment on their behaviour in life.

The right words were given to me to speak, I replied to her question by saying, "Your husband is as unfaithful to you as you are to him." A startled and alarmed look came over her face. They left quickly and quietly and . . . no charge!

HOW IT ALL STARTED

The libraries of the world are filled to overflowing with books containing religious outpourings. Rather than going into long and complicated theological issues that truly have no great importance in the scheme of things, let us try to keep our exploration simple.

The pathway to a belief in one God that did away with worshipping idols, gold or otherwise, was initiated by just eleven men.

A long time ago when God was just a bit of a lad, at differerent stages in history these eleven wonderfully enlightened souls were dispatched from the higher realms of spiritual life, to live in bodies and teach the true word that would be relevant to that particular society, civilisation and culture. They would prove to be the founders of the world's main religions, showing in the process there are an infinite number of ways to an infinite God.

Every religion without exception teaches the same thing using of course, different formats of words and language. The main points stressed were the immortality of the soul, a belief in a single supreme power, reverence for all life forms, love towards each other, and charity of mind as well as the pocket, personal honour and self-dicipline.

Religious expression is such an individualistic matter, responsible for so much trouble in this world caused by well-intentioned people trying to impose their own ideas of theology on others. A wise person once said, "The road to hell is paved with good intentions." The compulsion to prove that your particular beliefs are exclusive to the rest of humanity, can reach such an obsession that the issue of words becomes more important than the joy of people. Lesson number one: never be dogmatic and say, "Mine is the only way," because it isn't. Never, ever ridicule other faiths as being sheer nonsense.

The list of the world's main religions is impressive, I list them as follows: Judaism, Islam, Buddhism, Christianity, Hinduism, Taoism, Shintoism, Confucianism, Zoroastanism, Jainism, and Zen.

Every one of the initiators of these world's religions was a visionary; each one was also gifted with many sensitive awarenesses, setting them head and shoulders above their fellows.

The Hindu religion, at first sight, would seem to consist of the worshipping of many gods. When I asked a follower about this, his explanation was, that each god is a different face of the one God, each wearing a different expression and each concerned with a different facet of life.

This exclusive band of religious founders was each blessed with various gifts of the spirit that extended their influence far beyond the confines of this physical world of matter. They differed only in the fact that varying cultures and races demanded a totally different approach in the expression of the same divine truth.

As an illustration of what I have just stated, note the following. True spirituality is to love your neighbour as yourself. In the words of various religions it comes out as follows:-.

Judaism. What is hateful to you, do not do to your fellow man. That is the entire law. All the rest is commentary.

Christianity: All things that men should do unto you, do you even so to them, for this is the law.

Buddhism: Hurt not others in ways which you yourself would find hurtful.

Islam: No one of you is a believer until he desires for his brother that which he desires for himself.

Confucianism: Is there one maxim which ought to be acted on throughout one's whole life? Surely it is the maxim of loving kindness. Do not to others what you would not have them do unto you.

Taoism: Regards your neighbour's gain as your own gain, and your neighbour's loss as your own loss.

In all it's exactly the same meaning, just using different words.

Here is a rough guide to the spiritual qualities contained in any man of the cloth. Ignore his flabby flesh, dropped chest and unused muscles, for his labours reside in the mind. Just two innocent things reveal all – his eyes and his mouth. If his eyes are hard like two gimlets and his mouth displays thin, bitter lips, usually turned down at the outside, then he has not climbed far up the ladder of spirituality.

On the other hand, if his eyes are kind and compassionate, his lips relaxed and he smiles from the heart, then this particular cleric is in his rightful profession. Try running a spot check on the clergy you know and you will find I am right, for bodies always respond to the influence of the mind.

I am not about to express my opinion on any particular religious out-look for I respect them all. I also make no comment on the truths – or in the same cases the partial truths – that religious opinion has ehanged them into. The Master I serve has all religions under his surveillance, and looks on them all with great tolerance, like a kind father viewing the behaviour of the teenagers who regard themselves as grown persons. Perhaps the thought comes to him often, "They will learn" or perhaps, "When will they learn?"

It is sad, yet true, that over the years there have been untold millions of people slaughtered and persecuted in the name of religion. The fault lies not in the religion, but in a total misinterpretation of the teachings of that particular religion by its followers. Both politics and religion tend to raise great passions in their particular followers breast's. Countless wars have been fought and millions of people killed by avowed religious believers, who seem to revel in an unswerving viewpoint.

The intention of this chapter is to bring to an end the confusion that reigns in the average thinking person's mind as he desperately tries to make sense of the great gulf of inconsistency that lies between religious teachings and religious practise.

We find that many religions have dissolved into a combination of the perfect purity of truth compiled by the originator's visions, and the partially disguised integration of old pagan rites into their dogma and creed. Add to this, ceremonies that are specifically designed to impress the onlooker in a deliberate attempt to enhance the stature, exclusiveness and infallibility of the priesthood.

The world is composed of sheep and shepherds. Sheep accept and are led; shepherds demand some type of rational and logical explanation. You have just qualified as a shepherd by even bothering to read this age.

In practise it will be found that we are left virtually in the dark and must use our own devices to work out life's problems. Burning bushes, except on Guy Fawkes plot night, are a very rare sight in this day and night.

My approach to this subject can only be that of a down-to-earth Yorkshireman, with his inbred attitude of plain common sense. It is so very easy to be critical of religious bodies and institutions, for it is possible to quote thousands of incidents and peculiar actions by people claiming to be religious. Take Tamerlane the Great and hear what he was 'great' at. He had over two million people executed on the pretext he was following to the letter the teachings of the Koran. Then there was the infamous Spanish inquisition which resulted in an estimated nine million people subjected to a gruesome and cruel death in a futile attempt to convert the known world to the Roman Catholic faith, often by resorting to the great lengths of pulling out convert's finger nails and stretching them on the rack.

Nearly as bad was the bright young cleric bucking for the next vacant bishop's seat, who in a flash of inspired reasoning invented a little thing called income tax. This he thinly disguised under the name of 'tithing' with a proportion of all your income going to the church. Is it any wonder that this firm, with a branch in every parish, prospered and still does?

How is this for a nice little earner. One religious sect teaches that, everyone who has sinned during their lifetime has to spend a certain time in purgatory as a penance by God in order to work off the sin. Until quite recently it was possible for indulgences to be bought back from this church for cash. The bigger the sum, the less time spent in purgatory. No comment!

Just how did these various systems of worship culminate? It has always been obvious to the searcher that there is an element of great creativeness through all forms of life. It is only common sense to assume that somewhere there is an active intelligence to bring this about.

It is searching for a greater understanding of the particular force that creates life which has driven mankind into these many forms of worship. To gain an appreciation of these various philosophies, we must bear in mind how they all began.

It was our cavemen ancestors who, at the dawn of history, first felt the need to communicate with the force that created life. With limited speech – and even less knowledge outside his own survival – his whole life was controlled by fear, hunger and cold. He lay huddled in burrows or caves for safety. Dreading the dark with its unknown dangers, he fought a constant battle with the elements just to stay alive. Illness or injury often meant death. Only the fittest survived – just.

Is it any wonder he worshipped the sun as the benevolent giver of life? This source of light and heat – and its bonus of ripe berries and fruits, his sole variation from an all-meat diet, certainly lived up to the standards expected of a God. It gave in abundance.

As time went by and the animal called man increased, so he grew together with others of his kind, both for company and protection, and formed the first tribes. The strongest and cleverest became leaders and as such reaped the rewards by receiving various perks befitting their position. The same thing still applies today.

The basic laws of the 'dove and the club' had arrived. Be good and confirm to the tribal laws and the big God high up in the sky will smile on you and reward you with lots of life's goodies. Alternatively, be perverse by independently going your own way and he will give you a big clout. Strong stuff I agree, but it worked and still does today in a more subtle form. We now call it forcing a person to conform to the will of society.

The wise men of the tribe prayed for more children to make it larger and thereby stronger. They similarly prayed for greater luck in the hunt, and for increased crops to help them survive the winter. These prayerful acts and fertility rites were the forerunners of our present -day harvest festivals.

Disease, like the poor, has always been with us. Clinical examination of the remains of paleolithic man proved he suffered, amongst other things, from a tubercular condition of the spine. Arthritis was as common then as it is now.

Civilisations have risen and fallen. One puzzling and curious fact was the discovery of the remains of a mammoth, hundreds of thousands of years old, encased in ice, with a bullet hole in its skull. Historians tell us that the priesthood of the ancient Greek, Egyptian and Roman Empires had great knowledge concerning the treatment and cure of illness. There is masses of evidence derived from examination of ancient skeletons which proves that advanced surgery such as pre-frontal lobotomies, for the restraint of madness, were quite commonplace.

It was then – and still should be now – that good results were the hallmark of a successful healer-priest. There is no greater encouragement for quick learning concerning health recovery than if your life is on the line, as was once the case, for failure to bring health to your patients. As a result, poor quality medics never grew old enough to receive their old age pensions.

The ancient Chinese devised a good system to urge doctors to greater efforts. You paid a weekly sum of money when you were well and healthy but stopped when you fell ill. Payment only began again when the doctor had cured you. There certainly would be plenty of poor, starving doctors if that system were practised in our present society.

These old-time givers of health sailed under various different colours of beliefs. Many were forced to shroud their particular gifts of healing and knowledge of herbal remedies in mysticism and mumbo-jumbo, with assorted religious trappings thrown in, to give credence to their gifts and skills in their fearful, superstitious and ignorant followers.

Some of the early medics, in a desperate search for health recovery, adopted very peculiar methods. There was the time in Kashmir during a cholera epidemic, which was rapidly decimating the population, when bulls were driven through the streets of the city in the vain hope the beasts would somehow absorb the disease.

As man became more intelligent, learning first to produce fire and then the wheel, so he became more ambitious. He turned away from the elements as gods. Why not gods in the shape of himself?

Indeed, superhumans with great power over nature were more understandable to common clay, than a vague disc high up in the sky that was only in attendance twelve hours a day, and then only in good weather.

It was little wonder that this splendid idea caught on? It wasn't long before it was thought desirable to keep in these new god's good books by offering them the bribe of a human sacrifice. As a result of this new attitude, fair maidens were slung off cliffs or barbecued by the score in an attempt to appease these powerful beings.

Time passed. Man evolved. The age of the higher mind we call *our* civilisation began. I think it highly possible there could have been one previously. Dreamers dreamed their prophetic dreams; men of insight had visions of what could be; philosophers tried to crack the secrets of life; deep thinkers thought profound thoughts. Each added his quota to the overall picture of man's attempt to explain the unexplainable.

Strange men were born into the world, poor in the social scale for they scorned materialism, but rich in the wisdom that only belongs to elevated souls. Here were no intellectual giants, for book scholarship in those times was confined to the rich. But they were people whose perceptions went far beyond the confining world of three dimensions.

Each one of these wise men tried by personal examples and simple analogies, within the frustrating confines of words, to show in a manner understandable to their particular civilisations, the workings of the làws that govern all life. They emphasised that the force we understand by the name of God, could by its very nature, only be a singular thing applicable to all people everywhere.

They went on to explain that God was not an anthropomorphic creature full of brooding menace who demanded blood and sacrifice as his rightful due, but rather an integrated part of each one of us, linked always to Him and each other, by the inner spiritual soul.

Here then, were the founders of all the world's religions. They were united in their emphasis that the cosmic laws which bind our universe could be under our control because we were part of the whole. If only we could learn how to operate the law.

Their instructions to achieve this state of grace hinged entirely on a lifestyle motivated by loving compassion for others, charity in all things, and concern for everything that bore the stamp of life.

Unfortunately, the majority took the other path and opted for mechanical science, personal egotism and the gaining of personal power, thus making certain that materialism boomed and expanded into every avenue of life from the Church to the courts of kings. It was at this stage that medicine divorced itself from the priesthood and went blithely on a pathway of its own creation, confident in its own mind that man was no more than a quite modest creation of flesh and blood.

The outcome is that we find ourselves living in a world of artificial values, for the rush and bustle of today is far divorced from the inner peace that a person really needs.

People everywhere are being mentally manipulated by the power of suggestion. Couple this to HP demands, bank rates going up or down, exposure to such horrors on TV as the charred bodies of little children burned by napalm bombs: all tend to make spiritual matters somewhat unreal and far removed from the harsh reality of the present day.

Install in your mind once and for all the truth that these are conditions created by ignorant men. If you can but firmly grasp this fact, it helps to keep things in their proper perspective.

If you believe that anything goes, bar cheating at cribbage: if you think that pretty words, pretty songs and pretty settings make up a religion; if you look upon God as being a Father Christmas-type philanthropist, I feel sorry, because you are missing out entirely on what life is all about. These things are merely the icing on the cake, in other words top show, or as common folk say locally, "Fur coat and no undies."

I wish with all my heart that more people would realise there is no greater act of worship than the hand stretched out in the act of generosity; that *every* act of loving, unselfish, caring behaviour and sympathy, no matter the context, causes a gentle spasm of one-ness to vibrate between ourselves and the Universal Mind. So now you can see you have been religious many times in your life in the true sense of the word and never known it.

That little tag of religion you have placed around your neck doesn't mean a thing either. You can call yourself a Christian, Born-Again or otherwise – my mother did a good job on her first attempt – Jew, Muslim, Atheist, Humanitarian, Flat Earther or any of the other sects man likes to join, in order to make himself appear exclusive and to separate himself from the rest of the herd.

If you are living your life in a truly godly way to the best of your ability considering your circumstances, then you are a religious person for God doesn't expect you to be either a saint or a martyr.

I am by no means against orthodox religion for there is both comfort and peace to be gained by visiting any place of worship. This fact alone proves that the basic principle is right. However, the theme needs to be enlarged in people's hearts and minds. God is thought of by many as being a father-like figure, sitting on a throne in a Michaelangelo-type heaven, receiving petitions via prayer and dispensing justice only to the true believer. However, the present state of the world says otherwise.

Realise that God is everywhere, in every single thing that lives; in the good and the so-called bad; in the weeds and in the well-cared for garden; in the eagle that scours the skies for food; in the little hedgehog as he snuffles harmlessly along the hedgerows. You may say – and many do – that the law of the jungle is unkind. Exactly like you having to work out your own salvation, it is a necessary part of nature to ensure order, continuity and the correct evolution of each separate species.

In reality, it doesn't matter in the slightest what you believe; it's how you behave in life that is important. Accept that religion is one of the few subjects whereby two people with totally opposed views can both be right for I can assure you that in this area no human being has all knowledge, not you, and least of all myself.

Here in a nutshell is what most people do in their search for understanding of the great mass of intelligence that we mean by God. They shrink their concepts down to human size and adopt the ostrich technique by conveniently blocking out the less praiseworthy behaviour of themselves and their fellows.

Being overwhelmed by the complexity of life with its many false facades and questions that are unanswerable by personal experience, all thoughts regarding God, religion and dictates of conscience are crowded into a tight little mental box. The unexplainable facts regarding life are carefully sieved off leaving an unreal fairytale image dripping with sweet sentimentalities. These do not mean a thing and bear not the slightest resemblance to the true state or the nature of the force that created and controls our lives. Know that the timeless wisdom of God *is* always available if approached in the right way, and your pathway through life will be eased to a bearable level.

It should be realised the root purpose of religion is to give the believer a measure of faith in the infinite.

I would be the first to agree that very few people manage to achieve a full, strong measure of this belief business. A minority do. The results of their beliefs speak for themselves. Here is a true story of such a person. The effect it had on his health is remarkable.

A man in North America lived to a ripe old age of one hundred and ten years in apparent perfect health. He was loved and respected by all the community for his good humour, personal honour and caring good works. No one could remember him ever having even a single day's illness.

So amazed were medical staff at the region's hospital at his apparent perfect health and longevity that they asked him to donate his body to medical science when he died, to see if they could gain a clue regarding his wonderful condition.

Eventually the old man died. A post-mortem was carried out on his remains and doctors found to their utter amazement that he carried healed scar tissue of many potential terminal ailments.

They approached the old man's family and questioned them closely as to his habits. They were told that he had been a happy chap with simple beliefs who had worked hard and played hard for all his life. The only thing out of the ordinary was that every night he had spent a few quiet moments in earnest prayer, asking that all parts in his body which were imperfect should be taken away from him. Such was the power of his request that indeed they had been removed.

You may call his actions those of a person who had a secure belief and faith in the power of God, completely unhampered by any of the false ego which educated man has in such an abundance. The old man remained untainted by the stench of materialism. Lastly, his belief overcame that faith-stopper, fear, the totally negative emotion that places a rigid barrier against gaining the full natural health from God which is man's birthright.

141

If you are still clinging to the idea of God being in the shape of a man, you might well think, as I have heard it expressed many times, that life's pains and illnesses are imposed on us as some sort of divine punishment. If you do, shame on you. Surely seeing the bodies of little children, crippled as a result of some obscene drug or genetic failures that have arisen because of harmful medication during pregnancy, can only be regarded as the work of ignorant men, despite their worldy qualifications.

Come with me. Let us try once and for all to erase the idea of God as some type of 'Big Daddy' in the sky.

It's a warm summer's night, join me in the garden. There's not a cloud in the sky and as yet, the moon has not risen. Go on. Sit down. Relax and give your brains a rest. Just study the sky over your head with care. See against the dark blue heavens there are sprinklings of light, every speck of which is a sun. Astrologers tell us that at a rough estimate it is possible to see with the naked eye about four thousand five hundred stars, depending on how good your eyesight is, and that around these suns, for that's what they are, revolve planets, many similar to earth.

Our own sun, around which the earth revolves, is so large, that if it were hollow, it could contain one million worlds the size of earth. By the same yardstick, there are stars in space so huge they could hold five hundred million suns the size of ours.

There are about one hundred million stars in the average galaxy and at least one hundred million galaxies in known space. Makes you think, doesn't it?

By using modern technology, man has perfected an instrument called a radio telescope. Scientists have computed that within range of this instrument there are at least one hundred and eighty million earth-type worlds, each capable of maintaining life as we know it. Is your head reeling? Well how about distances then? If you have ever crossed the Atlantic by boat or air you may well consider yourself a bit of a traveller. Interstellar distances have the field to themselves for they are measured by how far a beam of light can travel in a year. We call them light years and the answer amounts to a long, long walk. For those of you with a mathematical turn of mind the answer is 5,875,083,800,000 miles. As an instance, let us take as an example the star cluster of Andromeda which, it has been computed, is ten million light years away. Multiply that with the first figure, and the answer on my abacus is a lengthy walk.

The human mind simply cannot visualise the term infinity, something that has no beginning and no end. Our brains just boggle at even contemplating the thought, yet this is the true extent of creation. It makes Bill Bloggs, with his expanding waistline and contracting imagination, look a bit on the puny side.

I often wonder, when I hear the clergy ranting on about God being in the shape of man, if there is a little blue skinned person somewhere on a world beyond Venus, with his eyes extending on long stalks, pounding away on his pulpit with one of his six hands, insisting that God must be in the shape of a Venusian, for how could civilisation prosper without six hands to make all its artefacts?

None of this detracts from the fact of there being an active intelligence linked to every living thing. Just as there is an ever – expanding universe, so there must be an ever-expanding God. Do carry the thought that mother earth is a relatively new creation in spacial terms, and that there could well be other worlds with cultures far more advanced than ours.

Let the last word on this subject be those of the Lord Buddha. He parried every request by his followers for a full description of the perfect state to be aimed for in the Buddhist religion, by saying it was "incomprehensible, indescribable, inconceivable, and therefore utterable in the format of words."

IN CONCLUSION

You must have fully grasped the fact by now, that church teachings and religious practise are two separate entities and cannot possibly be grouped together.

I find it curious that the various church leaders seem preoccupied with sin to such an extent that any thinking person could well assume they know more about badness than goodness.

Let us try to put the whole matter into perspective. All church's are founded on certain rules that demand a devotee observes a certain code of morality and adhere to the religions personal rules. If you break the code or are found out, then you are a sinner in that religion's eyes. Let us change the word sin to mistake. We all make mistakes in life, some little one's, some big one's. In fact it is only by making mistakes that we can learn life's lessons.

If we protect ourselves by living a cloistered safe life, that is far divorced from the reality of the everyday world, such as a monk or nun, then this escapism is leaving unfulfilled our purpose for living. It is a fact that nobody is perfect, nor were we intended to be. Exposure to, and the overcoming of life's problems, is a necessary part of our evolution as learning souls. Just bear that in mind next time you hear someone telling the world how perfect and untainted they are by life's pressures.

Chapter Eleven

HOW TO LIVE LIFE

IT is a concrete fact that full conviction of spiritual healing and the great implications behind it can only come from within yourself.

By the very act of opening these pages you are looking for explanations about life's mysteries.

These cannot be forced on your shoulders like a friend who has bought you a lifetime's subscription to a magazine whose views you do not care for. It is irrelevant whether you dislike my views because they do not fit in with your philosophy. Nevertheless, they are true.

I have one consolation. If you are an out and out materialist on your first journey through life, my explanations and deliberations will not mean a thing. Furthermore, you wouldn't be reading this book in the first place.

I find this attitude rather sad but unavoidable, for by your curious mental block, you may well miss out on your birthright of being able to link into this source of full physical, mental and spiritual health. As always in a life that has freedom of choice, the decision is yours.

Most of the experiences I have written of are personal to myself. In view of that, all I can ask of you is to treat my experiences as distinct possibilities. In other words a direction indicator in which you can delve and forage out the truth of my words for yourself. I will be happy enough if I have aroused your curiosity.

If you are chronically sick or have any condition that has not responded to orthodox medical treatment, then try healing and test the power of health recovery by the results gained. Don't be disillusioned if the response is poor. Try several healers until you find one developed enough to be able to help you.

If you are unhappy, sad, depressed or unable to make sense of life's inconsistencies, see if my writings have the answer for you.

By far the strongest persuasion to full acceptance of healing's wonders is to be cured of an ailment. This does not in any way automatically carry with it a full knowledge of healing, but gives you a reasonably strong base from which to explore further.

I know of many people who have been cured through my gift who have since become strong healers themselves.

There are many factors regarding ill-health and recovery that I have not touched upon in these pages, mainly because they would be beyond most people's understanding, except for a handful of experienced healers, and they know of these anyway.

If you are a potential healer, it must be obvious to you by now that much of the knowledge you are seeking can only be obtained by the actual experience of applying healing. Gradually, over a period of time, you will learn by your experiences, unlike a 'healer' I once met who told me she had always one hundred per cent success. Rather taken aback, for all healers have failures, I asked how many patients she had treated. She proudly replied, "Two!"

Whilst access to the upper portion of healing is confined to only a handful of practitioners, every sensitive person has it within them to grasp the concepts and practise a form of healing that will at least bring peace and tranquillity in its wake, even if sickness is not taken away from the patient.

My advice to you is that if you have the gift in an undeveloped form, for goodness sake try and use it. Follow your own impressions. Have patience. It takes time to develop any gift of the spirit. Do not allow yourself to be distracted by spiteful people with ideological differences.

Believe me, the world is literally starved of spiritual qualities. You have only to see our hospitals crammed to capacity, and the heavy onslaught of illness and disease to realise that this is man's own personal cry for help.

Never forget that the seemingly simple act of dispersing the arthritic adhesions in a patient's little finger is an action simply loaded with implications. Besides being a medical impossibility, it points a way for the observer to follow if he has the inclination. It reaches far beyond the mere removal of pain and distress for these are the important issues of the now.

Come for healing, whoever you are, and a price will be expected of you, not in monies but in general behaviour. It may take the form of yourself being kinder to workmates and neighbours. If you stay cynical and bitter even though your illness has been taken away from you, the healing has sadly failed.

We hope it will result in you having a more unselfish approach to life that will influence for the better those with whom you come in contact. Stay selfish and again the healing has failed in its purpose. It could take the form of a simple act such as spreading news of your recovery that will eventually reach the ears of someone who desperately needs the help only healing can bring.

If you remain secretive and hole-in-the-corner, as many do regarding the help received from healing, then your cure has been pointless and without worth. If you are not prepared inwardly to make concessions towards the healer in the form of being at the very least open minded, I wouldn't bother to even try healing.

The reason I say this is that some patients carry such strange and harsh vibrations I would willingly pay them *not* to come to me for treatment. The strain they impose on my well-being is so traumatic that I couldn't even begin to describe it in words.

Spiritual healing, like many other mental activities, has divine planning behind its formation. We healers know that all acts of healing are part of a divine plan for the progression and eventual evolvement of all mankind. If you think about it, that is quite a mouthful.

In other words, the divine plan is that, in the distant future, all mankind will find a happy balance with their fellows, their work, their religion and their home life. In my book, that can't be a bad thing or happen quickly enough.

At first glance, many of the subjects I have touched on in these pages may seem far removed from healing and health. Their importance has only been shown to me by experience. For instance, the great stress I place on the attitude of a truly open mind and a sane, tolerant and happy approach to life, provides a mental state that not only makes a person receptive but also to remain healthy afterwards.

Nobody except a complete moron is in a euphoric state of mind all the time. Every person has his ups and downs on the roller coaster of life. Consider yourself lucky if you have equal measures of happiness and depressions.

Often patients say to me: "I wish I could be like you, Mr Greenbank. You are always cheerful and full of life." They don't know how I am feeling inside, although the act of 'giving out' as we do when healing, brings a tranquillity and peace, to the inner person. I can truthfully say that when working, I am happy.

I am reminded of an Eastern prince who was given a large jewel by one of his followers. Sending for his goldsmith, he asked him to make a ring for the precious stone and to inscribe it with something that would humble him in times of plenty and give support in hard times. The goldsmith eventually returned to the prince with the completed ring. On looking inside he saw the simple inscription, 'It will pass'.

A healer walks a lonely path, mainly because of the exclusive nature of this work. Therefore when I mix with people of other interests, I have to act as a mental chameleon and talk only at their level of interest.

Whether you are aware of the fact or not, it is your emotional state that rules your glands. These have an effect on every function of the body. Cherish any overstrong emotion, like hate, bitternesss or resentment, over a long period, and I'll guarantee that your body will not function properly and you could well fall ill. Living in a body we tend to overlook what a complex mechanism it is. It is so easy for it to malfunction and fall out of phase. The answer is simplicity itself: stay happy. Saints are rather thin on the ground. You are not expected to be one. All that is expected of you by the chap 'Up There' is to try your very best. By doing that, you will find your body *will* stay healthy.

It is of great concern to me just how many people are anything but happy. It is possible that society, with its false values and its emphasis on materialism, is to blame, so that people become bored, envious, and depressed. Obviously, their health then suffers.

So we must face the fact that such individuals are missing out somewhere on what life is all about. Inertia has always been the enemy of progress in mankind. Just sit around and do nothing, waiting for another star rising in the East to lead you, and you will have a long wait.

The keys that will make your hidden powers within your mind are implanted in you at birth by our Creator. He doesn't want you to sit around on your bottom all the time bemoaning your lot. There's no gathering new soul experience by doing so. That's the reason you were placed in a body in the first place.

Be more enterprising. Start living instead of just existing, waiting for your old age pension. Do not stagnate. Start *now* and enjoy a constant stream of new experiences. Try activities you have never attempted before, be it hang gliding or even just going for a long walk. I can promise you one thing, if you allow yourself to become bored, you have taken the first step to becoming a total neurotic, and there are plenty of those around without you adding to their numbers!

146

Ignore completely what the world thinks of your performance in life, for it is of no importance. It's your personal rating of success to yourself that really matters. Be assured of one thing; whatever you attempt to do in life, it will never come easily. If it did, you would never gain any sense of achievement.

The true test is this. Can you – like me – sit down in the evening of your life, with a well satisfied and perhaps smug feeling of, "I did it my way." If so you have been a success to yourself.

You will have made plenty of mistakes. Everyone does but that's how you learn. There's a saying that the man who never made any mistakes, never made anything, or in fractured Yorkshire dialect, "The man who never lost any brass, never made any either."

For goodness sake, place great value on the life you have been given for it's a precious thing. Never blame the accident of birth for your troubles and failings. Dig right down to the core of matters and take a long, hard look at yourself.

If you feel that you are one of life's failures, study your weak and strong points carefully and then count your assets. You will have some, even if it's only good health. Then have another attack on life's problems armed with this new approach – and I would like to bet you will then win out.

Over the years, I have met hundreds who never did this. They have groused and grumbled, constantly saying, "If only this had happened," or "If only that had occured." Bounce back at life. Treat it as a game. Be prepared for some defeats. You can't win them all, but never anticipate defeat before you start.

For goodness sake, don't let one beating from life be the end of all your dreams, or even a dozen beatings for that matter. I can speak with authority for it has all happened to me. Then, like me, you can look down your life at those years of struggle and adversity and record them as the happiest times.

You have to learn to flow with life, just giving an extra nudge every now and again in the right direction, exactly the same as a wise man swimming across a fast flowing Yorkshire river. Instead of swimming upstream and tiring himself out, he heads for a point downstream on the opposite bank and allows the current do the work and help him across.

Here's a little tip that life has taught me . . . and it certainly works. If you have plans of action you intend taking, don't tell anyone who is not involved. I don't know why, but if too many people know your plans, they spoil them, and they never turn out as you wish them to.

Retain your sense of proportion by treating life and the act of living with humour. If you haven't a sense of humour, develop one quickly. Don't take yourself too seriously for there never was a farce as funny as this human comedy.

The keys to happiness in this life are these, treat life as a game, have a whale of a time. Do not stagnate. Be enthusiastic with both your work and your play. Develop humour and lo and behold, you will find yourself well, happy and "As fit as a butcher's dog."

Every word within these pages concerns that stubborn, enigmatic, twisted, confused, often frightened, kind and loving creature known as mankind. He's immortal and doesn't know it: he has within himself the keys to unlock paradise, yet his eyes are closed by ignorance and therefore can't find the lock. People similar to myself – and we are quite thick on the ground – plead, cajole, nudge, and sometimes give a darn big shove to help him in the right direction. For want of a better word we are called 'healers'.

We regard ourselves as channels through which a remedial health-giving energy flows to the patient. Partial access to the art we practise is within the scope of most sensitive people to utilise, but so few do.

If this book acts like a super oil to unlock those rusty, unused parts of you by helping to rid the artificial values – and I implore you to allow nature to regulate your life – if you do so you will have made one person happy – me.

I hope these writings prove of interest to student healers who are perhaps puzzled and perplexed over certain facets of healing as I once was, as well as to the fit and well person who has a natural curiosity about what makes the universe tick over.

If your doctor or specialist has closed his file on your case and ticked up a 'medically incurable' sign even if that is only in his mind, don't accept this yourself, but try spiritual healing's way back to health!

As a professional healer I do not issue any glossy brochures. Neither do I give patients any hot line of persuasive spiel. Everyone comes to see me on a personal recommendation. I make a charge, not for healing, but: for my time, skill and experience. Allowances are always made in cases of hardship.

Every treatment I give is in the nature of an experiment and patients must accept the result of that single treatment. Obviously, if the condition is vastly improved but not cured then a second visit would be indicated. I will try my very best, but you must never try and twist my arm to gain a definite promise of a cure. That I cannot do. Over years of healing, I have seen most sick conditions respond. I am very conscious of the fact that there are no incurable ailments. But there are incurable people.

The cause of non-response to healing can be outside pressures having a stressful effect on the patient. This can be wrong medication from a doctor or even the negative thoughts of a person's family. The list is endless.

Healers are what one can only term 'freethinkers'. We should not be bound or inhibited by any religious dogma. For us, healing should be recognised as an expression of a natural divine concern for all living things. In view of this, be assured that a healer should never use his gift as a rostrum from which to convert you to his particular way of religious expression. He should respect your personal religious opinions and never, ever tell you your illness is the direct result of sin imposed on you by a merciless God. As a very sick and kindly Jewish lady was told recently by a lady who considered herself a healer, that she had the "blood of Jesus on her hands," and that the only way she would be cured was to become a Born-Again Christian. There's is one person who has a lot to answer for when her time on earth is over.

In this present climate of too much emphasis on medical matter's many become preoccupied with illness. The latest surgical triumphs are spoken of with baited breath. One I heard of was related to me by a patient, with just a touch of envy. In all seriousness, she told me of her friend who had been fitted with a plastic heart! Another person wondered if I had any experience of treating arthritic 'Noodles'!

An air of complete innocence seems to be the answer, so keep far away from such people.

Chapter Twelve

EXTEND YOURSELF TO OTHERS

It has been my privilege over the years of healing to meet thousands of kindly, caring people, perhaps the one that sticks out strongest in my memories was a loving, sweet soul, a saint dressed in a tatty apron, with her wispy grey hair tied up in a bun. Her body was worn out and weary in service to others. To me she will always be 'the lady with love for others'. This lady – and I call her lady in its fullest sense – sent me a letter asking if I would call and give her healing's help when I could spare the time. Her main task in the evening of her life was looking after four dear old ladies. This she performed dutifully for many years in spite of having severe ailments herself.

At the time of my visit to give her healing's help, three of the ladies had passed away. The patient's one ambition was to be given enough strength to see the remaining old lady safely into the next world. Then she, in turn was ready to depart this life.

The physical condition of this frail and bent saint was nearly past description. She weighed no more than five stones in the rain, as we say locally. Totally blind in one eye, and with her sight failing in the other. A breast had been removed due to cancer and all of her body was misshapen by chronic arthritis. Yet in spite of all these handicaps, any one of which would have been sufficient for lesser mortals, her thoughts were on the welfare of others. By healing, help was given for her to bear the load. Later, she passed to a higher state as gently and peacefully as she had lived, her last old lady preceding her by just a week. One can visualise the happy reunion awaiting this shining soul. Doesn't it make a lot of people who are living totally self-orientated lives sound rather petty.

We live in a world of opposites, good and bad, negative and positive, love and hate, right and wrong. Great cruelties and acts of love are committed daily by people similar to ourselves. The majority manage to keep a pretty even balance between the two extremes. It is a critical matter simply because of the influence of other personalities in our lives. There is a right and a wrong way of living. Certain aspects of life can be quite frightening. Consequently many people drift into the wrong way so gradually that are not aware of it and withdraw themselves into a limited world and clamp themselves tight against any intrusion. It is not bad living, but it is not good for them at all.

Extend yourself to others. It is in service that the greatest of life's pleasures are to be found. It can fill an empty life with meaning and expression as well as mend a broken heart. It is often said in conversation: "So-and-so never did anybody any

149

harm," but did they do any good? There are thousands of ways that this good to others can be expressed – the wife or relation who looks after a loved one in a serious illness, people who nurse and really care for those in their charge, the foster mother who adores children so much she takes in and loves others. Examine them carefully and see for yourself that they have invariably found happiness and joy in an otherwise harsh life by the act of giving of themselves. That is the right way for you to live life.

So if your favourite tune is the 'Dead March' from Saul and your best reading confined to the 'hatch, match and dispatch' column of your newspaper, with the emphasis on the dispatch part, that's wrong too.

When ninety-six, my own grandfather studied with great interest the death's column in the newspaper every evening. One night he said to me with a smile: "You know, son, I haven't an enemy in the world. I have buried them all."

If the distress of a neighbour is looked upon as a spicy conversation piece for the church knitting circle or if you do your service with the air of a martyr that's another wrong. If someone asks how you are, like I once did to a patient, and she replies with a smarmy smile of a born martyr, "I can still smile, be it through tears," that is the wrong attitude. Just try forgetting the "I" part. Do you know who will benefit – *you*'

It is, of course, essential that you do have a certain amount of respect for yourself. I remember the advice of an old friend of mine, who over the years had met and overcame most of the difficulties life can throw at a person. His advice to me was, "If you go through life and treat yourself as a doormat, you can only expect that people will wipe their feet on you." It's all very well to think that in the eyes of God all people are equal, but perhaps the person who is trying his best to overawe you hasn't heard this.

Don't blame Him because life has appeared unkind to you. People have told me: "I have prayed for years to have a certain thing given to me. Now I have lost all faith because my prayers have not been answered." If that person had put as much active effort into going single-minded after what they wanted so badly, they would have had it long ago.

Mankind expects – and this surely shows the child in his make-up – that the answer to his prayers will not always be "YES," for just as equally, it could be "No".

Having only a confined view of life and being unable to see the full picture of our life span, we are unable to assess it. As an example, look at our children. If you give a child everything it requests immediately on asking, what happens? The child becomes a spoilt and pampered brat growing up to be a spoilt and pampered adult. Sometimes you have to say "No!" for the child's own good.

I am reminded of the story of the man who was bemoaning his lot because he had holes through the soles of his shoes. The pebbles were hurting his feet. Then he came across a man begging at the side of the road with *no* feet.

This is a plea from my heart to yours: alter and change yourself, especially if your outlook is pessimistic and narrow. You can only enjoy the fruits of the world if you lose all fear and negativity. Do not be too security conscious for you cannot protect yourself from every adverse occurance that may happen in life. You can only overcome fear by doing that which you are afraid of.

People are frightened of many things. These fears come with a thousand differing faces. Fear can mar and ruin lives that should be rich with happiness. Some people live in perpetual fear of losing their jobs, their friends, possessions and loves. Others have a fear even of facing life's problems, fear of what may happen and seldom does. There are even people who anticipate grave illness. They eventually *do* become ill. Does this solid thought of fear stimulate the body to bring this about by inhibiting its immune system?

On the other side of the coin, it is seldom that people such as nurses and doctors, who are in constant contact with grave and infectious illnesses, contract disease. Perhaps the concern for the sufferer cancels out and relaxes the defence system? As a further point of interest, the water at Lourdes is exposed to a constant flow of diseased patients. Does the faith of pilgrims nullify the ingress of disease?

The absence of fear in myself could possibly explain why I can treat wild animals and have never been attacked. The animals seem to know exactly who I am, what I do and accept healing with gratitude. In the Bible, didn't Daniel enter the lion's den without any harm befalling him?

I am not advocating that everyone attempts to crowd into a lions cage as a test of faith, but do try and be a little more adventurous.

The wrong attitude on how to live is perhaps expressed in the following verse. A Yorkshireman's advice to his son.

> *See all, hear all, say nowt,*
> *Eat all, sup all, pay nowt,*
> *And if tha ever does owt for nowt,*
> *Allus do it for thesen!*

Translated this means:

> *See everything, hear everything, say nothing.*
> *Eat everything, drink everything, pay nothing.*
> *And if you ever do anything for nothing,*
> *Always do it for yourself!*

Chapter Thirteen

ADVICE FOR THE SEARCHER

EVERYBODY who practices healing has their critics. They, like most people who give adverse comment, generally have no knowledge on the subject they are talking. Any critical views that are aired must stem from a complete ignorance of the subject as any serious thinker who examines the evidence available must agree that healing by spiritual means is completely proven.

These critics usually come by their strong anti-healing views not from investigating the subject thoroughly, but by accepting the views of one or two biased TV programmes they have watched or an article in the 'yellow press'.

Amazingly to my mind, most of healing's critics emanate from either the Christian clergy or medical doctors. The clergy's attitude is in the main purely an academic one for seldom do they practise what they preach. The doctor's attitude, on the other hand, is usually patronising. In general they are conceited enough to believe they have far superior knowledge concerning sickness and its treatment, than any other discipline and tend instantly to close ranks on any mistakes they make. Believe me they make plenty.

Doctors invariably fail to recognise that healing is a vastly different approach to illness recovery than the one taught at medical school. The only part of healing they are qualified to assess is the disappearance of the illness in a patient.

Psychiatrists, who as you know are qualified doctors, are probably the worst with their acid comments on my work. They invariably hint at the cured illness being of psychosomatic origin, attributing cures to the plausibility of the healer and the gullibility of the patient. The aspect which most amuses me, is that the arguments are not whether or not these cures take place, but how.

It all boils down to the fact that humans in general are a pretty conceited crowd, who think everything is explainable and understandable in worldly terms.

I find this attitude very curious. A person wouldn't under any circumstances profess to understand nuclear physics, quantum physics or the intricacies of advanced electronics without spending years in study. Yet they will pass completely biased comments on healing's wonders without any knowledge at all on which to base their opinions.

It is quite a unique position we healers occupy. On one hand we are deeply involved in sickness and disease: on the other, we stand on the outside of medicine with no conventional medical knowledge to blur our insight.

As outsiders, we see a society increasingly dependent on tranquillisers, pep pills, sleeping pills and placeboes in a futile race to remain sane in a world of false values. Healers differ from the formal medical view in the sense that we see a person as a personality, *not* just a very complicated machine. We fully accept that many ailments are a reflection of the inner discontent of the patient.

As a healer, I certainly have no strong bias against conventional medicine as a whole. Indeed, I seek ever closer co-operation with all those whose first interest is in restoring sick and unhappy people back to health.

Any criticisms I make are aimed at the small minority of medical personnel who play God by exerting the power of superior knowledge over frightened, sick people or of the few ignorant doctors who are in positions of authority, displaying neither tact nor diplomacy by using a completely negative psychology and seem to attain a personal sadistic kick out of so doing. This can take the form of explaining at great length to sick patients the possible course that their illness could take, telling them they have a limited time to live. One of my clients was told by a doctor in a particularly smarmy voice, "This is the ward where you will peacefully pass away!" Such is the power of negative suggestion that those told they have a short time limit on their lives will duly oblige.

I also protest strong and loudly at the policy of issuing addictive drugs as a short term answer to some ailments, knowing at the time of prescribing that all this will achieve is to submerge the symptoms at the price of uncertain and often very dangerous side effects.

One point that must have struck you after reading my views on healing is that many facets of this work are simply not understandable to the layman. Indeed several times every day I am asked for explanations where a full and detailed answer would be outside the understanding of the questioner. So I have to give a part answer, the one that's understandable by any reasonably intelligent person.

This difficulty in producing an acceptable explanation lies in the complexity of a healer's perceptions. It can best be likened to trying to explain to a man who has been blind all his life what the colour blue looks like or describe the emotional qualities of love and kindness. In other words, you can't.

On account of limits on the reader's experience I have had to keep my explanations simple. However I do hope that the curiosity aroused by the many healings described will urge you to explore deeper into this work.

If your interest has been aroused enough to research healing further and your investigations are via the written word, the only advice I can offer is to choose your author carefully. A practitioner's viewpoint is far preferable to second-hand gleanings picked out from an unknowledgeable writer's interviews.

You see, even an apparently unbiased writer with his 'how and why,' shares little common ground with the healer who practices his art on a level of spiritual consciousness far removed from the eager contemplation of piles of meaningless statistics, often compiled by an austere and perhaps spiritually ignorant analytical mind. The end product and effect of such writings is nothing less than boring. In fact, reading train timetables can often prove to be far more interesting.

Let me put the whole question of being a healer in a nutshell by reversing the roles and asking *you* how you would react if you discovered that the energies of healing flowed through your mind and body. Imagine that in certain circumstances it was possible for you to read people's centres of pain, the emotional pressures they were undergoing and their deep sadness and hidden motivations. Also imagine that the veil beyond life was occasionally drawn back so you were aware of people supposedly dead.

There would only be two courses of action open to you: one would be to consult a psychiatrist and deny the evidence of your own senses, in the firm belief you were going insane and that you might soon be issued with a generous supply of 'giggle pills' and a strait-jacket. The second would be to accept this wonderful gift and use it for the good of humanity.

I rather fancy you would plump for the second option and exercise your new-found gift. You would give the comfort of your awareness to someone who had lost a loved one and was distraught with grief: you would remove pain from those in agony: you would find yourself maintaining a sympathetic attitude to any of the victims of our selfish, affluent society, who came your way asking for help. That, dear friends, is exactly what I did and still do.

I have tried to give you an insight into healing from the healer's side of the fence. You will perhaps realise by now that being a healer is possibly the best job in the world. It is also one of the hardest for healers are in a particularly vulnerable position, having no worldly protection from barbed words and people's ignorance, only the positive knowledge that they are doing God's will.

Age should bring a certain maturity and wisdom. From their teens onwards into being grown men and women, young people are by inclination so full of themselves with clearly defined views that everything is either black or white. Only with maturity do we become more tolerant and accept the fact there are vast areas of grey regarding most areas of knowledge and experience.

One famous American writer explained in a different way. He said: "When I was fifteen years of age, my father was a complete idiot. It is amazing what that man learnt in the next six years."

As the years of healing roll by, one gains a deep insight into human behaviour, probably best recorded in that Yorkshire saying, 'There's nowt as queer as folk and nowt as nice as folk.'

As this is an advice chapter, my final condensed comment is for you to gain wisdom by examining nature. Revel in your gift of life. Give affection and love wherever and whenever possible. Draw freely from the well of healing for your every need. Lo and behold, I can promise you that your life will be full, rich, and complete.

HAVE YOU FOUND YOUR SOUL'S LEARNING PLAN FOR THIS LIFE?
It is a very good thing if you have for I have pondered hard and long as to what mine was. Only as I am approaching the end of these writings has it become crystal clear to me what my particular plan of life is? The application of healing has been only one facet of my learning plan. The other main one is, that I have not to lose a single one of my good principles. By that, I mean those I had as a child.

In retrospect, that sounds easy, but in actual practise it is the most difficult task you could possibly attempt. Earlier I wrote of the forces of chaos most people would be completely unaware that there is such a force. That is mainly because this force has been ingrained into every facet of our society since time began, so it has more than a head start on poor little innocent you. Its servants are to be found in the ambitious, the selfish, the hard, the ruthless and the cruel. Many of the heartless heads of industry, who are more interested in profits that people, carry

154

more than their fair share of this quality. The whole system is encouraged to make it permanent by the teachings of our education system.

It is the young who are the victims – and they do not realise it. Remember when you were youthful and idealistic. Your head was full of dreams and goodness that your elders called rubbish. You believed in the Tooth Fairy, in Father Christmas, in Robin Hood who robbed the rich to help the poor, in King Arthur and his Knights of the Round Table, who toured the countryside performing great deeds of chivalry. Miracles, you believed were not only possible, but they happened all the time whilst knights did come on white chargers to rescue fair maidens in distress. Do you remember the sheer delight when you first fell deeply in love, and of how that literally changed the world for you?

Gradually, as people grow older, each of these lovely comforting beliefs are stolen from you one by one. Our education system, famed throughout the world, is deliberately geared to teaching people to become competitive in life generally.

You are initiated into the wrong belief that you must beat the other man by whatever means at your disposal, be it fair or foul. This applies both in business and leisure. One is taught that the decadent word 'honour' should be looked on with contempt: that you must never help lame dogs over stiles but learn to kick them over; that you must always have a really good personal reason for doing good works; that you must cultivate a, "What is in it for me?" attitude; that you are far better than the other chap, if you have gained more of life's goodies. Love, honour, personal integrity and helping your brother humans are relegated to secondary importance to the main aim of life, which is being a worldly success.

All this negative and ungodly advice was thrust at me. I never did change a single one of my childhood ideals that my inner instincts told me certain teachings were wrong . . . and my instincts proved right. As a result of my unswerving belief in my inner feelings, it now gives me great personal delight to have survived a lifetime in this manner and proved to the world that *my* way is the *right* way.

A very wise man once said that, "Until you become like a little child, the Kingdom of Heaven is closed to you." I know exactly what he meant. I have two sons who swear they are older than myself.

So if you are young, do not allow yourself to be side-tracked from the nice inner person that is endowed with the same idealistic instincts you once enjoyed in your pre-birth life in the spirit world. This world of ours would much prefer you to be changed and moulded into a stereo-typed, robot-like person with the fixed conventional ideas that materialists enjoy and know how to handle.

If you are an older person, it is odds on you have been moulded, at least in part, to the system of false values we call civilisation. In your case, it is a much harder task for you to lose a lifetime of wrong values, but you must at least have become disenchanted with them to be reading this book.

Delve deep into your early memories. Try and recapture your lost idealism and all those values you carried in the secret parts of your mind.

Reject the false facade the world likes to impose on people. Be eccentric, be a one off job. Do not consider what the world thinks of you. It's far more important what you think of yourself. If your values are right, it can only follow that every action you perform in life be ethically right also. The outcome of your mental cleansing will result in a change, to a condition known as a complete inner happiness.

Read slowly and deliberately the following, each morning. If I were asked to compress all my advice on living into just a few words, I could do no better than offer the 'Desiderata' which was written centuries ago.

Go placidly amid the noise and haste and remember what peace there may be in silence. As far as possible without surrender, be on good terms with all people. Speak your truth quietly and clearly and listen to others, even the dull and ignorant. They too have their story. Avoid loud and aggressive persons, they are a vexation to the spirit. If you compare yourself with others you may become vain and bitter for always there will be greater and lesser persons than yourself.

Enjoy your achievements as well as your plans. Keep interested in your own career, however humble. It is a real possession in the changing fortunes of time. Exercise caution in your business affairs for the world is full of trickery. But let this not blind you to what virtue there is.

Many people strive for high ideals. Everywhere life is full of heroism. Especially do not feign affection. Neither be cynical about love, for in the face of all aridity and disenchantment it is as perennial as the grass.

Take kindly the counsel of the years, gracefully surrendering the things of youth. Nurture strength of spirit to shield you in sudden misfortune, but do not distress yourself with imaginings. Many fears are born of fatigue and loneliness. Beyond the wholesome discipline, be gentle with yourself. You are a child of the universe no less than the trees and the stars. You have a right to be here and whether or not it is clear to you, no doubt the universe is unfolding as it should.

Therefore be at peace with God, whatever you conceive him to be, and whatever labours and aspirations you have, in the noisy confusion of life. Keep peace with your soul. With all its sham, drudgery and broken dreams. It is still a beautiful world. Be careful and strive to be happy.

Follow this advice to the letter . . . and I can guarantee you a happy and healthy life. Good luck be yours.

EPILOGUE

You may think this is a strange place to insert an epilogue, but then this is an unusual book, one that is completely against the usual format of writing. I hope that my sincerity will have outweighed any discrepancy you find in literary convention.

The world is full of men who have great book learning, yet of these there are only a handful that can be termed wise. Such a person was Professor Murdo MacDonald-Bayne. To honour his wisdom and his memory, for it is one of the most moving and truthful documents I have ever read, I can do no better than quote you the foreword of his book, *I Am The Life.**

In it, he gives a format for the perfect way for a person to live life. It should be a blueprint for every human being as it was given to him from a high spiritual source. It is a code of living that every advanced healer tries to emulate. I would be the first to concede that few people will be able to follow to the actual letter the guidelines given, for many allow the world with its false values to intrude on their privacy, but trying is the thing. Here is his foreword:

**By kind permission of the publishers L N Fowler.*

He who lives in Truth is not afraid to proclaim the Truth. He is strong. He is full of optimism. He looks for the bright side of all things. In the darkest corners he makes the sun shine. He walks through life with a smile. He sings the song of joy. His faith is in the Absolute who lives in and through him. He carries a message of hope and courage and loves all life. He gives where and when it is needed. He helps others to help themselves. He is free from fear and worry, always forgiving, always tolerant. He is devoid of hate, envy, and malice. He radiates love to all the world and minds his own business and expects others to do the same. He goes joyfully through life. Things that drive others to despair and misery leave him in a calm undisturbed state of mind. His peace comes from within. He is like the ocean which receives all streams and rivers, yet the ocean's mighty calm is unmoved. Those who contact him feel his presence and receive encouragement.

He attracts love and friends, not that he desires them because he does not depend on people and things, but those things come to him as his right. He acknowledges the Law and the Law responds. He is at home with all classes of people: the rich and the poor are all alike to him. He does not favour one more than the other; he is not interested in what they have. All are equally at home with him. He is welcome in all homes. Children cling to his hand and coat.

He loves life and life responds. Sinner and saint are the same to him; he sees the good in the sinner and does not look for the weakness in the saint. He knows that he himself is not without sin and so never casts a stone. The outcast recognises him as a brother. The woman who has passed through the furnace of life trusts him. He gives of his love and wisdom and points a way to happiness.

He heals the heart and relieves the troubled mind. God never holds 'His' love from 'His' most disobedient child, neither does he hold that love of God from his brother or sister. He neither pities nor condemns because he knows that all are conquerors if they will but conquer. He finds joy in his work. He never hurries nor can he be rushed. He knows that time does not control him: he is attuned to the eternal.

He has absolute faith in the absolute power of which he has become aware. He knows that he is one with all life, and behind him is the power of the Universe. He believes in the all good. Divine justice is his key to all situations. He is simple, loving, and kind. He recognises that to attain wisdom one must be humble and when wisdom is mastered one must be humbler still. He is the future's promise of a better world to come.

You will join in this promise too. Open yourself. Do not resist. Receive the blessing of wisdom and understanding, through your love and service to others.

Then You Will Become As He Who Knows.

You have read of my personal beliefs and the strange pathway I have been made to walk through life. Now for the proof. The following written testimonies prove the power of healing and will endorse everything that I have said previously. In many respects regarding recovery from serious illness, spiritual healing can be far superior to any accepted orthodox medical method. All these quoted cases have been through the usual medical channels with little or no benefit given to them. The patient has then tried healing and been cured by this agency of spiritual love.

I have in my files tens of thousands of other testimonies to the sheer power of healing, but here I have mainly concentrated on either the pain aspect or the unusual character of the patient's ailment.

It is most important you remember that these quoted cases are *not* testimony to the power of Don Greenbank, but to the power of God. They give only a slight indication of the tremendous caring energies that are readily available regarding man's welfare.

If just one single sick person recovered from a serious illness by virtue of my gift, that would prove the validity of healing. Multiply the cases I have quoted in this book by thousands and you will have gained an idea of the full extent of my ministry.

So you have now heard my 'Song of life' or is it 'Swan song'? What a wonderful and exciting life I have had, with an endless variety of ups and downs, happiness and tears, poverty and plenty, loves and losses, and great kindness that has been showered on me as compensation.

It has never been boring for it's been an action-packed life, both to man and God. My reason for telling my story is a simple one. It was written because I was told to by the fates that control my life. It certainly hasn't been compiled to make you look up to me as some sort of superman. That I am not. I class myself as ordinary as fish and chips. They are tasty, aren't they? The real reason for this book is to tell the world what one person with a dream and an ideal can do in a lifetime – provided he is completely dedicated and has a surplus of love for people. I can assure you that some people are so sour and envious they sure take a lot of loving!

My orders to write were given specifically to serve as a signpost to all humanity, to give direction to those sensitives who are searching for reason in this chaotic melee we call civilisation. You will find that these writings contain divine truths rarely exposed to man in such a raw form. These should not only give enlightenment to the open-minded searcher, but will serve as an encouragement to those who have an inner urge to heal. It is a truth that what one person can do, another can follow.

With regret, for I have enjoyed confiding to you just a few of the experiences life has thrown at me, I now put down my one very sore finger and write the last words. Let us hope that this will be the beginning of a brighter, happier future for you. Pucker up your little lips and give me a big smile.

Now read of other people's impressions of healing's wonders. The testimonials which appear come not only from those in this country, but all over the world, including Italy, America, Australia, Belgium, Switzerland, Hong Kong, New Zealand, Israel, Crete . . . the list is almost endless!

THE PROOF
Testimonials to the power of healing.
HERE are just a few of the cures that have taken place through my gift. They have been taken purely at random from my visitors books and are therefore in the patient's own words. Often the height of understatement, they also include many interesting and medically impossible cases.

Amongst them I have selected many cases of animals that have been cured, which fully answers critics who insist that suggestion by the healer is the reason people become well.

All of the cases quoted have previous to healing been through the hands of orthodox medicine, with little or no benefit.

Miss B Steele, BEM. (Ex Senior Nursing Officer at the Bradford Royal Infirmary.) The following letter was her response to an article published in a local newspaper, written by a reporter commenting on my work of healing. She wrote. "I have often had the privilege of being present as an observer at many of Don Greenbank's healing sessions. With my own eyes, I have seen what must be surely considered miracles, events that as a trained nurse I would have termed medical impossibilities. I have witnessed cures, such as curved spines becoming instantly straight and perfect, within minutes.

I particularly remember one, a child who came for healing with a withered arm that she had suffered from birth. The arm became straight on her first treatment. After several weeks, the child was able to use it perfectly. Obviously, less spectacular cures take place all the time. The essence of healing, and indeed of this man's life, is love, surely the basis for all miracles."

Mr Bridge. "I must confess that I was neither enthusiastic – nor even hopeful that you would be able to alleviate all my aches and pains when I first came to see you. It is not that I am a pessimist by nature, rather a realist. Few people, as they approach middle age, expect to be free of some kind of trouble or another. I was quite reconciled to living with mine.

I must express my gratitude for your wonderful skill, or do you prefer to call it a gift? I now feel absolutely marvellous. I have no pain whatsoever. It is a great comfort to me to know you are there if I ever need you in the future."

Mrs Rushton. "Thank you very much for curing our Yorkshire Terrier, Brandy, of his hip trouble, in just two healing sessions."

Mr Dennis. "The tingling pain in the shoulders has gone straight away. Thanks for curing our little dog two years ago of spinal trouble that made him walk lame. He has had no more trouble since you treated him."

A Woodhead. (Perforated eardrum in right ear since a teenager.) "Perfect hearing was restored in my right ear immediately. Thank you for other benefits given on my one visit for healing."

Simon Lowcock. "After my first visit for treatment of asthma twelve months ago, healing achieved a big improvement. Following the second treatment, my chest is completely clear."

Mrs Greenwood. "Rebel, my daughter's horse was written off by the vet because he was suffering from the potentially fatal 'Grass sickness', for which there is no medical cure. In just two healing treatments, he was fine and well, and has stayed well to this day, eight years later."

Mrs Close. "I first went to Don for healing nine years ago suffering from cirrhosis of the liver having been told by doctors I had just two years at the most to live. I am happy to report I have had no further liver trouble since. I was also suffering from three slipped discs which he cured at once. I have had no further trouble with my spine since. I must pay my grateful thanks to Don for all he has done for me. This letter is written ten years later."

H G Craven. "Having been three times for healing. I have gained a complete cure from an hiatus hernia. I also had a long-standing painful condition of the pelvis. This was cured immediately."

Mrs Hird. "I have not been able to walk outside for years because of the intense pain in my back, legs, and feet. I am now so well that I have taken to wearing high heeled shoes again after a lapse of several years."

Mrs Jones. "I can now eat anything after healing, with no ill effects." (This client had been unable to eat solids for many years, suffering from what the hospital described as gall stones. Just one healing treatment removed all symptoms of pain and discomfort.)

B Guy. "I came for healing because of bad migraines. This was cured immediately. I also received a bonus in the fact that my hearing improved dramatically."

Mrs J Bell. "I have suffered for the last fifteen years with a very painful back. In just one visit for healing all the pain went completely. Previously no other form of treatment was of any use.

Andrew Skelton. "I have had a very painful and swollen knee for the last twenty years, with very restricted movement. Full mobility and all pain has gone in one healing treatment."

Before Healing.

161

After Healing, no need for the walking stick now.

A Robson. "I have been suffering greatly with Reynaud's Disease, which inflicted great pain in my hands. Thank you for curing me completely."

Mrs Davies. "Severe dizziness vanished immediately after receiving healing, much to my delight."

Mrs McKenna. "I had a large, painful cyst on my knee for several years and intense stomach pains of long standing. No medical explanation could be given. I was cured in one visit."

Mrs M Sykes. "Intense pain of long-standing in my spine was cured in just one visit. Hospital doctors said I would probably end up in a wheelchair, for they wanted to perform a laminectomy operation on my spine. I can only say, 'Thank God I came to see Don.'"

J Mann. Arthritis in the hip. "Wonderful relief from pain on this my first visit for healing." (This patient also had intense pain in his right shin and his big toe. This was also cured. The hospital told him it was hardening of the arteries and nothing could be done to help except amputation.)

M P Keighley. "I have suffered with colitis for the past ten years. After only two visits for healing, everything is working all right again!"

Mr Hobson. "I suffered from gall stones and warts in the bladder, I was bleeding internally as well. After two treatments all pain has gone. I have stopped bleeding. I feel fine and well."

Mrs Illingworth. "I have had pains in my back and neck for seven years. All pain was taken away from me in just one visit for healing. I feel wonderful."

Rose Logan from Leeds. (Cancer of the womb and pelvis.) Sorry over the delay in writing to you but I have been waiting for the results of medical tests at the hospital. I finally received the results a few days ago and we are delighted with the news. The specialist says that I am now completely cured of the cancer and that the previously active cells are now dead. As you are aware, I was very ill on that first visit to see you for healing. I was suffering from cancer of the womb and the pelvis and I was in great pain and having to take fourteen pain killing tablets a day and there was no other medical treatment for my condition. I had not eaten any solid food for three weeks previous to seeing you and even a drink of water would make me constantly sick!

The hospital had only given me a few weeks to live. After the first treatment, on my way home afterwards, I had a fancy to eat some fish, so my son stopped the car at a fish and chip shop and bought me some, which stayed down and I wasn't sick. After a few days, I found that I could eat just what I wanted and I had no pain at all. I came four times for healing to gain this wonderful cure! (Actually this lady was cured on her first visit, I saw her three more times for her reassurance, as she found it very hard to accept she was cured, which is quite natural after being told she had only a short time to live by the doctors at the hospital. Later when closely questioned by the doctors over her remarkable recovery, she refused to admit that she had been for healing and told them she had taken, in her words, "Some stuff that I bought at a chemists shop.") When I asked her why she had shown such reticence in speaking about healing she said, "Well it might come back, and I need to go see them again." People, I will never understand!!!! DG.

M Thorpe. "A very painful spine that had a curvature since early childhood, has been completely cured after only two visits for healing. All my thanks."

M A Mars. "I have had a large, painful swelling on my leg for eighteen years. After two visits, all pain has gone. The leg has returned to normal size."

Mrs D Lewis. (nurse) "I was told by a consultant I had arthritis of the spine, and that the condition was incurable. After just one visit for healing, all pain has gone, I have regained full mobility and feel like a new person."

B Martell. "I was told by the hospital that my condition was incurable yet I was healed on my first visit and have been fine ever since. I shall always be eternally grateful."

Mrs Longley. "I have suffered from asthma and bronchitis for the past thirty years. I feel great now. For the first time in all those years, I can breathe easily."

M Denison. "I have suffered from pain in the spine for the last twenty-seven years, I was told by the hospital that two vertebrae were disintegrating, and that there was a deterioration of the spinal tissues, plus arthritis of the spine and a very painful shoulder. All these conditions were cured by Don on my first visit."

D Bentley. "I feel very much better after this first healing treatment. All the pain and discomfort, that was the result of a parachute accident thirty-six years ago – and I have suffered ever since – has gone. I had pain in my back, legs, feet and hips. Previously I had been told by doctors that three discs had rotted away."

Mr A Charge. "The hospital wanted to operate and give me an artificial knee joint. I just came for healing just the once. All the pain has gone. My knee is now fully mobile. The pain I was getting in my hands and feet has also gone. Even my eyesight has improved from the cataracts that I had. I have now got the feeling back in the two fingers that were dead."

A Hewson. "I twisted my back and knee six months ago and have been in pain ever since. Just one visit for healing was enough to get rid of all my pain and give me full mobility.

D M Fearnley. "All the pain I had in my back and legs has now completely gone. The feeling has come back into three toes that were dead. Previous to healing, I attended hospital for ten month's treatment with no improvement. I went for healing just once. Isn't Don amazing!"

Marrion Myers. "I am absolutely amazed. It is impossible to put into words my thanks to this wonderful gentleman. I literally crawled into his clinic and walked out tall and straight and with no pain at all. Previous to healing, I had pain in my knees, back, shoulders, neck, hands, fingers and elbows. All the pain was removed from me in just one visit!"

D Bailey. "I had a large lump in my breast. Mr Greenbank dispersed it in just one treatment."

B Cawood. "I am leaving Don's clinic feeling very much better. I am very glad I came for healing. I had a painful spine, suspected stomach ulcer, impairment of breathing. I was told by doctors I would have to learn to live with these conditions. All pain and discomfort has been taken away on this first visit for healing."

E Sugden. "After twenty-five years of suffering migraines daily they have gone completely. This is written three months later."

A Mortimer. "Six months ago, I came to see you for severe back pains and black depressions. The back pains went immediately. Within a short time, the depressions lifted off me. Life is really worth living now."

Allison Damant. (nurse at Sheffield General Hospital) "Instant relief from intense pain in my spine. I can now do many things that previously I couldn't. Many thanks."

M Holroyd. "I was issued with a surgical collar by specialist at the hospital, who said that I had cervical spondylitis. All pain went and full mobility was given to me on my first visit for healing. No collar is needed now."

B Brooke. "I was waiting to go into hospital for an operation on my knee, for what specialists said was a cartilage fault. All pain was removed. I could move my knee easily on my first visit for healing. No operation needed or required." (Written six months later.)

A Rowley. (nurse) "Came on this first visit for healing with a very painful back, the result of lifting patients at work. The hospital where I work were unable to help me in the least, except to give me pain killers. It feels wonderful now."

K Haigh. "I have had constant back trouble for the last ten years and pains in the chest. During those years of suffering I received all forms of treatment. All of it was non-effective. This is my first visit for healing. All the pain has gone and I feel one hundred per cent better already."

D Gott. "Feel very much better after just one visit. Mr Greenbank has straightened my twisted pelvis, which has troubled me for the last thirty years. All the pain has gone."

Mrs Garside. "My first visit for healing, and I feel a lot more relaxed. All my pains have gone after eight years, suffering." (This patient has just come out of hospital, after having been given traction for one month with no benefit or decrease in the pain.)

Mr F Firth. "I was told by the hospital I needed a laminectomy operation on my spine. This is my first visit for healing. The pain has gone. I can walk easily now."

E Wright. "My pain really began when I had a laminectomy operation twenty-two years ago. I also had pain in my shoulder and neck. All my pains have gone. This is after all those years of seeing doctors and consultants, who told me that no help could be given for these painful conditions."

Mark Whiteley. "I am just nineteen years of age. This letter is written five months after receiving healing. I attended for healing after being told by a hospital specialist that I needed to be put in a plaster cast for my painful spine. After Don had treated me, all the pain went, I am now able to play sports again. Two weeks ago, I was able to run in a marathon, which is twenty-six miles, with no ill effects. Needless to say, I am delighted."

Mr, Mrs Goodall. "My wife and myself wish to thank you for all the help and relief from pain you have given us both. I had pains in my left arm and could not lift my left leg up at all. After just three visits for healing we are both fine. I am fit and well. My leg is back to normal. My wife was suffering from angina and could only walk a short distance before being out of breath. After you treated her, she is pounds better and has no chest pains. Her breathing is fine. She can walk a long distance without having to keep stopping to get her breath back."

Doris Wright. "I have waited some length of time since you treated me before writing. Now I am delighted to tell you I am perfectly fit, well and happy. I have not had the slightest sign of cystitis or colitis since my last visit to see you for healing. This, after years of suffering, is indeed a wonderful feeling. I do thank you for all your kindness and understanding, but most of all for your healing hands!"

J Holdsworth. "When I first came to see you about three months ago, I was in agony. I had been wearing a steel corset for eighteen months. I never thought I would be able to stop wearing it. After you had treated me and removed all my pains, you told me I did not need to wear it ever again. Now I have no pain and no trouble."

A Hobson. "I spent my fifty-first birthday in Leeds Infirmary, where medical tests and X-rays proved I had arthritis of the spine and that two vertebrae were badly worn. I was forced to spend five weeks flat on my back. There was no improvement in the pain at the end of it. Then the hospital fitted me with a steel corset. I was issued with lots of pain killing tablets, and told to go home and learn to live with the condition for there was no cure.

Through a friend, who told me of your wonderful healing gift, I came to see you for healing. We only needed to visit three times to gain a complete cure. That was fifteen months ago now. I had to return to hospital with stones in my bladder. Further X-rays were taken of my spine. These proved that healing had rebuilt it back to normal. The specialist said there was no sign of arthritis, and that my spine was in a remarkably good condition for a person of my age."

Mr Kershaw. "My dog, Charlie, being unable to express his thanks on any other way than his usual tail wag, leaves it to his master to write and say 'Thank you very much'. Your healing resulted in a leg joint being freed of all pain and restoring the fleetness of foot that is normal for a seven-year-old border Collie.

After you treated him last week, Charlie enjoyed a restful sleep for most of the evening. The next day I took the two dogs for a walk on the footpath near Skipton golf course. Much to the bewilderment of the younger dog, Kattie, Charlie outstripped her in a five-times-round-the-field sprint. We jumped a four feet wall and condescended to let the younger dog catch up for a rough and tumble, considerably rougher than we have seen him do for years. Our joint thanks."

E Draper. "For several years, I had bad pains in the calf of my leg and shoulder. My doctor said it was rheumatism. Whatever it was, it went immediately during the healing. Now I have no pain at all."

Mrs Kilgollen. I am a geriatric nurse, and have been suffering greatly with bad pains in my spine. My GP recommended that I went for traction to the hospital. I didn't. I went to see Mr Greenbank. After his first treatment, I am cured."

Mrs Forest. "I last went to see Don eight months ago for just one visit of healing. Since that day, I have not taken a single one of the various nerve tablets I've taken for years. The chest and throat pains all went the same day."

Mrs Baxter. "I went to see Mr Greenbank, only able to walk on crutches. After three healing treatments, I do not need them any more and am back to normal. The hospital was unable to diagnose the cause of my trouble."

Julie Firth. "My little girl had fourteen months hospital treatment, seeing various doctors and specialists, was put into plaster casts, and had two weeks of hot wax treatments, with no improvement. Then aged three, she was brought to Don for healing. Afterwards, she ran out to play with her friends – cured. I thank you with all my heart."

Patricia Hartley. "Thank you, thank you! After months and months of pain, I walked into your clinic like a semi-cripple . . . and walked out free from all pain. I will spread the news, soon all Rome shall know." (This lady works for the United Nations in Rome.)

Audrey Greenwood. "How wonderful it is to be without pain. As I told you earlier, I have suffered pain for the last fifteen years. During that time I saw numerous specialists, which resulted in me having four operations to no effect. When the pain, caused by trapped nerves, or so I was told, still continued, I was referred to the Bradford Pain Clinic. I underwent even more unpleasant treatments, all to no effect. I was then informed nothing could be done, was prescribed powerful classified drugs, and told that I would have to live with the conditions forever.

Consequently, these last few years have been indescribable, causing migraines and tension pains daily. That continued until I visited your beautiful sanctuary. After only two treatments I am pleased and happy to tell you that at long last I am free of pain. I feel absolutely wonderful. I can do my own housework, plus being able to work full time. I can look after others and do shopping for them. May I express my gratitude. You are indeed my saviour. May you long continue to do your wonderful work."

Mrs McCarton. "I have suffered from blinding headaches and vertigo since the age of sixteen, also I had clawed toes. Both these conditions were cured in just one visit for healing."

Mrs Joan Kelly. (tutor nurse) "I received three months treatment in Woodlands Orthopaedic Hospital with no improvement at all in my condition, prior to coming for healing. This cervical neck trouble has now gone on for three years. A full cure was given me after two visits for healing and now I have thrown the surgical collar way."

(Written several years later.)

Mrs B Featherstone. "Came for healing, suffering from Mythenia Gravis an illness that is medically incurable and is usually terminal.

I was dying from this creeping paralysis, unable to walk without aid. This condition has been getting gradually worse over the last nine years. After healing, I am back to normal. I can walk, run and eat anything. My weight has gone back to what it was previous to being ill."

Mrs Hartley. "Just two visits required for the full healing of long standing and painful neuralgia of the face. Now I am free from all pain after suffering for twelve long years. I feel absolutely marvellous and thank you."

Mrs Marple. "I am able to walk out of the clinic a different person to the one that went in. I have been waiting to go into hospital for an operation on my hand. This is no longer necessary as my fingers came free and the pain left me during healing."

Mary Humpreys. "Incredible!!! I have suffered for years with severe back problems. The hospital performed an operation, to no benefit. Don has put me right immediately. This gentleman sure is incredible."

Mrs Robinson. "I brought my dog, Toby, for healing after he was knocked down by a car two weeks ago. This left him paralysed in his back legs. The vet advised us to have him put down as his bladder and bowels were paralysed; he said Toby would need a catheter permanently. After his visit for healing, Toby's bladder and bowels started to work normally. Following his second visit, he started to walk on three legs. After the third visit, he is fit and

167

well and running again."

Diana Meadows. "I am aged forty-five years and I have had a curvature of the spine since I was a little child, my back is now straight, all thanks to Don.

Mr Brayshaw. "Thanks Don, for taking away all my pain. I would also like to thank you on behalf of my friend Mr F Balmforth. He came to see you ten years ago with a circulation problem in his leg, and you saved his leg from being amputated, for that is what the hospital wanted to do. He has been fit and well ever since. You achieved this cure in only two treatments."

C King. "I came to see Don nine months ago with what the doctor said was a spastic colon. Since that visit, I have had no further trouble with my insides. I came this visit with a whiplash injury caused by a car crash. All pain and distress were removed immediately, many thanks!"

T Rawmarsh. "The pains in my shoulders and the right arm were caused by war wounds I received forty-one years ago, since then I have not been able to raise my right arm in the air. After healing, I can now lift it straight up with no effort and no pain at all now."

D Atkinson. "Since receiving healing, my eyesight is nearly back to normal. Previously it was deteriorating rapidly. In fact, it got so bad I could no longer work. After healing, I was able to start work again."

Mrs Dowler. "For many years I have been treated by doctors at the hospital for arthritis, they confirmed their diagnosis by X-rays. I came for healing over two years ago and was immediately cured of all pain and immobility. Recently I was again X-rayed at the hospital, regarding another complaint, and they imformed me that my arthritis was cured completely and was no longer visible on the X-ray plates. I shall always be grateful."

Mrs Brooksbank. "Mr Greenbank laid his hands on our parrot who had been blind for many years. Immediately, the bird could see. He flew across the room and landed on my shoulder, and he is flying around all the time now. Previously he could not fly!"

Mrs Mann. "I cannot thank you enough after healing me of severe internal pains for which the hospital could find no cause. Surgeons even performed an investigatory operation and admitted they could not find the source of my intense pain. After healing, all my pains have gone."

Mrs K Bailey. "My mother, of ninety, was screaming in agony before Mr Greenbank arrived at our house. Within minutes, she had no pain at all."

F Granger. "Unbelievable! I have had arthritis in the neck and knees for the last twenty years, and noises in my head. It was all put right by the remarkable man in just one treatment."

Mr Stoney. "After thirty-eight years of suffering with bleeding haemorrhoids, for which I have been having hospital treatment with no improvement, in just two treatments with Don they have all gone. Thanks, and God has blessed you."

Mrs Begal. "A one hundred per cent improvement in my varicose veins. They have now completely disappeared."

Mabel Mills. "Many thanks for making me able to walk easily after ten years of pain. I can now walk without my stick and have no pain. Previously I attended a physiotherapist for ten years, after I had an accident. I came to see you only twice – and you cured me."

Mrs Walker. "I brought my small grey cat, Kipper, for healing. She had

168

received a terrible injury to her eye, so bad the vet thought that he would have to remove it. After you gave her healing – to which she responded at once – I am pleased to inform you that the eye is almost perfect and she can see perfect. Kipper is full of life."

Miss Dollietasch. "I had a bad fall when I was a child, resulting in my spine becoming crooked and very painful.

Hospital consultants and doctors all said nothing could be done to help this condition. My back is now straight. I have no pain. It's wonderful – and all in just one healing treatment."

E Robinson. "My long-standing back pains have all gone, in just one visit. This is after five years of ineffective hospital treatment."

Mr E M Williams. "For two years, I have had angina pains. After just two visits for healing all the symptoms have gone. This is written four months after my last visit. I was forced to retire because of the pains I was getting. After healing, I was able to get a full time job with the City of London Police Department. (Ten years later he is still working and in good health.)

Alice Yates. "This is the third time that I have received healing from you, each time with great success. Some four years ago I came for healing for a duodenal stomach ulcer. Previous to healing this showed on X-rays. It was cured immediately by you and later this was confirmed by further X-rays. Later you cleared a blocked artery above my left eye, and now after a nasty 'menieres' or similar attack, you have instantly relieved me of head and digestive problems.

Each trouble was medically diagnosed but without any benefit being given me by medicine. Each was healed in one visit by you and your helpers.

The mystery of spiritual healing causes much discussion Don, and in the end to most people it is still a mystery, but the earthly dedication and discipline practised by the healer, is both tangible and obvious to all. Thanks be to both of you, for all the effort which must be entailed in creating and keeping that lovely atmosphere, which means so much to inner healing."

Benita Harris. "Thank you for giving me hearing in my left ear, it is getting louder every week that goes by." (This child has been totally deaf in one ear since birth.)

S C Stephenson. "The medical profession diagnosed that I suffered from multiple sclerosis. They kept me in hospital for several weeks and gave me cortizone injections, all to no avail. I visited Don for healing when I left hospital. After only one treatment, all the MS symptoms disappeared. I now have full feeling in my hands and legs. I now have a healthy son. Life is very sweet and beautiful since I saw you three years ago."

Mr J Stanley. "I have suffered from Crohn's Disease for six years. I was cured in just one visit for healing, I write this letter twelve months later."

Mauchheri Mockouity. "What a relief after all those years of pain. I have suffered for years with ankylosis of the spine. This was diagnosed both by doctors in this country and in America. You have given me complete freedom from pain and gained me full mobility in just one visit."

Mrs Betts. "My grand-daughter's feet turned inwards. She was aged six months. Doctors said it was a dislocated hip, caused by a difficult birth. They intended to operate when she was older. Don put it right in a few moments of healing."

Mrs Walker. "I first went to see Don eight years ago with an extremely painful neck with a large lump on it. Three days after having healing, the lump disappeared and the pain went. I have had no more trouble since."

Mrs Swift. "One morning I scalded my foot with boiling water, right from my toes to my ankles. I normally have very poor healing flesh the district nurse had to come every morning to dress the scald while I was waiting for a skin graft operation. I went to see Don for healing. Within seconds he was even able to slap my foot and it did not hurt. When a few moments before, it had been untouchable. I no longer had any pain or soreness. The next day, the district nurse came to dress the scald as usual, and was amazed to find that it was nearly completely healed. Within a further seven days, it was perfect, with no scar. Of course I do not need an operation now."

Irene Hill. "I am delighted to tell you that my arthritic joints are still free from pain and that I have not had any angina pain's since I saw you now two months ago. Having been in pain and had my joints locked up for twenty-five years, you will realise how wonderful it feels, to walk normally again.

Mr Baluam. "About six weeks ago I brought my dog, Pedro, for healing. He is a large Dalmatian. A large wart developed on the lower lid of his left eye, but I was loath to have the dog operated on, though the vet said this was necessary. I am delighted to report that following our first visit to see you, in a matter of a week a large portion of the wart had dropped off. Following our second visit for healing, the wart has disappeared."

Mr Walker. "I have suffered from a hiatus hernia for the past ten years. During that time I was unsuccessfully operated on, and the surgeon wanted to operate on me again. Instead I came for healing, afterwards I was able to eat solid foods, which I have not been able to do for several years previously. Now I can eat quite normally, this letter is written eighteen months after receiving healing."

Mrs Green. "I have suffered for the past thirty-nine years with spinal troubles. Over those years I have received all forms of medical treatment, all to no effect, such as traction, plaster casts and so forth.

After healing, for the first time in all those years, I can run up the stairs with no pain at all now."

R Sheer. "I have suffered for eight years with a thrombosis in my leg. Just one visit for healing, and all the pain and discomfort have gone from my leg and my back."

Norman Orange. "On a trip to England from Mallorca I brought my wife to see you suffering from severe nerve pains caused by an attack of shingles two years before. The pain disappeared while you were treating her. Ever since she has been completely without it. And that was four years ago."

Mrs J Scott. "Many thanks for taking away the pains I had for the last seven years. I walked into your clinic wearing a calliper. You took all the pain away. I was able to walk out without it."

Mr H Jackson. "I have suffered from rheumatoid arthritis for the past nine years. At one stage I had to go into the Royal Bath Hospital in Harrogate for a five-week treatment. When I came out, I was no better than when I went in. After another five weeks just sitting around at home doing nothing, I found that I had 'locked up' and was only able to go upstairs on my hands and knees. I couldn't walk at all. When I rolled out of bed in a morning, my wife had to dress me. The arthritis had expanded into my shoulders, neck, arms, hands, hips, feet, knees, back and ankles. Those who read my letter and know about this dreadful illness will also know how much I suffered.

At this stage I honestly thought I would be confined to the house for the rest of my life, together with early retirement at the age of forty-two years. One day, I was lucky enough to meet a person whose wife had been in a similar condition, and who had been treated and cured by Don Greenbank. He gave me his phone number. It was to prove to be the most important call of my life.

It took a few treatments to bring me back into a normal state again, but completely normal I am. I have been working for several months and not had any time off work on account of illness. I am enjoying life to the full and will always be grateful to this wonderful man."

Jean Hake. "Eleven months ago I lost my voice. After several weeks, I consulted a throat specialist, who gave me little hope of my voice ever returning at all. As the weeks and months passed, I found vocal communication extremely tiring and as a result tended to avoid meeting strangers. I then visited you for healing two weeks ago. The very next day there were signs of my voice returning. Now I have fully recovered and my voice is normal. I still find it hard to accept that I can now talk normally."

Mrs Dunnara. "I was told by the hospital specialist that both my hips and back required operating on. I came for healing. You immediately gave me full mobility and took away all my pains. On returning for another examination by the same specialist, he confirmed that everything had been put right, and that the operations were no longer necessary."

Mrs L Deakin. "Thank you for healing my sick horse, Grey Dawn, she is now in excellent condition, the bursa having gone completely from her front leg. I rode her for the first time this weekend, taking it gently, trying not to tire her too much. It is lovely to be able to ride her again after so long."

Mrs D Brownhill. "I am delighted to tell you that Blackie, our Labrador dog, is fine. He can now get into his basket with no help, run upstairs and jump about. When we brought him to see you, we had to lift him into the car, but after you treated him, he jumped in by himself to go home. A friend told me about you. Her dog was also lame and crippled when she brought him to see you. You also healed it immediately.

Risy Roselic. "I feel much better now. You have made my thyroid work properly. My weight is slowly coming off. This is without medication."

Miss Currie. "I feel that a big weight has been lifted off me. All the rash has gone completely." (This girl had an unsightly skin condition. The hospital dermatologist admitted he was unable to help the condition. After two treatments, the rash disappeared completely.)

A Adams. "Many thanks for all your help. We are moving out of the area, but will always remember you. I had an unsightly skin condition on my shoulder. Thanks to healing, it has gone completely. I could not wear off-the-shoulder clothes because of the rash. Well, now I can!"

"Thanks Mr Greenbank, for making my pony, Fudge, fit and well. You have done the same for some of my friend's ponies. My pony was covered in warts. Only three hours after you gave her healing, they had all disappeared. My friend's horse had 'Grass sickness'. The vet advised them to have it put down, as it was medically incurable. Three weeks after healing, the same horse was pronounced fit, well and fully recovered by the same vet. It has put on weight. Its coat is gleaming with health."

Mrs M Chambers. "You have made me a different person. For six months I suffered from a heart defect whilst for twenty-one years I had back and neck pains. All this has now gone after receiving healing from you."

F Moran. "After an unsuccessful operation on my spine, I was in agony, but immediately on having healing from Don, all the pain left me. I now feel great and wish I had gone to see him before going into hospital. I have not felt so fit and healthy for years."

Mrs Rodber. "I am writing to tell you of my little bird Peter, who you were kind enough to see out of your usual clinic hours. He was unfortunate enough to knock his leg, the one that had a ring on it.

The leg became very swollen whilst the ring prevented the blood from reaching his foot. He was in tremendous pain so I took him to the vet. He removed the ring, and said he thought the leg would be all right, but there was a possibility the condition has gone too far and that the leg would need amputating.

As the week progressed, we saw the leg turn from blue to black. Peter was obviously suffering greatly. We rang you up, and you agreed to see him straight away for healing. When you had finished treating him, he was able to put his foot down on the floor and stand on it. It had started to turn its usual pink colour.

After just that one treatment, Peter began eating and drinking again, and in general he seemed a lot happier. The pain had obviously subsided. He has started to chirrup once more. He is now nine years old. We do thank you for your kindness. Even small birds are not overlooked by you and the Master for whom you work."

Mrs Butterfield. "After enduring a most distressing bladder and uric acid complaint for the last twenty years, you will be pleased to hear that after just one healing treatment from you, I no longer have any trouble at all. To me and my family this is in the nature of a miracle, if only I had heard of you before, I could have spared myself years of misery."

Tom Aleer. "Feeling a lot better after healing, which dispersed a large, painful lump in my groin in just three visits."

Deborah Kent. "I am fifteen years of age, and I had lumps in my breasts for the last six months and I was getting very worried over them. In just one visit for healing, Mr Greenbank dispersed them and they just vanished, thank you so much."

Mr Bates. "Thank you for sending healing to my little girl – photo enclosed – after she scalded her arm so badly. It was thought at the time she would have to undergo plastic surgery. It has now healed perfectly with no sign of any scar tissue forming. No operation is now necessary."

Mick Kelly. "Just a line to say thank you, for enabling me to play hockey and tennis between the ages of sixty-six to seventy-two years of age. As I am still playing them both, my thanks are somewhat overdue. I can think of no one else who could have achieved this."

Mrs Hainworth. "I would like to thank you for curing my little girl's warts. Previous to seeing you she had to go into hospital at regular intervals, to have them removed surgically. They always came back within a very short time. Since that one visit four years ago, they have not returned."

Jackaline Batt. (This letter is written three years later.) "You treated my grandson, Dean, for asthma. Up to that time, he had been attending hospital every fortnight. The medicine intake they gave him was huge. It included drugs, puffers, and tablets. After seeing you just once for healing, he is now off all medicines. There is not a trace of asthma with him. It is like a miracle to him."

Carol Vaugn. "This letter is written three years after you cured me. After suffering many years with a capital 'S', from Reynaud's Disease. This included being confined to hospital, both as an in and as an outpatient. I found that after just one visit for healing, my circulation was restored and I have had no trouble since that day. Many thanks."

M Brown. "I thought that I would let you know there is now no sign of the large lump that had formed on my appendix scar. The doctor was amazed when I saw him and showed him it had vanished under the healing."

Isobel Gilbert. "I am happy to report that the healing that you gave me for the severe migraines, I have been pestered with since I was in my teens, has been successful. I have not had a single attack since I came to see you five months ago."

Pauline Kilburn. "From being about eighteen years of age – I am now forty years old – I had a troublesome back. This reached its peak two years ago when I had to spend several months in bed. I gradually learned to walk in a crab-like fashion. My future sounded grim for the medical prognosis was either an operation to remove part of one vertebra, or an endless intake of pain-killing drugs, along with anabolic steroids to build up muscle strength. A colleague at work, which is part of the medical establishment, suggested that you may be able to help me.

After visiting you for healing, I am now completely free of pain. I am able to enjoy my great love of gardening once again. I have also walked for fifteen miles on the Pennine Way – in boots. A miracle? Yes. As a bonus, I have also been cured of a skin condition on my face that I had for nine years. Radiation was given at the hospital, with no success. My friends cannot believe what they see. Thank you for giving me good health."

Mrs Lambert. "Thanks a million. I have been crippled with arthritis for twenty years and could barely walk, even with the aid of two sticks. After just one treatment I was able to walk without them and I have no pain at all now."

Mr Wright. "I have been meaning to write for some time. With each week that passes new experiences seem to occur to me. I came to see you twelve months ago because I had suffered with numbness between my left hip and my knee, numbness between my left shoulder and elbow, and pain over my left eye. Just one fifteen minute healing session was all you required to put those things. right. My father-in-law came into the healing room with me. You inquired about his health, and you cured him of arthritis in the neck in seconds. He has had no reoccurrence, after being forced to wear a surgical collar for the last five years."

M Stott. "For twelve months I have been in severe pain from my head and neck. The hospital took dozens of X-rays, but could not come to any diagnosis. This is my first visit for healing . . . and all the pains have gone completely".

Mr Morrison. "My father-in-law was the first of our family to come to see you for healing. He had suffered for years with reoccurring back pains and was seldom out of pain. He went to see various specialists who told him he had bone

173

damage in some of his lower vertebrae, and that there was nothing they could do to help. He was given a surgical corset and a lot of pain-killers and advised he should get out of his trade and find a new one. He is a motor mechanic.

But you Don Greenbank, have cured him. So when my father hurt his back at work and as a result had pains in his back and legs, we did not hesitate, but brought him straight away to see you. Poor Dad limped into the healing room . . . and literally danced out after you treated him. I came to see you for help, not knowing what exactly was wrong.with me. Doctors seemed to think that my troubles were connected with glandular fever and hepatitis, which I had contracted ten years ago. My body felt as though it was burning up. I was constantly tired. My whole system did not feel to be working properly.

You treated me last week. I can honestly say I have not felt so good for ten years. I suppose cynics would say that you use auto-suggestion or some such nonsense, but I have proof that this is not so. I have had many urine tests in the past, and for the first time in all those years my urine is clear. Now, that must prove something."

Miss Whitham. (WAAF)."I suffered one year of pain and made countless visits for physiotherapy, plus time spent in a rehabilitation unit. All this was to no effect, and must have cost thousands of pounds. I am now pain-free in just one visit for healing. (This lady was also cured of the fact that her knees knocked together, a condition she had since she was a child.)

Mrs Easthorpe. "I was told by the specialist I had glaucoma in my right eye and had developed a cataract on the other. He then put my name on a list for an operation. My brother brought me to see you for healing. You said the improvement in my case would be gradual. I found it easier to see in the months ahead. I visited the specialist again for a routine check-up before the operation date was decided. However, after the check-up, the specialist said there was no sign of the cataract, and my name was taken off the operation list. He also said the general condition of my eyes was excellent."

Tim Ross. "After nine years of visiting doctors, they finally diagnosed me as having Osgood Achletter's Disease. Specialists at the hospital wanted to insert a steel pin in my shin bone. The condition was cured by Mr Greenbank in a matter of moments."

Frau Curting. "I came for healing with pains in my stomach, groin and legs. Previously I had been hospitalised for over a year all to no benefit and the doctors could give me no medical explanation for my pains. Eventually a sympathectomy operation was performed on my groin and leg nerves with still no improvement. I came to Don for healing and all the pain and full mobility was given me within the space of a few moments.

Ann Bryant. "My visit for healing was for a pain in my left side, that Don put right immediately. I last came to see Don for healing eight years ago, after having a total of three laminectomy operations with no let up in the pain or benefits given. The pains immediately went during the first treatment and I have had no trouble since that day. Now I have taken up rock climbing and I have grown so fit that I have run the Bradford Marathon race twice, I didn't win but I finished the course.

J Lindon. "I was told by the specialist at the hospital that I had a fused pelvis and that nothing could be done for the condition as it was of such long standing,

174

possibly from my birth. It was put right on my first visit for healing and all the pain went. This letter is written years later."

Mrs Ellison. "I have suffered from migraine since I was eighteen years of age, I am now fifty-three years old and I have not had a single migraine since I came for healing. This letter is written ten years later."

Pamela Harris. "Still can't believe what has happened in the space of a few short moments. I went in to see Don all twisted up and in terrible pain. Now I am leaving with no pain at all and walking straight and tall."

T Wilson. (SR Nurse) I came for healing for trapped nerves in my neck, I was unable to move my neck at all to one side and I was experiencing pins and needles all the time in my hand and arms. I am now perfect after just one visit for healing. The hospital consultant told me five years ago, that nothing medically could be done for this condition."

S Barret-Symes. "My symptoms were severe pains in my stomach and lower abdomen, having previously seen several doctors and other medical personnel from whom I could gain no medical explanation. I attended only once for healing and every pain left me immediately and as a bonus my long standing sinus trouble cleared up at once."

A Prichard. "For two years I had severe pain in the back of my right knee due to trapped nerves, so I was told by the doctor at the hospital. Another doctor said that he thought I had a thrombosis in my leg. So I came to see Mr Greenbank. All the pain has gone and my back is completely relaxed, and all the stiffness has gone also."

Mr Simpson. "After three years of pain and suffering words cannot express my gratitude to you for curing my pains. Following an accident I saw no less than nine doctors and had endless hospital treatment that was all non effective. At this time I was having to take up to twelve pain killer tablets a day, just to keep me going. I also had to wear a surgical collar and could only walk with the aid of a walking stick.

I did not think anyone could help me after being told by my doctors that I would have to learn to live with the condition. The day came when I visited you for healing. Just one session was all that was necessary, now I no longer have to wear a collar or walk with a stick and I have not taken a single pain killer since that first treatment. It takes some believing after three years of pain, it's just wonderful; once again I thank you from the bottom of my heart.

Mr Abrahams. "I suffered a stroke eighteen months ago, and since then I have not been able to walk properly until I attended for healing. I also had a speech problem. Now after healing I can walk and talk properly and I feel wonderful.

Mr Hanno. "My wife has suffered greatly for two years with painfully sore eyes. No specialist could do anything for her, nor the doctor's treatments. I brought her for healing in a desperate state but it took Don only twenty minutes to put everything right. Words cannot convey what a tremendous change has taken place."

Mrs Farrell. "In just one visit to receive healing, you have removed all pains from my back, legs, arms and neck. It must be of interest to you that I have been under medical specialists for the past thirty-two years. Now after healing I can move about without pain, like I can never remember before."

Mrs Waterhouse. "After suffering with a prolapsed disc for the past twelve months, to be free of pain is simply wonderful. I have been to see an orthopaedic specialist four times and eventually after having a bone scan. I was told to rest and do nothing at all and if that did not work the only possible solution left was an operation with a very high risk attached to it. After two visits I am a different person with no pain, so much so, that I am going to Tenerife for a holiday."

Lai Kong Clan. "Thank you for curing my mum and dad's severe back pains in just two visits. Their pains have persisted for over three years and no doctor could help them. Your healing is just like magic."

R Dickenson. "Dragged myself in to see you, then ran out and round and round your garden with no pain. Yes, it definitely works.

Deb Sufrin. "Just a few words to thank you for curing me from a large ovarian cyst. Doctors said that they would need to operate to remove it. Being pregnant they would have had to abort the child. After healing, when they took another body scan they searched all over, but could not find the slightest trace of the cyst – much to their astonishment and my delight. 'It's gone!' they said. You will be pleased to hear that the pregnancy went well. Now I have a fine healthy son."

Mrs Bonnington. "Thank you for curing my very painful elbow. Doctors said the only thing they could do was give me a series of cortisone injections, and that there was some risk of paralysis. I am now completely cured in just one visit for healing."

Mrs J Hoyle. "I am now forty-six years of age and have been deaf since I lost my hearing as a child. Since then I have had to rely on lip reading. I am overjoyed to tell you that my hearing has returned after all that time. Thank you for healing my painful back. I never expected that anything could be done for my ears."

Mr Motrom. "This is my second trip for healing. Within forty-eight hours of my last visit, a big difference was noted in the volume of air I was able to breath into my lungs. Prior to my first visit to see you, I was told quite definitely by both a doctor and a specialist that no improvement could be expected as the air vents to the lungs were closing up. Many thanks for this vast improvement."

Mrs S Whitall. "It is very hard to put into words the gratitude I feel towards you and your heavenly helpers for curing me. I received healing from you two months ago. I had been suffering considerable pain in my left leg for seven months and was hardly able to walk. No doctors or consultants could find a cure. As an active person who first lost mobility and then my job, I felt hopelessly lost and depressed.

After just one healing session from you, I was able to run round your garden. I was so happy I could not stop crying as I had not run for seven months. My favourite hobby has always been ballroom dancing so you can imagine how pleased I was when the weekend after seeing you, I was able to dance again. I have an exciting new job as a design assistant for the Burton Group which offers me lots of experience and a new challenge."

Mrs Mullarky. "I was waiting to go into hospital for an operation to have artificial knee and hip joints fitted. I came to you in great pain from all or most of my joints, in particular my felt knee. I walked in with the aid of a hospital walking stick – and walked out unaided, without my stick and no pain at all."

Mrs Kinvig. "My horse, Sporting Sam, was diagnosed by my vet and the Cambridge University Veterinary College as having sinovitis. He became lame as a result. They both wrote a report to the effect that in their opinion the horse would not recover and for me to think about having him put down. Mr Greenbank treated the horse and after the very first treatment, he was sound. Subsequently, Mr Greenbank came again a second time, and the horse made a complete recovery. He was placed at county shows all that season and actually qualified for the 'Horse of the Year' at Wembley! He is now perfectly all right and has started jumping again. He owes his life to Mr Greenbank. Thank you!" This is written several years later and the horse is still well and active. The insurance company paid the owner out as in the vet's opinion, the horse was ruined and needed destroying. No comment!

Mr Dwyer. "I was diagnosed as suffering from multiple sclerosis. My sincere thanks for the healing and hope given to me for the future after many years of suffering. To be able to take an active interest in life once again is simply wonderful."

Mrs Jorden. "After receiving healing from Don, my husband's leg ulcers showed a great improvement. He also had some very bad, protruding veins in his leg, which now are a lot less prominent. The very next day, there was a definite 'healing ring' round the ulcers that had not been there previously."

Mrs West. "I came for healing seven years ago, having previously been put into a plaster cast, with no improvement in my condition. This was very bad back trouble. I have been completely free of pain since. I am able to do my own housework and even play badminton."

Mrs Thorpe. I came for healing suffering from what was medically described as a 'nervous stomach,' only to find – or rather Mr Greenbank found – that the condition was caused by a trapped nerve in my back which was running pain into my stomach. After healing, I felt relaxed. The pain went after just one session. I now realise that I was not imagining it, as was implied by the doctors at the hospital who could not find the cause of my trouble."

S Wilmer. "After just one healing treatment, I was cured of nasal polyp, from which I have suffered for the last thirty years. During that time, I have had operations and hospital treatment all to no avail. Absolutely incredible. This is written years later."

F Hobart. "You are incredible, Don. The last time I came to see you I was cured of sinusitis that had troubled me for years. After this treatment all the pain and tension has gone from my body."

Mrs Lawn. "Thank you for healing my young horse, who was very lame. This was caused by a terrible accident when he ran into a wire fence six months ago. The vet has now – with much amazement – pronounced him A1."

C F Needham. I have received unbelievable relief from severe pains in my jaw that defied medical help. It all went right after two visits for healing."

A Enright. I brought my son to see you when he was twelve years old. His right foot was pointing inwards as he walked. He had trouble running at school. Since you cured him, he has been awarded 'Footballer of the Year' twice on the trot, 'Rugby player of the Year' and 'Golfer of the Year.' He has also broken the school record for discus throwing – and that record has stood for the last thirteen years. All this would not have been possible without your help."

John Lindley. Fifteen years of age. (Written by his mother. John was in Leeds General Infirmary and is a good example of healing from a distance.)
"Problem, a broken neca-femur. The accident was caused by a mugging. It was

deemed so serious by the hospital that the father was told the boy would be in a wheelchair forever as the bones would not knit.

Help was asked via absent healing. After the hospital discharged John, he was treated further in the clinic. Eventually he was declared fully fit and well. John had an isotope nuclear body scan of his hip area, and tests for blood supply to this area, and his body. These tests showed that there was no evidence of any disruption to the blood supply at all in the original fracture.

In fact, when I saw the photograph, the left side of the pelvis appeared to be better supplied with blood than the good side. The surgeon confirmed that the blood was managing to supply, the neca-femur with 'healing' blood. Yesterday the surgeon arranged another X-ray to see the extent of the repair that had been achieved to the fracture since the original X-rays were taken seven weeks before. Everyone who saw the original plates and compared them with the latest one taken, were amazed at the transformation.

It was obvious that the surgeon was a little open mouthed. He was so surprised at the wonderful progress that he simply did not know what to advise concerning the next stage of treatment. There were some in John's ward with far less serious injuries who were not making even normal progress. Indeed compared to John, they made slow progress.

I saw the X-rays and admit that the plates, side by side, make interesting viewing. The X-rays taken yesterday showed that the neca-femur and the ball joint were almost back to a normal state. This vast improvement has come about since we asked you for help."

Jane Shaw. "I brought our Labrador for healing last year. He was unable to stand and in constant pain due to a long-standing problem in his hips. We had to lift him into the car to bring him to see you, but after forty minutes he was able to jump into it for his return journey home. He has had only minimal trouble since. Needless to say both my husband and myself were thrilled to bits, and amazed.

To finish this letter of thanks, I rang you three weeks ago to ask for help via absent healing. My father, George Newhill, was dying of renal failure in the hospital, and I wanted your help yet again. You will be pleased to know that he is now at home and recovering well."

Mrs Wilson. "Thank you for your healing last year. Within two weeks of seeing you, all the pain in my back had left me. It was just like a miracle. After three years of intense suffering and being almost helpless, I am now able to say I am my old self once again. I have gained weight and am enjoying my meals. It feels lovely to go out and catch a bus to town, this after being told by doctors that I would have to learn to live with it. Thank you again from the bottom of my heart.

Edna Laycock. "I find it unbelievable. Never did I imagine when I walked into your clinic with my walking stick that I would not need it when I walked out. There is no pain at all now."

Sue Newgarth. "One thousand thanks, I came with a very painful spine that I had been receiving treatment for, over the last thirteen weeks at the hospital, from all this treatment there was NO improvement in my condition. I came just once for healing and was cured immediately.

D Millom. "I have got back my hearing after fifty years of deafness, in one visit for healing. Thanks a lot."

R Hersal. "I am able to see normally following healing from Don, after having double vision for several months!"

Helen Gill. "I am writing to thank you for all your help and kindness. My back problem has responded to healing. I must admit I was very depressed when I came to see you because my back had been very painful and incapaciting for the last eight months. I was beginning to wonder if it would ever be normal again. As you know treatment at the hospital and from an osteopath did not have any effect. As a result, I was a prisoner in my own home for many months. It's absolutely fabulous to be able to get around without pain, and without being bent over like the dame in a pantomime. My husband is delighted to have a fit wife again – it must be something to do with me being back in the kitchen! You are a gem!"

F Williams. "Two years ago I came for healing. My hands were always breaking out in a rash whilst my skin was forever cracking and weeping. Today I have come as a taxi driver for my wife. I am pleased to report that my hands are still OK after two years. And all that in just one visit for healing."

Mabel Brooksbank. "I am writing this letter as a testimony to the power of healing. Little Paul was brought to you for healing twice six years ago. At the time of his first visit, he was about eighteen months of age, and unhappy and uncomfortable because of a skin condition caused by a bone marrow deficiency. Following his first visit to see you, he became happier and started to walk. On his second visit, I remember holding his hands. He walked round and round your waiting room. Ann, his foster mother, told me that between those two visits she took him for his usual check-up at the Great Ormond Street Hospital in London to see specialists who were treating him. Their remarks were to the effect that 'natural healing' was doing a better job than the treatment they were prescribing. When he was about three and a half years of age, Ann was told by them that he needed no further medicines. The latest report, when he went for a check-up is that he is cured.

Paul is now, apart from the scarring and the skin discolouration, a normal, bright and healthy schoolboy. This is indeed a miracle of healing because medical specialists, just before she brought him for healing, had said that Paul's liver and spleen were enlarged due to his body trying to combat the bone marrow deficiency. You will be pleased to learn also that my eye, that was giving me pain and nearly closed when I came to you for healing, is now normal and gives me no trouble at all. Thank God for your ministrations."

Angela Hartley. "After years of pain from trapped nerves and pain in the neck and spine it took just one treatment to cure it all. It has never reoccurred in the slightest since I came for help just the once, twelve months ago."

Mr Diou Mistry. "Thanks for helping me to face life again. When I came to see you I was a nervous wreck, intent on committing suicide. Now thanks to you, I am a happy, lively young man. May God bless you."

Trevor Jones. "For years I have suffered with nervous troubles and light backache. I had literally tried every possible treatment, then heard about Don. From the very first visit, the change was miraculous. Thank you."

Silvia Haigh. "I have suffered from migraine for the past thirty years. Now, after receiving healing from Mr Greenbank, I am delighted to say they have disappeared, I have not had a migraine now for over ten years. If only I had known of him forty years ago a lot of my life would have been much better."

S Rispon. "After being in hospital for one month on traction with severe pain, there was no improvement. I came for healing just once, and now have no pain and feel wonderful."

Brenda O'Connnel. "One visit for healing. I can now run upstairs and down with no pain, something I have not been able to do for months despite thirteen non-effective sessions of physiotherapy, just one visit for healing."

Mr Greenwood. "I injured my eye on twigs in my hedge. Three days after Don had treated me, the red discolouration of the eyeball cleared away.

After one week the haze cleared away and I could see perfectly. Thanks Don. Sight is so precious."

A Glegg. "I came for healing with a septic gland in my mouth, plus stones in a gland. It is OK now after healing."

Hamish Waugh. "Shot in the foot as he tripped up climbing over a fence. Shot one toe off completely, and had wounds and burns to the rest of his foot. Responded immediately to healing. All pain was taken away from him at once. The foot was healed perfectly within three weeks."

Mary McCorgen. "Internal growth was dispersed at once. I will be ever grateful for making me feel like a human being again."

B Wilmott. "I have had a pain in my side for the past thirty years. No doctor could help me. With Don I gained instant relief. Healing has to be experienced to be believed."

Julie Wall. "I visited Don about a year ago with perforated eardrums, causing deafness. After receiving healing and my hearing being restored to normal, my doctor found two large white scars on my eardrums. Don said I had received a psychic operation. I have been going to the hospital for many years now with my hearing trouble, all to no effect. I can hear perfect now after one treatment."

S Ryams. "I came for healing with neuralgia and long-standing pressure in my ears. This was put right for me within the space of a few moments. Such peace, such power, no pain at all now."

Mrs Ward. "May I take this opportunity to thank you for healing my dog.

About five years ago he had a bad painful leg and did not respond to the vet's treatment. However, you treated him and he has walked normally ever since."

Mrs Howard. "I walked in to see you with a sailors gait, complete with hand splint and the need for built-up shoes and, of course, a lot of pain. After just that one treatment I was able to walk out straight and upright, with no pain. I squeezed my husband's hand harder than I have for a long time."

Mrs Lambert. "I brought my little boy aged nine for healing. He has been totally deaf in one ear since birth. He is cured with perfect hearing in both ears now after just two visits for healing."

Sally Cardwell. (nurse) "I would like to say a big thank you for healing me of a large ovarian cyst, which the specialist at the hospital told me was the size of a tennis ball. I was supposed to go into hospital the following week for an laparotomy operation to have it removed. However, when the surgeon had a look inside me with a microscope, prior to operating, everything was perfectly healthy, including all other organs. I was discharged from the hospital the following morning, no operation being necessary."

Mrs Tomlin. "My weight was only four and a half stone fourteen months ago.

After a visit from Don at my home, I was cured of the malnutrition from which I was suffering. Since then I have put on weight, and am back to my normal weight! (At the time of my visit, this patient was in the course of arranging to go into a hospice for the terminally ill to pass away. She was also confined to a wheelchair.

Within one month of my visit, she was able to return the wheelchair to the hospital, as it was no longer needed. This is written some five years later – and she is still active and in good health.)

Mrs Jones. "After my very first visit for healing, I have not used my walking stick or needed my wheelchair. I am looking forward to returning my disabled badge. Life for me now is much fuller and more pleasant, with no pain at all. This is written two years later."

Mr E Askew. "This letter is written several years after my wife was cured by Don. She was diagnosed as having cirrhosis of the liver and pernicious anaemia, by the hospital. My wife was down to six stone in weight. She went to see Mr Greenbank three times for healing. That's all. She has been well ever since and now weights ten stone. Both her sick conditions have gone completely. This has been confirmed by the hospital, which cannot explain it. She is enjoying life, a life for which we give thanks to God and you."

Mrs Bullen. "I tried to have a family for two years without any success. The specialist at the hospital said my fallopian tubes were badly blocked, and that even after a long involved operation there was only a ten per cent chance of conceiving a child. Thanks to the healing by Don on two occasions, I went back to the same specialist, who confirmed that I was seven weeks pregnant. No operation was performed. Bless you Don, for as you give so shall you receive." (Not only has this lady a healthy child, but since then has had another one.)

Mr Earnshaw. "Thank you for making my leg warm again and the pain go. After suffering for many years with a deep vein thrombosis, it is cured.

Ann Lewis. "I came for healing with Don four years ago. I was in terrible trouble, with intense pain in my back and neck. The doctors at the hospital told me that X-rays showed that it was rotten. Nothing could be done for me. Mr Greenbank put the trouble right immediately. I have not had any trouble since that one visit. This is written many years later."

Mr Tomlin. "I went to see Don six months ago with faulty vision. Hospital specialists said it was a scarred retina, and that the condition could not be improved by medicine. After receiving healing from you, within a period of three months the vision was perfect and has remained so ever since.

Last week I brought my grandson for healing. He had a large lump on his foot, which the doctor said would need an operation to remove. Within half an hour of Don treating it, the lump had gone completely."

Mr Eagleton. "After attending hospital as an out patient for the last twelve months with no success. In just one visit for healing all the pains went."

Susan Halliday. "I have been attending hospital for the last four years, with no benefit or relief from the intense pain. During that time I was issued with no less than three steel corsets and the specialists wanted to perform a laminectomy on my spine. You Don, cured me on my very first visit for healing and I have had no trouble since.

181

Mrs Jones. "On my one visit for healing, one month ago, Don healed a deep fissure I had in my foot. This was the result of an operation that went wrong fifteen years ago. Until now, it had never healed."

Mrs Taylor. "I had a trapped nerve in my wrist, causing me intense pain. Doctors said it needed operating on, and even then it would be a considerable time before I recovered to normality. Don released the nerve immediately and the pain went in just one healing session."

F Betts. "I had a malignancy of the face that was removed surgically. Later according to the specialist it was showing signs of returning. After healing was given, my face returned to normal. Also pains in the back and leg were removed."

Mrs Cawood. "I suffered from very high blood pressure. Immediately Don treated me, a calmness came over me. On my next visit to my GP for a check-up, the reading had gone down so far that the doctor said that he did not want to see me for two months. Great delight was expressed by the doctor at this new condition."

R Haley. "Continuous bleeding from the bladder. After seeing Mr Greenbank, the condition completely cleared up at once. Later I was admitted into hospital and given every form of test, including X-rays and a full examination. They revealed there is nothing wrong with me now."

Mrs Fieldhouse. "Fifteen years ago I attended the hospital with arthritis. I was told that I should return home and do nothing but rest as in a month I could be confined in a wheelchair there being no cure for the form of arthritis that I had. I came to Don for healing and was completely cured. I am now eighty years of age and lead a normal and very active life. Needless to say I am very grateful."

C Birstal. "Don cured me of angina fourteen years ago. I have had no trouble since that date with my heart."

Mrs Scofield. "I have been through the ordeal of medicines, drugs, acupuncture and physiotherapy. From none did I receive any improvement at all. I came for healing just the once and was cured instantly. Written months later."

B Wallbank. "I have never felt as good as this for years. Previous to receiving healing, I have suffered severe pains in the spine for a period of twenty-six years. Over that period of time I have had all forms of treatment, none of them helped my condition. All pain and discomfort were taken from me in just one treatment by this man."

B Lowe. "I was told by the hospital I was suffering from Padget's Disease, a condition of the bone marrow that is very painful, in my leg and spine. Just one visit for healing was all that was necessary to remove instantly all the symptoms I was showing."

S Lowe. "I went to see a specialist at the hospital who said that I had a spastic leg and that I was lopsided. After healing, I feel so much taller and straighter in the body."

A Gardner. "Many thanks for curing my condition. Now I can actually stand up straight. All the blurring has gone from my eyes. I had been told by one specialist that the condition was caused by an attack of meningitis while yet another specialist said my symptoms were just nerves."

Paula Agnew. I would never have believed that the pain I had in my knees could go in seconds, especially after the doctor told me it was caused by arthritis

182

in the hips and knees."

Voemie Parr. "One visit only for healing. I have been deaf in one ear since I was a child. Now I can hear perfectly. Previously, I was told by doctors I had a perforated eardrum."

Mr Savage. "After fifteen years of stomach trouble. I can now eat everything. Cured on my one visit for healing three months ago now."

Mrs R Newby. "I have no words in me, to describe what I feel like to be suddenly lifted free of a very painful hip displacement, after thirty-six years of pain. Your very special."

Joan Brierley. "Three years of pain, sixty-four treatments at the hospital that were useless and sixteen months of weekly treatments from an osteopath. After just one healing Don, took away all the pain, making me feel wonderful straight away."

E Elis. "Very many thanks. I have been suffering from pain and vertigo for a total of forty-seven years. This remarkable freedom from both was achieved in just one treatment."

H Hendrick. "Thanks a million. I am feeling marvellous after just the one treatment. I have been in pain for fifty-six years following a bicycle accident when I was a boy. I am walking out of this clinic without any pain and carrying my walking stick under my arm and I have used this stick for most of my life."

J Pickard. "I have suffered for many years with arthritis. After just one treatment, my blood count has improved from over one hundred, down to twenty, and I am now able to walk at least one mile each day."

Mrs Leiberman. "My seven year old daughter suffered from her back not growing properly. Her shoulders were hunched forward, and she had a curvature of the spine. She claims wonderful new freedom of movement after just one treatment. Her spine has visibly straightened whilst her shoulders are back now. She has been put down for a lengthy physiotherapy course of treatment by the doctors. Weekly swimming lessons were recommended and special exercises prescribed. The consultant at the hospital confirmed the vast improvement in her condition so much so that he has ordered the treatments by the hospital to be discontinued."

Michael South. "I came to see Don a month ago with jaundice, after being told by a surgeon I would have to attend for an operation at Leeds General Infirmary. I subsequently went to see the consultant, who admitted me for surgery. Preliminary tests were carried out to get more accurate details of the stone which had been identified before my visit to Don. After many tests and a full body scan, I was told the stone obstructing the duct to the liver was no longer there, thanks to Don Greenbank."

Mrs Wooler. It is now several months since I came to see you and I am still feeling as fit and well as I did when I left your clinic. In just one half hour I changed from being an unbalanced, weak legged person, being unable to do the ordinary things that most people take for granted. I had been diagnosed four years before as having multiple scerosis. Now I am totally co-ordinated, confident, and a unbelievable new me. In fact Don, a new friend has recently renamed me, the new GT model turbo charged.

Anyway the reason for this letter is to thank you from the bottom of my heart, for through your experience and wonderful gift of healing, I am now

183

fighting fit again. I will always be grateful and cannot stop telling people about you."

Maurice Batley. (Roman Catholic Priest.) "He brings good news and instant relief from pain."

The end of this book, but by no means the end of my story!

The address of Don Greenbank is:

Oak Lee Hall,
Greenbank Road,
Allerton,
Bradford, BD15 7LU
England.
Telephone 0274 490710